The Master Musicians Series

BEETHOVEN

Series edited by Stanley Sadie

THE MASTER MUSICIANS SERIES

BEETHOVEN

by
Marion M. Scott

Revised by Sir Jack Westrup

With eight pages of plates
and music examples in the text

J. M. DENT & SONS LTD
London, Melbourne and Toronto

Printed in Great Britain by
Biddles Ltd · Guildford · Surrey
and bound at the
Aldine Press · Letchworth · Herts
for
J. M. DENT & SONS LTD
Aldine House · Welbeck Street · London
First published 1934
Last revised 1974
Paperback edition 1974
Last reprinted 1979

Hardback ISBN: 0 460 03149 X
Paperback ISBN: 0 460 02140 0

PREFACE

WHERE so great a man as Beethoven was content to send the majority of his works into the world without preface, it might well be that a mere biographer should follow his example. Yet I could not rest happy were my thanks to remain unspoken —thanks to friends for the loan of books; thanks for the permission to reproduce the Beethoven manuscript in the library of the Royal College of Music and for the music facilities I enjoyed there; thanks also to Mr. C. B. Oldman of the British Museum for reading and revising my Beethoven Bibliography—which, indeed, had been already founded on his valuable bibliography in the Beethoven Centenary number of *Music & Letters*. To the editor of that periodical I owe the kindly permission to quote from some little-known Beethoven letters, and acknowledgments are due to the Beethovenhaus Archives for permission to reproduce some pictures and a page of the 'Moonlight' Sonata which are among the treasures at Bonn.

I should also like to express my thanks to the editor of this series for his consideration, patience, and many helpful kind-nesses over the putting together of the book—indeed, he made the Calendar and Index—and for having allowed me such entire freedom to develop and express my own views. When I began the work, I sternly conditioned myself into re-studying Beethoven and his music afresh from the beginning, in a chronological order and correspondence. It was an enthral-ling experience. That I had to change some preconceived views during the progress of my mental journey only heightened the almost passionate absorption and excitement.

Preface

When writing I tried to select from the immense wealth of material such historic and aesthetic elements as might be interesting for all music-lovers, irrespective of whether they were professionals or amateurs; and where the technical aspects of Beethoven's music were under discussion, I again endeavoured to choose the features which could be readily recognized by any one with some knowledge of music, not necessarily a theorist or musicologist.

MARION M. SCOTT.

LONDON, 1934

THE principal revisions in the present edition (1974) are as follows: 1 In the interests of uniformity quotations from Beethoven's letters have been taken from Emily Anderson's translation (*Ludwig van Beethoven. Letters.* Published by Macmillan, London & Basingstoke, 1961). 2 The list of works has been completely revised and re-arranged in categories. 3 The bibliography has been brought up to date.

J.A.W.

TO MY FATHER AND MOTHER

CONTENTS

BEETHOVEN'S LIFE

I.	Antecedents	1
II.	The Child	11
III.	Boy to Man	22
IV.	The Grand Mogul	35
V.	The Unhappiest of God's Creatures	44
VI.	Lover and Lion	59
VII.	The General of the Musicians	73

BEETHOVEN'S PERSONALITY

VIII.	Beethoven the Man	89
IX.	Beethoven the Musician	109

BEETHOVEN'S MUSIC

X.	Works for Piano Alone	127
XI.	Orchestral Music	150
XII.	Dramatic Music	190
XIII.	Vocal Music	209
XIV.	Chamber Music	230

APPENDICES

A.	Calendar	278
B.	Catalogue of Works	294
C.	Personalia	310
D.	Bibliography	318
	Index	328

ILLUSTRATIONS

Between pages 150 and 151

BEETHOVEN'S BIRTHPLACE, BONN (*Beethovenhaus, Bonn*)

BEETHOVEN AT THE AGE OF THIRTY-ONE (*Neidl's engraving after Stainhauser's portrait, reproduced by kind permission of the Austrian National Library*)

LYSER'S SKETCHES OF BEETHOVEN

REPRODUCTION OF A PAGE OF BEETHOVEN'S MS.—THE 'MOONLIGHT' SONATA

BEETHOVEN'S 'CREED' (*facsimile of MS. in Beethoven's own hand-writing, reproduced by kind permission from the collection in the Royal College of Music*)

BEETHOVEN'S HOUSE IN HEILIGENSTADT (*photo: Max Jacoby*)

BEETHOVEN, BY FERDINAND WALDMÜLLER, 1823 (*reproduced by kind permission of the Archiv für Kunst und Geschichte, Berlin*)

PORTRAIT OF BEETHOVEN BY SCHIMON (*Beethovenhaus, Bonn*)

BEETHOVEN'S LIFE

CHAPTER I

ANTECEDENTS

BEETHOVEN, during his last illness, was given a picture of Haydn's birthplace. It afforded him extraordinary interest. 'To think,' he exclaimed, 'that so great a man should have been born in a common peasant's cottage.'

To visit Beethoven's own birthplace is a strongly moving experience. Now, as then, the traveller approaches Bonn through a green country-side, bright in spring with the flowering orchards for which the Rhineland is famous. Now, as then, the Seven Mountains show their lovely contours against the south-eastern sky, and the great Rhine pours northward swift from the snows of Switzerland. The little town stands on its western bank just at the point where the river, flowing faster than a man can walk, has emerged from the wonderful Rhine gorge with its mile upon mile of winding hills, rocky cliffs, ruined castles, orchards, vineyards and romantic legends, and slowing its pace, here spreads out into the green plain that stretches ever onwards to the distant sea.

From pre-history the Rhine has been one of the world's great highways. Its ebb and flow of travellers kept Rhenish cities alive when such a town as Salzburg, Mozart's birth-place, lay stagnant. And history says the Romans founded Bonn. One cannot doubt it. They had an unerring eye for a key position. They remain in the background of its being, as they stand in the background of Beethoven's thoughts—the Romans with their stern code of courage and citizenship, and their great literature linked with that of Greece.

1

To-day, passing through the little town to its centre, one arrives at a modest well-to-do house flush on to the street, No. 20, formerly No. 515, Bonngasse. It is the Beethovenhaus —now dedicated in perpetuity to the memory of the great man who was born there. The rooms are filled with relics and pictures from every part of his career; glass cases enshrine the manuscripts which he valued so lightly, but which are almost beyond price; his piano stands for the pious to see, his ear-trumpets for the pitiful to bemoan. It is all a monument of devout hero-worship and national homage. A monument too of the way of the world, for at Beethoven's birth only the poorest corner was rented by his parents. Clasen, the owner, occupied the parterre and first floor with his family, he being a worthy gold-lace maker to the electoral court. The second floor (after 1771) was let to the Salomon family, already reputable as musicians and later to be remembered for their son, Johann Peter, the fine violinist who brought Haydn to England in 1791, and who now lies in the cloisters of Westminster Abbey.

Behind these flats in the main house was a small wing on the garden side. To-day it is regarded as the inner shrine. Reverently one ascends the back staircase to the top and there, under the roof, one gazes through an open doorway into a little box of a room, its ceiling so low beamed, its dormer wall so slanted, its space so tiny, that one marvels how people ever lived in it. Beethoven's birth-room! A bust of Beethoven, some dingy laurel wreaths and a shaft of dusty sunlight alone inhabit it now. The silence and humility strike at one's heart, just as later, in another room, the sight of Beethoven's death-mask stabs at one by his look of a mute conqueror over mortality.

Going about the house, one slips back into the eighteenth century and that December of 1770, when Beethoven was born. Did the Clasen family glance out of their windows at the baby being carried on a pillow to his baptism in the church of St. Remigius near by? Or did the Salomon family waken with annoyance in the night to complain of him howling as he cut his teeth? Or when it was summer-time, did they see the unsmiling young mother take her boy into the garden to roll upon the grass and gaze upon the blue skies and the brightness of the leaves? Not a pretty baby—perhaps even black-avised and defiant—but with a beautiful understanding between himself and his mother.

Whatever Beethoven missed in childhood, he had the thing that means most of all in the formation of a boy's character —he had a good mother. And whatever he missed in daily comfort and schooling from lack of money, he was surrounded from the beginning by a wealth of natural beauty in the Rhineland and by a good taste and culture in Bonn itself that went far to offset poverty.

Heredity and environment (which is a kind of mental heredity) do not play so large a part with Beethoven as with some men of genius (for example, J. S. Bach), but they are worth considering in any serious attempt to understand his character and development.

Bonn, as he first knew it, was a town dominated almost entirely by ecclesiastical influence. From 1257, when the Archbishop of Cologne was dispossessed of his privileges in that city by the turbulent Colognese, Bonn had become the capital of the electorate, and since it was a town without trade or manufactures, everything centred upon the little court of the archbishop-electors. These rulers were nearly always picked from the younger sons of royal or semi-royal houses. They were elected by an ecclesiastical chapter, the choice of this chapter having to be confirmed by the Pope and the Emperor of the Holy Roman Empire, who, as over-lord of the confederation of small states, was in his own turn elected by the three ecclesiastical electors of Cologne, Mayence and Treves, and the four lay rulers of the Rhenish Palatinate, Saxony, Brandenburg and Bohemia, joined later by Hanover and Bavaria. Hence the title of 'Elector.' A clumsy and unsatisfactory system, in which none of the electing parties considered the good of the subjects to be ruled. But this much could be said—the ecclesiastical principalities were generally better to live in than those under secular control, though the Free Towns were happiest of all. Lady Mary Wortley Montagu, who travelled much and observed well, wrote to her daughter from Nuremberg in 1716:

I have already passed a large part of Germany, have seen all that is remarkable in Cologne, Frankfort, Wurtsburg and this place; and 'tis impossible not to observe the difference between the free towns and those under the government of absolute princes, as all the little sovereigns of Germany are. In the first, there appears an air of commerce and plenty. The streets are well built and full of people, neatly and plainly dressed. The shops are loaded with merchandise, and the commonalty clean and cheerful. In the other, a sort of shabby finery, a number of dirty people of quality tawdered out; narrow, nasty streets out of repair, wretchedly thin of inhabitants, and above half of the common sort asking alms.

She gives no names, but since she surely passed through Bonn on her way from Cologne to Frankfort, one concludes it supplied some of her evidence.

Apart from this dependence upon the electors in general, Bonn had recently suffered heavily for the French proclivities of its elector in particular, the Archbishop Joseph Clemens, ruler from 1689 to 1723. A large part of that time was spent by him popping in and out of exile, and his capital was a shuttlecock between the warring nations. It is strange how, even before Beethoven's birth, those French armies which, near or far, always trampled through his life, already threw their prophetic shadow across the ways he was to tread. Three times Bonn was wrested from the French.

At the third rescue, in 1703, such was the state of the town that it 'aroused indignation, grief and compassion on all sides.' Joseph Clemens, however, did not return till 1714, after an agreeable exile spent largely in France, where he had indulged his tastes for music and display. He dabbled in verse-making and composition, and built better than he knew when he laid the foundations of the new palace at Bonn (which his successor completed) and established the musical *Kapelle* (or chapel) on lines more generous than was then the custom. He was followed by Clemens August, a typical prince of the eighteenth century, worldly, urbane, artistic, a great ladies' man notwithstanding his ecclesiastical vows, a grandiose builder with a passion for Italian taste, an enlightened patron of opera and drama. His immense capacity for acquiring money was equalled by his energy in spending it. Under him Bonn grew architecturally hand-some and genuinely artistic. He enlarged his *Kapelle* and raised its status by employing really good musicians. He may even bear an honour then quite unsuspected by every one concerned—he may have been instrumental in bringing the Beethovens to Bonn. Clemens August had travelled much. Tradition has it that at Louvain or Liége he heard a young church singer with a pleasing voice and good musical education whom he invited to enter his service. The young man came of a family that called itself variously Biethofen, Biethoven, Bethofen, Bethof, or, as we now know it, van Beethoven, a name that had an aristocratic sound, with the prefix *van* so like the noble German *von*, but in reality meaning nothing more than 'of the garden of beetroot.' This Flemish family was settled in the eighteenth century in the districts of Louvain, Rotselaer Leefdaal, Berthem, Maestricht, Tongres, Tirlemont, Antwerp and Malines, one of the two last-named being the home of that branch of the family to which the young singer Louis belonged. Until lately he was believed to have been the son of Henri-Adelard, a master-tailor at Antwerp. More recently M. van Aerde claims to have identified him with certainty as the son of Michel van Beethoven, a master-baker at Malines. The evidence is involved; when sifted it reads like the plot for a Comedy of Errors. To be brief, both Henri-Adelard and Michel van Beethoven had among their numerous offspring two sons named Louis, Henri's couple being born in 1712 and 1728, and the couple belonging to Michel in 1710 and 1712. In each case the elder Louis is presumed to have died in infancy, while the younger ones are known to have survived. What is indisputable about Louis the singer is that his forbears and relations were trading folk with a tendency towards art and letters, that he was born in 1712, held posts as a church musician at Louvain and Liége in 1731 and 1732, went to Bonn, and in March 1733 was appointed by decree court musician to the Elector with a salary of four hundred florins. Thus at the age of twenty-one young Louis became established for life. Behind him lay the Low Countries which he was never to see again. Ahead lay more than forty years of responsible and respected work, the rise to the dignity of *Kapellmeister* and the glory, near the end, of becoming grandfather to one of the greatest composers who ever lived.

Grandfather Louis—or young Louis, as he then was—did not lose much time after his appointment in marrying, on 7th September 1733, Maria Josepha Poll of Bonn. Unfortunately for her, Louis augmented his income by carrying on an export wine business. It was a profitable trade in that vine-growing district, and perhaps the only one possible in a town where everything else revolved round the electoral court, Bonn being fed, so the saying ran, from the elector's kitchen. But wine was the disaster of Louis's home; Maria Josepha drank; her last years had to be spent under restraint in a convent said to have been in the Kölnerstrasse, Bonn. Of all her children only one lived to grow up.

6

The Grandfather

The *Kapellmeister* was of stronger stuff, 'a man short of stature, muscular, with extremely animated eyes . . . greatly respected as an artist,' said one who knew him. The description tallies with the portrait by the court painter Radoux which now hangs in the Beethovenhaus at Bonn. It shows the *Kapellmeister* wearing a furred robe and the sort of turban affected by the *cognoscenti* of the time. The face is smooth, plump, wise, Flemish—the face of a man who impresses one as having fulfilled all his duties with punctual zeal and skill, a man who had raised himself to an honourable position by his exertions and thereafter was disposed to stand upon the dignity of his calling.

His son, Johann, born about 1740, was of another sort. Some writer has said wittily but unkindly that Johann's sole function in life seems to have been to provide a biological link between his father and his son. Physically taller and more handsome than the *Kapellmeister,* Johann did not approach him in musicianship, while in character he followed his mother. Nevertheless, he had sufficient ability to sing soprano at twelve years old in the elector's chapel, and at sixteen he was appointed a *Hofmusikant* in consideration of his ability in the art of singing, and also for his 'proved experience.' More probably he was given his chance out of consideration for his father; but let that pass. So long as Johann had his father's firm hand to force him along the way he should go, he was, if not a triumph, at least not a failure. He managed to work up a good teaching connection and was 'of fair deportment,' as an official report of him states. Once, and once only, he flew flat against his father's counsels: ironically enough it is the one deed which gives them both their claim on our remembrance. Johann fell in love with, and insisted upon marrying, a young widow named Maria Magdalena Laym, daughter of the late chief cook, Heinrich Keverich, at the castle of Ehrenbreitstein. She was the widow of

Joseph Laym, late valet to the Elector of Treves. *Kapell-meister* Louis van Beethoven was greatly disturbed. The prince archbishops of that time might see no social distinc-tion between musicians and cooks, all alike being their ser-vants, but to *Kapellmeister* Louis the difference was marked. His sense of personal and professional dignity was really aristocratic (a trait which his grandson inherited as a sort of royal republicanism), and Johann had affronted it. More-over, the *Kapellmeister* had suffered much in his own marriage. He was anxious to save his son from a similar fate.

'I would never have believed or expected it of you that you would thus lower yourself,' he said to Johann, when the latter unfolded his plans; adding, when Johann persisted: 'Very well. Do what you will. I shall do also what I ought; I abandon to thee the lodging, and I shall remove.' And off went *Hofkapellmeister* van Beethoven to live in the Kölnerstrasse, in the ancient Gudenauer House. At least, that is the account given by Gottfried Fischer who, if not very accurate in his reminiscences, was at least a life-long resident in Bonn. The story ought to be true, for one traces in it exactly the same intransigence that cropped out in the great Beethoven.

According to Fischer, the *Hofkapellmeister* would not even attend the wedding. The ceremony took place at St. Remigius's Church, Bonn, on 12th November 1767, and it is perhaps evidence of his absence that the register was signed by two colleagues of Johann's from the electoral orchestra—Joseph Clement Belseroski, the viola player, and Philipp Salomon, the violinist. After the marriage, the bride of twenty-one and bridegroom of twenty-seven spent a short honeymoon at Coblenz and Thal-Ehrenbreitstein, and then settled into the little lodging, at No. 515 Bonngasse, which has been already described.

They were a taking couple—Johann tall, handsome, with powdered hair; Maria Magdalena also tall, with a slender figure, face somewhat long, nose a little aquiline, and earnest eyes. Johann was a rattle; his wife a clever woman who could 'give converse and reply aptly, politely and modestly to high and low, and for this reason she was much liked and respected. She occupied herself with sewing and knitting. They led a peaceful and righteous married life, and paid their house-rent and baker's bills promptly.'

So at the beginning things went well, and even the *Hof-kapellmeister* was won over to a reconciliation. His own integrity led him to recognize that of his daughter-in-law, and she had a gravity that suited well with his dignity. Cäcilia Fischer, sister of Gottfried, both of whom as children knew the Beethovens, could not recall that she had ever seen Madame van Beethoven laugh. Though this gravity may have been assumed out of deference to her father-in-law's social code, it also emanated from an inner sorrow and hope-lessness that grew upon her during the years spent with Johann. He was one of those people who make no one happy but themselves; his wife, handicapped in the family counsels by her supposed social inferiority, had not the power to keep him sober. She once said to Cäcilia Fischer: 'What is marriage? A little joy, followed by a chain of sorrows.' And in that sentence she summed up her life-experience of Johann.

Such then were the environment and ancestry of the great Beethoven—a petty, ecclesiastical court in a wide country; Flemish *bourgeoisie*; Rhenish peasants; and two generations of music immediately preceding the genius.

But another possible strain in his heredity is one of Spanish blood. Spanish occupation and influence had been long and fierce in the Netherlands, longest of all in those Catholic districts from which the Beethoven family came. M. Ernest Closson, in *The Fleming in Beethoven,* writes:

We know that his swarthy complexion and coal-black locks earned for Beethoven the nickname of 'the Spaniard,' '*der Spanjol,*' in his

9

family.* It is well known, too, that, just as the Italian type is met with among the Austrians, so one often sees the Spanish type in Flanders, a relic of the Spanish rule in the Netherlands. This hereditary phenomenon is in fact generally spoken of in Antwerp as *spaansche bloed* (Spanish blood). And certainly there was no lack of Southern fire in Beethoven.

Beethoven's face, as shown in his miniature by G. von Kügelgen and in the portrait by Stainhauser, is distinctly southern, just such a typical Spanish peasant as one may find again and again in the pictures of Murillo. This ancestry might account for some of the characteristics which neither the Flemish nor Rhenish strains in Beethoven quite explain; for example, his tremendous pride, and anger as quick as lightning. Coincidence is a strange thing. When he came to die in Vienna, it was in the Schwarzspanierhaus—the House of the Black Spaniard.

CHAPTER II

THE CHILD

IT is a mark of the hero in folk-lore that mystery should attend his birth and portents announce his death. Beethoven, by a curious chance, fulfilled both conditions.

The earliest confusion arose because Johann and Maria Magdalena had *two* sons named Ludwig. Their eldest child, Ludwig Maria, born in 1769 and baptized on 2nd April, bore the names of his grandfather and Frau Courtin next door, who were his sponsors. The poor little mite lived but six days: babies had barely a dog's chance in the eighteenth century. Twenty months later, December 1770, a second child was born. Again the baby was named Ludwig in honour of the grandfather, who again stood sponsor, the godmother being Frau Baums, wife of another next-door neighbour. She also gave the baptismal feast—a kindly act.

The record of the christening reads thus in the parish register of St. Remigius:

Parentes :	*Proles :*	*Patrini :*
D: Joannes van Beethoven & Helena Keverichs, conjuges	17ma Xbris Ludovicus	D. Ludovicus van Beethoven & Gertrudis Müllers dicta Baums

(The mistake of Helena for Magdalena is easily explained by their common contraction, Lena.) The date, 17th December, supplies strong evidence that Ludwig No. 2 had been born on 16th December, since in Catholic Bonn the custom was to baptize infants on the day after birth. The presumption is strengthened by a note made by a clerk in Simrock's publishing establishment fifty-six years later on the back of an announcement of Beethoven's death:

'L. v. Beethoven was born on 16th December 1770.' The significant link here is that Simrock was actually living in the Bonngasse at the time the Beethovens were there. He later became one of Beethoven's publishers.

Further confusion over the date of Ludwig's birth was deliberately engineered by Johann v. Beethoven. The father observed little Ludwig's gift for music and hoped, with his stupid cleverness, to make of the child a second Mozart—a *Wunderkind*—who would bring in money and fame to the family mill. Ludwig was not sufficiently precocious for that purpose. Happy thought! Johann took a short cut by knocking a couple of years off the child's age. This plan was practicable because Ludwig was short and naturally could not remember his own beginnings. He believed for a large part of his life that he had been born in 1772. The matter was only cleared up when he was about forty, after most tiresome investigations which included having a copy of his birth certificate sent from Bonn to Vienna. As to Johann, the evidence of his duplicity is damning.

Last, and most fantastic strand in the mystery surrounding the hero's birth, was the rumour started by someone that he was the illegitimate son of King Frederick William II of Prussia. Why in the name of wonder any one should think that only the highest social position can produce genius—in short, that Bacon wrote Shakespeare—is incomprehensible. The evidence, if any, is in the other direction. Yet the silly story, put into circulation in 1810 and carried on till 1826, caused Beethoven and his friends keen annoyance. One of them wrote to Beethoven on the subject, who answered: 'I have made it a principle never to write anything about myself nor to reply to anything written about me. For this reason I gladly leave it to you to make known to the world the honesty of my parents, and of my mother in particular.' Beethoven was right; the story was scarcely worth the words to refute it.

Of the first three years of Beethoven's childhood not one morsel of information remains. But that he already observed and remembered the life around him is proved by his loving recollection of his grandfather. Many children cannot remember things before the age of four or five. The *Hofkapellmeister* died suddenly from a stroke on 24th December 1773. Ludwig was then three.

The grandfather had been the good guardian of the family. After his death nothing went well. Johann sent in a petition to the elector, hoping to get his father's post, which the elector refused. The little family moved to a house, No. 7 or No. 8, 'on the left as one enters the Drieckplatz in passing from the Sternstrasse to the Münsterplatz.' Here another child, Caspar Anton Karl, was born in April 1774 and baptized on 8th April with the names of his sponsors, the Minister Belderbusch and the Countess Caroline von Satzenhofen, Abbess of Vilich. Johann no doubt felt he had done a fine stroke for himself by securing the interest of these aristocrats, the two most puissant people in the electorate next to the elector himself. Clemens August no longer reigned; he had been succeeded in 1761 by Maximilian Friedrich, 'a little, hale, black man, very merry and affable . . . easy and agreeable, having lived all his life in ladies' company, which he is said to have liked better than his breviary.' Max Friedrich, though he founded the university at Bonn, was indeed no saint. He carried on the governance of his people through a minister whom they detested (the very Belderbusch Johann secured for Carl's godfather), while he devoted himself to his religious duties and an intrigue with the Abbess of Vilich, who stood in but too intimate relations to both the elector and his useful minister.

This was a peculiar situation, and unedifying for the Bonners. I have little doubt that Ludwig van Beethoven's aloofness towards organized Catholicism—and indeed towards all organized religion—originated in his clear-eyed contempt for what he saw at Bonn in high places.

Music being the business of the Beethoven family, Ludwig was put to it early. His father began teaching him the violin and clavier when he was either four or six years old, an uncertainty in date for which the blame lies at Johann's door. But whether four or six, 'to scarcely anything else did he (Johann) hold him.' The wretched child was given his daily tasks of practice and kept to them, willy-nilly. Had he been older such discipline might have been useful. But Johann generally put the cart before the horse. Our hearts revolt, as did those of the neighbours, at the picture of poor little Ludwig standing in front of the clavier, weeping and playing. To rob a child of its childhood is a theft nothing can repair. Only the grace of God and the genius in him saved Ludwig from loathing music.

Before Ludwig was six the family removed from the Drieck to the Fischer house in the Rheingasse 934 (now No. 7), a stone's throw from the river. It was almost opposite the old Gasthaus zum Engel. Here, in October 1776, another little brother, Nikolaus Johann, was added to the family. Soon after came another home-removal, this time to the Neugasse 992. In all these changes one perceives a controlling factor; Johann had to be near the palace so that he might go and come from his daily work with the least loss of time. Before long he had reason to find the Neugasse altogether too near.

At three o'clock in the morning of 15th January 1777 a frightful fire broke out in the western wing of the elector's palace, the powder magazine blew up and the Bonners wakened to feel their town rocking. They rushed out horrified, a seething, distracted mass of people, who congested all the streets in their efforts to save their homes and see what was happening. The elector, scantily clothed, had but just escaped with his life; the wildest rumours spread everywhere.

For the Beethoven children it must have been a night of hideous terror. As time went on, the fire raged more fiercely. At six in the morning the tall clock-tower, with its fine carillon, crashed down as the bells were beginning to play Monsigny's overture to *The Deserter*. They had done so every morning—now they were dumb, yet we may still hear their echoes (if the French author, M. Cucuel, is right) in the thematic similarity between the final chorus of Monsigny's *Deserter* and the finales of Beethoven's ninth Symphony and *Fidelio*. For five days the fire and fear continued. Owing to a high wind, the whole town was in danger. Thirty different outbreaks occurred. It was a nightmare time, its horror only illuminated by the heroism of Court Councillor von Breuning, who lost his life attempting to save those of others. Little Ludwig must have heard the story often then, and years later von Breuning's family became his dearest friends. The fire unnerved Johann. He removed himself and his family back to their old quarters in the Rheingasse, and one gets the measure of the shock the poor children had suffered by their pathetic rejoicing that 'it is better we have returned because here there is enough water in the Rhine to put out the fire.' Poor little urchins! Seven years later the Rhine overflowed and the Beethovens had to escape for their lives out of the first-floor windows. *Götterdämmerung* indeed, strangely symbolic of the coming destruction of the old order!

That, however, is to anticipate. In 1777 the family settled again into the Fischer house, and the wretched routine of their days recommenced. Johann was already drinking too much; his wife moved unsmiling through her dutiful toil. Money was an increasing anxiety: household goods had to be pawned. In fine weather the maid took Ludwig, Karl and baby Johann to walk by the Rhine or in the palace gardens, where they played in the sand with other children. When the weather was bad, they kept a rendezvous with the

Fischer children in the courtyard. Those boys were a turbulent trio; their father would not have them in the house
when he received visitors. Upon which the enraged infants,
sent into a back building, revenged themselves by scrabbling
furiously up the house door on fingers and toes, determined
at all costs to see in. 'So Fate knocks at the door.'

'The Beethoven children were not brought up with kindness; they were often left to servants: the father was very severe
with them,' records old Fischer dryly. So it seems true that
Johann beat Ludwig and locked him in the cellar at times.
Besides the annoyance caused by his rampageous children—
magnified by his irritability as a habitual drinker—Johann
had business reasons for forcing Ludwig into obedience.
Ludwig *must* be a prodigy. By 1778 Johann thought him
ready for the role. He produced him at a concert on 26th
March in company with another of his pupils, Mlle Averdonk,
contralto singer of the court. The young lady sang arias, the
'little boy of six years old' (only he was really eight) played
clavier concertos and trios. The performance took place at
five o'clock in the hall of the Academy. Of the result of
the concert no word remains. We only know that about
this time Ludwig had his first lessons from a teacher other
than his father. It is traditional that old van den Eeden,
the court organist, a friend and colleague of *Kapellmeister* van
Beethoven, had offered to give his grandson, Ludwig, some
lessons gratis. There is also a tradition that the elector,
struck by the child's promising abilities, paid van den
Eeden to teach him. Both versions of the story may be true.
What more likely than that van den Eeden should offer to
coach Ludwig for the concert, and that after it the elector
might have given some small grant (perhaps at van den
Eeden's own suggestion) towards continuing the lessons?
The arrangement did not last long, and its breakdown was
no loss, for the old man was apparently futile as a teacher.

Johann realized that Ludwig had got beyond his own efforts and those of van den Eeden. He now turned him over to a certain Tobias Pfeiffer, a brilliant musician, but a thorough bad lot, who came to Bonn in the summer of 1779. Pfeiffer lodged in the Fischer house. He and Johann forgathered like birds of a feather. Together they would return late from the taverns, Pfeiffer wakening the poor Fischers in the middle of the night by tramping about overhead in his great boots (Hessians, I suppose), and when Fischer told him he ought to take them off, Pfeiffer removed one and kept on the other. Worse than all, when Pfeiffer had omitted Ludwig's lesson in the day, he would haul him out of bed and keep him at the piano all night. Yet Ludwig bore no resentment, possibly because Pfeiffer was a true musician. To an artist bad art is almost the one unforgivable thing. It is we who cannot forgive him for ill-treating a child. That Pfeiffer had the real gift is sure. On the rare occasions when he could be persuaded to play the flute, with Ludwig making variations upon the piano, people used to stop in the street to listen and applaud. Happily for Ludwig's health Pfeiffer's regime lasted only a twelvemonth, by which time Pfeiffer had made Bonn too hot to hold him.

In this same year Ludwig's cousin, the charming Franz Rovantini (son of Madame van Beethoven's sister) became an inmate of the Fischer house, and he gave Ludwig lessons on the violin and viola. The child was thoroughly over-worked, for simultaneously with all this music he was ploughing through the only schooling he had, first at an establishment in the Neugasse, then at the Münsterschule, and finally at the Tirocinium, a lower-grade school that prepared pupils for the Gymnasium. Small wonder his health was uncertain in after-life; he can never have had sufficient sleep or recreation, and quite possibly he was short of nourishing food.

One of his schoolfellows, Wurzer, afterwards President

of the Landgericht, recalls 'Luis' at the Tirocinium thus: 'Apparently his mother was already dead at the time, for Luis v. B. was distinguished by uncleanliness, negligence, etc. Not a sign was to be discovered in him of that spark of genius which glowed so brilliantly in him afterwards.'

No. Ludwig's mother was not dead; she was merely unable to cope with her family. It is said to be a fact, supported by the evidence of the Society for the Prevention of Cruelty to Children, that where the neglect of a child is due to the laziness of the mother, the mother's apathy is due to the father's disregard of home and family. That very thing happened here. But the blackness of the picture is relieved by some gleams of affection and fun. Each year when Madame van Beethoven's nameday came round, on the feast of St. Mary Magdalene, the children and Johann used to organize a little festival for her as a surprise, with a flower-decked canopy, a draped chair, special music, supper and dancing.

In 1781 Ludwig removed from school to concentrate entirely on music. It is difficult to get an ordered idea of his studies, because they were anything but orderly. He began the organ under Brother Willibald Koch, of the Franciscan monastery, an old friend of Johann's and a very capable musician, who presently 'accepted' Ludwig as his assistant. He also made friends with the organist of the Minorite church, got lessons from him and a tiny post as organist for the six o'clock mass each morning. A little later he appears to have studied with Zenser, the organist of the Münsterkirche.

Ludwig had already an inclination to compose. It is said that his first composition was a cantata to the memory of George Cressener, the English ambassador at Bonn, who had been kind to the Beethovens, and who died on 17th January 1781. If so, how strange that an Englishman occasioned his first composition and an English society commissioned that last symphony which he did not live to write!

First Professional Activities

In September 1781 Franz Rovantini died, and his sister, at that time governess in a Dutch family at Rotterdam, came with the lady who employed her to visit his grave in Bonn. They stayed with the Beethovens for a month and invited them in return to Holland. Johann could not leave, but it seemed a chance for Ludwig to follow in Mozart's footsteps as a travelling 'wonderchild.' So the boy and his fragile mother were packed off with the Rotterdam party in October or November of 1781. They travelled by Rhine boat. Mme van Beethoven said afterwards the weather was so bitterly cold that she only prevented Ludwig's feet from being frost-bitten by keeping them in her lap. (Another sign of under-nourishment and overwork. A boy of eleven should have a better circulation than that.) Whether Ludwig gave a concert in Holland is unknown, but he played at private houses and obviously did not relish his role of prodigy. Nor did he like the Dutch. On his return, when Fischer asked him how he had fared, he replied: 'The Dutch are skinflints (only his word *Pfennigfuchser* was more forcible)—I'll never go to Holland again.' He never did.

Running through Ludwig's earliest years there was a strong vein of resentment. One gets an impression of the child prisoned within himself, chained-dog-like, savage with captivity, glowering out from his kennel upon a world that seemed to him infested with fools whom he never learned to suffer gladly. Only his mother understood him as a human being: no one comprehended him as a musician. Yet he recognized already that music was for him, even more than religion, a supreme proof of the reality of God—that it *was* his religion—and that (as Browning's Abt Vogler says):

The rest may reason and welcome: 'tis we musicians know.

Two stories dating from this time illustrate the point.

There was a Father Hanzman, monk in the Minorite

19

monastery, and a competent organist, who, whenever there was chamber music at the Beethovens' house, insisted on coming to it. Ludwig could not endure him. 'This monk, who always turns up here, ought to stay in his monastery and tell his beads,' said the boy.

On the other hand, in Brother Willibald Koch, his old friend, Ludwig recognized a true musician. 'Why,' he asked, 'when you are so good a musician, have you vowed yourself to solitude?' To Ludwig such an act seemed a sort of apostasy. Music was the highest vocation he could conceive.

Things were in this state when a gifted and thoroughly trained musician, Christian Gottlob Neefe by name, came to Bonn in 1779. Here at last was someone who understood the young genius. At what date he undertook his tuition is unknown, but by June 1782, when Neefe (now court organist) went to Westphalia and Frankfort, he left Ludwig, aged eleven and a half, in charge as his vicar. Strictly trained himself at Leipzig, Neefe gave Ludwig the mental and musical discipline he needed, and though a stern critic, he was a constructive one. 'If I ever become a great man, yours shall be a share of the credit,' Ludwig wrote to Neefe some ten years later. Neefe deserves our thanks also because he was sufficiently impressed by Ludwig to make contemporaneous notes on him. As a correspondent for *Cramer's Magazine,* he wrote in March 1783 (and the passage has been often quoted):

Louis van Beethoven . . . a boy of eleven years and of most promising talent. He plays the clavier very skilfully and with power, reads at sight very well, and—to put it in a nutshell—he plays chiefly *The Well-tempered Clavier* of Sebastian Bach, which Herr Neefe put into his hands. Whoever knows this collection of preludes and fugues in all the keys—which might almost be called the *non plus ultra* of our art—will know what this means.

So far as his duties permitted, Herr Neefe has also given him instruction in thorough-bass. He is now training him in composition and for his encouragement has had nine variations for the pianoforte written by him on a march—by Ernst Christoph Dressler—engraved at Mannheim. This youthful genius is deserving of help to enable him to travel.

Besides the historical value, there are two points in this document linking it with Beethoven's future. One is his training in Bach's preludes and fugues, the tradition being that Beethoven first made his fame in Vienna by his masterly performance of the 'Forty-eight.' The other is his first published composition, the Variations upon the march by Dressler. The theme wears a curious look of having been the seed from which grew Beethoven's own superb theme for his thirty-two Variations in C minor, composed in 1806.

By 1783 Beethoven was sufficiently advanced to become deputy cembalist in the elector's orchestra, and he was further 'encouraged' by the publication at Speyer of three piano sonatas dedicated to the Elector Max Friedrich. In the first half of 1784 things began to happen rather fast. Beethoven, maturely aged fourteen, applied for the post of assistant court organist (15th February). In this same month the Rhine overflowed (as already mentioned). The hated minister Belderbusch had died in January, and in April the elector himself died. The old order was passing. His successor, Maximilian Franz, youngest son of the Empress Maria Theresa, was to be the last elector of Cologne. He was already touched with new ideas, and in his short reign went far towards making Bonn one of the intellectual and artistic centres of Europe. In June he appointed Ludwig assistant court organist with a salary of one hundred and fifty gulden. One can almost hear Johann's sigh of relief. Ludwig had become a wage-earner.

CHAPTER III

BOY TO MAN

OF the period from 1784 to 1787 not much precise information remains. But in general terms we know that Ludwig was living and working in surroundings where music was the warp and woof of his life. The professional musicians were all near neighbours, a coterie who met daily over their work. In the elector's chapel and in the churches Ludwig became thoroughly familiar with church music; in the elector's palace, at the concerts and daily *Tafel* (table) music, he learned the business of an orchestra backwards and forwards; in the opera theatre, where there were occasional opera performances, he heard contemporary works; while in the constant music-makings at the houses of wealthy amateurs he had a remarkable field for first-hand experience—quite the best way of learning. In short, he heard, thought and talked music; lived, moved and had his being in it. He was already adept in the modern harmonic style of composition. Boy-like, he enjoyed shocking his seniors. One exploit has come down to us. Beethoven, during the course of his duties in the elector's chapel, had to accompany on the piano those portions of the Lamentations of Jeremiah which are sung on a reciting note in Holy Week. In Holy Week, March 1785, the singer was Ferdinand Heller, an excellent musician, who, when Beethoven asked leave to try to put him off his note, assented very readily. He did not know his boy! That young monkey, while persistently striking the reciting note with one finger, improvised such daring harmonic excursions in the accompaniment that Heller became too bewildered to find the closing cadence. Tableau! The musicians of the chapel dumbfounded at Beethoven's skill, Heller furious to the extent of complaining to the elector, and the triumphant youngster 'very graciously reprimanded' by that exalted person. If in after years Beethoven showed himself awkward in church music, or undramatic in opera, it was not because he was without opportunities for learning in Bonn, but because his genius was fundamentally symphonic.

With the accession of the new elector, Max Franz, this little Bonn world was suffused by a steadily growing brightness of culture. 'The church and cloister ceased to be all in all.' Wegeler, who lived there, wrote that 'it was a beautiful and in many ways active period in Bonn.' The young elector encouraged science and education: he established a botanic garden, opened a reading room in the palace library, improved the theological instruction within his principality, obtained the charter for the university and in November 1786 inaugurated the new institution. Men of high intellectual standing settled in Bonn. The dawn of the new epoch had come and no one then realized that the day it heralded would contain the hurricane of the French Revolution. But already those forces were preparing: Beethoven, sensitive beyond the ordinary, was not insensible to them. There was to be observed 'through all his life a certain breadth and grandeur in his intellectual character, owing in part, no doubt, to the social influences under which it was developed,' says Thayer, his greatest biographer.

In the late spring of 1787 Beethoven's genius received a fresh impetus. He went to Vienna—whether sent by the elector or friends, or whether at his own expense is unknown—but he spent several weeks there, possibly even two or three months, and had a privilege that all succeeding generations must envy him—he met Mozart. Long afterwards some old acquaintance of Beethoven told Schindler (who became in a sort his Boswell in later days) that in Vienna 'two persons only were deeply impressed upon the lifelong memory of the youth of sixteen years: the Emperor Joseph II and Mozart.' The significance of the first lies in the fact that the emperor was that liberating prince who wished to abolish the death penalty, who restored the liberty of the press, and who actually suppressed the monasteries in order to give better amenities to the people. The story of the meeting with Mozart has often been told. Taken to visit the famous musician whom he so admired, Beethoven was asked by his hero to play to him. He obeyed. Mozart, thinking it 'a show piece prepared for the occasion,' praised it in rather a cool manner. Beethoven observing this, begged Mozart to give him a theme for improvisation. He always played admirably when excited. Inspired now by the presence of the master, he played in such a style that Mozart, whose attention and interest grew more and more, finally crossed to some friends in an adjoining room and said vivaciously: 'Keep your eyes on him; some day he will give the world something to talk about.'

It seems likely Mozart himself talked about the boy, and that it was through him that Haydn's curiosity was roused to write to Artaria the publisher (in a letter from Esterház): 'I should like to know who this Ludwig is.'

Mozart gave Beethoven some lessons, and it is supposed they were in composition. They confirmed the lad in his love of that Mozartian style which influenced many of his early works.

In June or early July Beethoven left Vienna. Most people do so still to escape the hot weather, but his reasons were more urgent. Madame van Beethoven was dangerously ill and his money was running out. At Augsburg he was obliged to borrow from Councillor Dr. von Schaden: and at each succeeding stage he found letters from Johann urging him to hasten. He arrived in Bonn, very unwell himself, to find his mother 'still alive, but in the weakest possible state: she was dying of consumption, and the end came about seven weeks ago, after she had endured much pain and suffering,' as he wrote to Schaden in September. The actual date of her death was 17th July. To Ludwig the tragedy must have seemed as ghastly as needless. She was only forty —still a young woman as years go—but so exhausted by the long struggle of life with Johann that there is no need to doubt the authenticity of her portrait merely on the ground that in it she looks eighty. Beside three sons living, there was also a baby daughter, Maria Margaretha Josepha, born as recently as 1786. Three other children had died when very young, from malnutrition, one supposes, due to insufficient food, due to insufficient money, due to Johann's drunkard habits. Johann, of course, ascribed his poverty to misfortunes and to his poor wife's illness. But for the help given by good Franz Ries, a friend, things would have been desperate. So little money was available that Maria Magdalena's grave could not be secured to her in perpetuity. For over a century it disappeared. At length in 1932 Herr Heinrich Baum, a great-grandson of Beethoven's godmother, was found, who recollected some details of the grave in the Alter Friedhof; these indicated a spot close by the wall that abuts on the Bornheimerstrasse, marked by the headstone of an Italian priest or professor named Matari, who died at Bonn in 1826. Digging down, the investigators found it was indeed his grave, but digging deeper they came upon the skeleton of a woman—Maria Magdalena van Beethoven. Thus the mother of Beethoven rests in the same cemetery as Robert and Clara Schumann, Mathilde Wesendonck and Schopenhauer's sister. A monument has been erected by the authorities of the Beethovenhaus. It is a plain stone, bearing her name, the date of her death and her son's words: 'Sie war mir eine so gute liebenswürdige Mutter, meine beste Freundin.'

Beethoven had loved his mother profoundly. Her loss nearly wrecked his health. What passed between them at the end has never been told, but his after-actions make one think she confided to him the care of those other near and dear ones in whose service she had practically laid down her life. If so, he took the trust from her as sacred. Biographers have marvelled at his assuming responsibility for his father and brothers, have commented on his strong sense of the blood tie, and have condemned his possessive interference with his brothers' affairs later in Vienna. Tepid generalities are of no use in explaining any warmly alive, sensitive human being: how much less a Beethoven! The true explanations of his actions lie locked in his heart. But the probability of his having promised his mother to guard the moral and physical well-being of the family is strengthened by the charge his brother Karl laid upon him many years later in the guardianship of young Karl, the nephew whom Beethoven watched over with cyclonic affection and despotism, and who, in return, nearly broke his uncle's heart.

For some time after Maria Magdalena's death Beethoven remained in a troubled slough of sorrow. He wrote to Schaden on 15th September: 'For the whole time I have been plagued with asthma; and I am inclined to fear that this malady may even turn to consumption. Furthermore, I have been suffering from melancholia, which in my case is almost as great a torture as my illness. . . . My journey has cost me a good deal and I cannot hope for any compensation here, not even in the smallest way. Fortune does not favour me here at Bonn.'

Johann van Beethoven had meantime sent a petition to the elector for an advance of a hundred *Reichsthaler* on his salary, since 'he has got into a very unfortunate state because of the long continued sickness of his wife, and has already been compelled to sell a portion of his effects and pawn others.' The elector took possession of the petition: there is no record that he did anything. He probably thought Johann's poverty had other causes. At any rate, when Johann died six years later, the elector wrote sardonically to the Count Marshall von Schall: 'The revenues from the liquor excise have suffered a loss in the deaths of Beethoven and Eichoff.'

If the portraits of Johann and Maria Magdalena now in the Beethovenhaus at Bonn are genuine, they must have been painted not long before Frau van Beethoven's death, for they show her as wasted by illness, and Johann with that indefinable coarsening and slackening of the features that follows upon drinking or fast living. Some authorities do not admit the pictures as authentic. But this much may be said for them: the painter, Beckenkamp, is known to have lived in Bonn in 1784 and 1785; he was a friend of the Beethovens, and the fact that the portraits were not in Beethoven's possession at Vienna is inconclusive, because many of the family effects were sold or pawned before he went there.

After Madame van Beethoven's death a housekeeper was employed to 'do' for the strange household of a drunken father, three sons, aged seventeen, thirteen and eleven, and the baby daughter of one year. Margarethe must have pined for her mother, for the poor mite died in November 1787. Johann went downhill steadily and by 1789 affairs had reached a point at which Ludwig, not yet nineteen, was compelled to become legally, as well as morally, the head of the family. In reply to a petition the elector issued a decree, dated 20th November 1789, that 'having graciously granted the prayer of the petitioner and dispensed henceforth wholly with the services of his father, who is to withdraw to a village in the electorate, it is graciously commanded that he be paid in accordance with his wish only 100 *Reichsthaler* of the annual salary which he has had heretofore, beginning with the approaching new year, and that the other 100 *Reichsthaler* be paid to the suppliant's son besides the salary which he now draws and the three measures of grain for the support of his brothers.'

Johann had lost the power to stop himself spending every' thing on drink. He dragged his sons through humiliation. Stephan von Breuning, one of Ludwig's friends, recollected seeing Ludwig 'furiously interposing to rescue his drunken father from an officer of police.'

Through all this black time the friends were the bright spot. Bit by bit, thanks to their efforts, Ludwig was brought back to cheerfulness and health, and it needs no clairvoyance to see that they were quietly active behind the scenes in securing for him opportunities to earn money—his great pride making charity intolerable. Foremost among these friends were the Breunings, a charming family. Since the death of her heroic husband, Madame von Breuning and her four children, Christoph, Eleonore, Stephan and Lorenz (Lenz), had lived with her brother Abraham von Kerich and her brother-in-law Lorenz von Breuning (canons of Bonn and highly intellectual men), in a house on the Münsterplatz. They drew Beethoven right into their family circle. The young people's ages ranged just below Beethoven's, and their avoca' tions were inextricably intermixed—Beethoven in his grown-up capacity teaching them music, while, as a boy himself, he shared their classical and literary studies. Franz Gerhard Wegeler, a young doctor, some years Beethoven's senior, was already an intimate of the household. Later he became the husband of Eleonore, and still later a biographer of Beethoven. Madame von Breuning mothered them all. She was a rare woman, with intuition to recognize Beethoven's inherent greatness and the wisdom to prevent him believing himself already a great man. It was Madame von Breuning who coined the phrase, when Beethoven was in one of his impossible moods: 'He is in a raptus'; and he said of her quaintly, when she showed him the worthlessness of flatteries: 'She knew how to keep the insects off the flowers.'

Eleonore was as fine a character as her mother, or even finer, and as true a friend to Beethoven. I have sometimes wondered whether it was a welcome coincidence that the magnificent Leonore in his opera *Fidelio* came so near to bearing her name. Indeed Beethoven actually began a letter, written on 2nd November 1793, with the words: 'Adorable Eleonore! My dearest friend!' One might push the speculation a long way. Did Beethoven see himself in the captive hero Florestan? If he had not known that Wegeler was in love with her, might he have allowed himself to become a suitor as soon as he made his place in the world? That he and Eleonore later had a violent misunderstanding disproves nothing; anger never flames more swiftly than when love burns beneath.

But in these early days at Bonn such difficulties had not arisen. The happy group of young people made music, scribbled poetry and went for long rambles in that lovely Rhine country of which Beethoven wrote to Wegeler in 1801: 'My fatherland, the beautiful country where I first opened my eyes to the light, still seems to me as lovely and as clearly before my eyes as it was when I left you.' His transient, romantic adorations for Fräulein Jeanette d'Honrath or Fräulein Wester- hold but added to the enjoyment. They were pretty girls.

It was all an extraordinarily civilizing experience for Beethoven, counteracting the tumults of his home and the servitude of the elector's court.

Most young people pass through a stage when their sym- pathies are entirely with the revolutionary element and against the conservative; just as the majority of people become con- servative in old age. Beethoven's sympathies were peculiarly liberal, and his youth coincided with the greatest movement for freedom the world had known. This little volume has no space to deal with the French Revolution and the tremendous forces unloosed by the ideas of liberty, equality and fraternity; but they must be taken into account, for they affected Beethoven profoundly. Had they not done so, he would not have been Beethoven. Their noblest results were seen later in the chain of heroic works, beginning with his *Prometheus*; their less admirable effects in his rude assumption of equality with his princely patrons—a type of self-assertion as unnecessary as undignified. Beethoven was great enough to hold his own as peer of any man by simply being himself.

Reading the stories of Beethoven's behaviour to the Viennese nobility in the last decade of the eighteenth century it is impossible to acquit him of deliberately adopting a tone similar to that of the French patriots towards their aristocrats. One recognizes the same cadences of speech, though with Beethoven they were less vitriolic and mixed with a kind of pose intended to impress people. In his Bonn days these traits were only sufficiently developed to put him at his ease with his first aristocratic intimate, the Count Ferdinand von Waldstein—now famous as the dedicatee of Beethoven's Sonata, Op. 53, but then a young Maecenas who came to Bonn in 1787 to enter the Teutonic Order. Beethoven had been introduced to him, possibly by the Breunings, or he may have attracted Waldstein's attention during the performance of his duties in the electoral band, as Waldstein was the favourite companion of the elector. He was a keen amateur of music and but eight years Beethoven's senior. Considerations of rank were forgotten; the two young men struck up a great friendship. Waldstein would come round to Beethoven's room in the Wenzelgasse and together they made glorious noises for hours on end and were as gloriously happy. Waldstein gave Beethoven a piano; he also contrived to help the proud Beethoven under guise of gratuities from the elector. Beethoven, on his side, was willing to 'ghost' for Waldstein. The music of the *Ritterballet*, produced by the nobility on

Carnival Sunday, 6th March 1791, was ostensibly by Waldstein, but in reality by Beethoven.

During these last years of the old regime a new vitality had come into the orchestra at Bonn. The elector had recruited a number of brilliant young musicians, including the two Rombergs, and the playing was now so good as to approach that of the famous Mannheim orchestra. A chaplain, named Junker, who saw and heard the band in 1791, describes it thus:

It would be difficult to find another orchestra in which the violins and basses are throughout in such excellent hands. . . . The members of the chapel, almost without exception, are in their best years, glowing with health, men of culture and fine personal appearance. They form a truly fine sight, when one adds the rplendid uniform in which the elector has clothed them—red, and richly trimmed with gold.

Beethoven in red and gold! Yet no doubt he wore it, for he was now a viola player in the opera orchestra, which Max Franz had organized in 1789. He found his colleagues stimulating and congenial, and in turn he was popular with them. They rightly regarded him as a great pianist. Junker, who heard him extemporize, refers to him as 'the dear, good Bethofen' (Junker's own spelling), and speaks of 'the greatness of this amiable, light-hearted man' with his

almost inexhaustible wealth of ideas, the altogether characteristic style of expression in his playing, and the great execution he displays. . . . Yet he is exceedingly modest and free from all pretensions. . . . His style of treating his instrument is so different from that usually adopted, that it impresses one with the idea that .by a path of his own discovery he has attained that height of excellence whereon he now stands.

Beethoven, in fact, was enjoying life at this time. He had professional colleagues worthy of his steel, to whom such a meeting as that arranged between himself and Sterkel—the famous pianist — was intensely interesting (especially as Beethoven had much the best of it). They were all good fellows, ready for any game. When the elector took them to Mergentheim, they whiled away the long days of the journey up the Rhine and Main by keeping a mock court on their barge among themselves. Bernard Romberg and Beethoven were appointed scullions!

Socially they made the most of any excitement that offered. For example, when Todi, the charming *prima donna,* visited Bonn, they gave her a serenade; and when Haydn passed through on his way to England, they entertained him with a Mass of his own in the church and a right royal dinner (at the elector's expense) in his own lodgings, 26th December 1790. On his return visit, in the summer of 1792, the orchestra gave Haydn a breakfast at Godesberg, a lovely spot opposite the Siebengebirge.

For Beethoven these Haydn visits had more than common importance, and at Godesberg Beethoven laid before him a cantata 'which received the particular attention of Haydn, who encouraged its author to continue study.'

Most biographers agree in thinking that the plan for Beethoven to go to Vienna as Haydn's pupil originated about this time. It is a mistake to suppose that Beethoven had composed little up to now, or that his music was that of a tyro. Inexperienced, partially self-taught, undisciplined he might be, but already the authentic Beethoven was to be heard in his Cantatas on the death of Joseph II (1790), the accession of Leopold II (1790) and the string Trio in E flat major known as Op. 3 (1792). By a fantastic chance this last found its way to England with the refugee chaplain of the elector—the Abbé Dobbeler—in 1793. It so transported with delight good William Gardiner of Leicester that when he went to London he inquired for other compositions by

Beethoven, 'but could learn nothing more than that he was a madman and his music was like himself.'

Many things belonging to Beethoven's Bonn period have been unearthed, or identified from among his later publications. There is even ground for believing that the first idea for the Choral Symphony came to him here. One marvels that he composed so much in these years. A man who is doing daily work as orchestral player or organist, to say nothing of the drudgery of teaching, has a drain upon his vitality that few composers are strong enough to carry. Composition is no light pastime to take up or put down at leisure; it is a tremendous, concentrated demand upon a composer's whole being.

By the autumn of 1792 the plan had become settled that Beethoven should go to Haydn in Vienna, with leave of absence on a salary granted him by the elector. Public affairs, however, were anything but settled. For two years the French Revolution had been disturbing Bonn. The sound of French armies was already audible. Aristocratic refugees kept casting themselves on the unfortunate elector, who as continually strove to pass them on and to remain neutral. His struggles grew frantic after the declaration of war between Austria and France (April 1792). By October 1792 a French revolutionary army was marching on the Rhine. German refugees began to roll in from Coblenz, the people of Bonn formed a citizen guard, the Treasury removed to Düsseldorf and on 31st October the elector himself fled to Cleve.

In this hurly-burly Beethoven packed up and bid adieu to his friends. He took with him an autograph-book in which they wrote their greetings. The dates show that the Breunings were the last people visited. Waldstein's entry is made on 29th October 1792, Eleonore von Breuning's on 1st November. She inscribed some lines from Herder: 'Friendship, with that which is good, grows like the evening

shadow till the sun of life sinks. Your true friend, ELEONORE
VON BREUNING.'

The post left Bonn for Vienna at 6 a.m. In the dark of
the morning on 2nd or 3rd November Beethoven set out,
travelling with a companion who may have been Libisch,
the oboe player. At Coblenz Beethoven noted in his pocket-
book that he gave the postilion as *Trinkgeld* one small thaler,
'because the fellow drove like the devil right through the
Hessian army at the risk of a cudgelling.' The French army
was advancing upon Mainz and Limburg. Travelling in
war-time is an unchancy business. In haste and shadow
Beethoven began the journey from which he was never to return.

CHAPTER IV

BEETHOVEN arrived in Vienna on some date between 4th and 10th November 1792. From now onwards the Austrian capital became his home. At a period when music was fashionable in most great cities, Vienna stood high above all others by the splendour of its professional musicians, the cultivation of its connoisseurs and the prodigality of those princely patrons who vied with each other in the maintenance of house ·orchestras and chamber-music organizations. If public concerts were few, opera was a constant factor, and the private concerts in the palaces of the nobility were an ideal ground on which to make music and meet musicians. Some idea of the prizes open to composers may be gained when we remember that Haydn's oratorio *The Creation* and Beethoven's *Eroica* Symphony both had their first performances in private, one at the Schwarzenberg Palace, the other by Prince Lichnowsky's orchestra.

This was the world in which Beethoven proposed to make his way, leaving his father and brothers in Bonn provided for, as he thought, by his father's pension. Nothing worked according to plan. The hundred ducats Beethoven had counted on finding at Vienna were not there. On 18th December, two days after Beethoven's twenty-second birthday, his father died at Bonn. The discovery was then made that Johann had embezzled (no doubt for drink) the portion of money allocated to maintain Karl and Johann junior. Political affairs went from bad to worse. The movements of French revolutionary armies kept poor Elector Max Franz fleeing or returning to Bonn and his electorate like an episcopal

parched pea on a plate. His exchequer was jeopardized.
By June 1793 his payments to Beethoven had ceased. By
1794 Max Franz too had left Bonn for ever, and in 1797 the
electorate was incorporated in the French Republic.

For Beethoven the situation would have been desperate
but that here, as in Bonn, the right friends came at the right
time. Someone—probably the Elector Max Franz or Count
von Waldstein—had given him valuable introductions which
took him straight into the best circles. Another helping
hand, I feel sure, was that of Haydn, who had fought poverty
himself for eight dreadful years. If an entry in Beethoven's
pocket-book—'Haidn 8 groschen'—relates to a lesson, then
the famous man was taking his pupil for a peppercorn fee;
eight groschen being about ninepence-halfpenny English
money. There is something too very Haydnish in Beethoven's
choice of a lodging—first an attic, then a ground-floor room
of the same house where Prince Lichnowsky lived. I suspect
Haydn of telling Beethoven to adopt the policy (or was it
strategy?) he himself had employed forty years earlier,
when he planted himself under the same roof as Metastasio
the poet, and secured thereby a good address and (presently)
a patron. Such things were possible in old Vienna, for the
great buildings were palaces on the *bel étage*, official dwellings
on the second floor, and then dwindled in distinction as they
rose, till almost any poor wretch might rent a garret under
the roof. Once again the charm worked: before long Prince
Karl Lichnowsky had taken Beethoven into his own lodging.

For us, Beethoven the composer is so important that he
rather blocks our view of the beginning of his career. But
during his first years in Vienna he was esteemed mainly as an
executive artist—a solo pianist of extraordinary skill and
daring, a mighty extemporizer and a teacher who soon
attracted pupils from among the most brilliant young professionals and the most elegant young ladies of the *noblesse*.

The tradition runs that he made his reputation by his 'superb playing of Bach's *Well-tempered Clavier*,' a reputation enhanced by his performance of his own piano works. He clinched it by his contests with the renowned pianists Gelinek, Wölfl and Steibelt. Gelinek emerged from the experience completely 'debounced,' and reported afterwards: 'He [Beethoven] is no man; he's a devil. He will play me and all of us to death. And how he improvises!' From which it will be seen that his fellow-pianists hardly loved him.

This sort of thing only added to the zest of life for a young man living as an honoured guest in Prince Lichnowsky's house, with a horse and groom of his own (which he forgot!), a salary of six hundred gulden a year and his feelings so considered that the servants had orders to answer his bell before the prince's. Further, Prince Lichnowsky specially practised Beethoven's piano works to prove to the world they were playable, and placed his string quartet of fine professional players at his service.

Prince Lobkowitz, another *magnifico* of music, and about Beethoven's own age, also became intimate with him. The Freiherr van Swieten (friend of Haydn and Mozart), Count Moritz Lichnowsky (brother of the prince) and Baron von Gleichenstein were personal and patronal friends. The Freiherr Zmeskall von Domanowecz, a precise official in the Royal Hungarian Court Chancellery, fell for life beneath Beethoven's spell and was perfectly happy to be his butt and to cut his pens for him, Beethoven being clumsy with his hands over everything save music. Schuppanzigh and Krumpholz the violinists, Hummel the pianist, Häring, Eppinger, Kiesewetter the singer, Amenda the young theologian, formed a second circle of devoted friends, to which presently were added intimates from Bonn days: Wegeler, Reicha, Stephan and Lorenz von Breuning. Few men have ever been so rich in friendship.

Meantime Beethoven was studying hard. He had begun his lessons under Haydn on arrival in Vienna; they continued for over a year, Haydn showing his pupil more kindness than biographers have been willing to admit. That the lessons were not a success and that relations were strained between the two men supports my statement, since Beethoven seldom accepted obligations with a good grace. We know from a letter of Beethoven's own that Haydn took him for a long visit to Prince Esterházy's country seat at Eisenstadt in the early summer of 1793, a most useful trip for a young man making his way. Haydn also wished to take him to England. The latter project fell through, and Haydn departed in January 1794 with Elssler as a valet-copyist (imagine the sort of a valet Beethoven would have made!), leaving Beethoven free to betake himself openly to the famous pedagogue, Albrechts-berger, just as, *sub rosa,* he had already gone to Schenk in search of stricter tuition.

The lessons with Albrechtsberger continued till 1795. Beethoven also began an intermittent course of study under Salieri, Mozart's old rival, in vocal composition, verbal accent, rhythm, metre, etc., and later learned a good deal about quartet writing from Aloys Förster.

Ferdinand Ries (son of Franz) came to Beethoven as a pupil while still a lad. He knew these early years at first hand and recalled the relations between Haydn, Albrechts-berger, Salieri and Beethoven thus:

I knew them all well; all three valued Beethoven highly, but were also of one mind touching his habits of study. All of them said Beethoven was so headstrong and self-sufficient [*selbstwollend*] that he had to learn much through harsh experience which he had refused to accept when it was presented to him as a subject for study.

And Thayer adds: 'Particularly Albrechtsberger and Salieri were of this opinion.' Haydn, as the greater man, saw deeper.

Beethoven was bound to be a difficult pupil, for his work, though far advanced in some directions, was very backward in others, a result of his haphazard training in Bonn. This had to be corrected. The amount of elementary counterpoint he ground through before passing on to fugue would horrify modern students, but Beethoven wanted it, and knew he wanted it. Funny as it seems, like Satan reproving sin, his complaint against Haydn was that the lessons were too slack!

It is no use employing a razor to chop wood! Haydn was a great composer, not a pedagogue. The mistake lay in expecting him to give Beethoven's unplastic technique the heavy malling it needed before it could become an obedient tool. But in free composition Haydn may well have been one of those best teachers who make pupils do things for themselves. Judged by that criterion he succeeded brilliantly with the 'Grand Mogul,' as he called Beethoven. But Beethoven refused point-blank to be named his pupil. 'Though I had some instruction from Haydn, I never learned anything from him,' said he.

He did owe much to Haydn. Any one can see it who compares their compositions. If in matters of form and style Beethoven's early music was modelled on that of Mozart, Haydn was the starting-point for some of his boldest harmonic strokes, even in his mature work. Too much has been written of the differences and not enough of the debts between the two men. Admit that Beethoven was impatient and suspicious of Haydn's advice over publication; admit that Haydn was self-complacent and displeased by Beethoven's arrogance: what does the affair amount to when a couple of anecdotes crystallize the worst and best of it?

In the one, Haydn (whose *Creation* was still in the first flush of its success) met Beethoven just after his ballet *Die Geschöpfe des Prometheus* had been produced. Haydn stopped him and said: 'Well, I heard your ballet yesterday and it pleased me very much!' Beethoven replied: 'Oh, dear Papa, you are very kind; but it is far from being a *Creation*.' Haydn, surprised at the answer and almost offended, said after a short pause: 'That is true; it is not yet a *Creation*, and I can scarcely believe it will ever become one.' (Which is even more witty when one knows German and the scenario of *Prometheus*.)

The other story belongs to 1808, and is the last moment at which history shows Haydn and Beethoven together. Haydn, old and helpless, had been taken to the gala performance of the *Creation* at the university. Intensely moved by the music and his reception, he was being wheeled out at the end of the first part. The nobility thronged round him with praise and greetings. Beethoven came among them and, stooping, fervently kissed Haydn's hand and forehead. By now he was great enough to be humble.

Humility is the last word, however, that could be assigned to the Beethoven of 1792–1800. Rather was he like Lucifer, a son of the morning, glorying in his power. And what a morning! The world had once again that dawn look of being new-made. Democracy and its ideals were mounting to full tide in France, and the young Napoleon was rising as the greatest leader in a millennium. Beethoven watched, knowing that in himself too lay some such capacity to conquer the world. His interest intensified after General Bernadotte arrived in Vienna in 1798 and became an intimate acquaintance. Noble ideals had always attracted Beethoven: now *power* became predominantly his creed. There is bare truth behind his banter when in a letter to Zmeskall (1798) he says: 'The devil take you, I refuse to hear anything about your whole moral outlook. *Power* is the moral principle of those who excel others, and it is also mine; and if you start off again today on the same lines, I will thoroughly pester you until you consider everything I do to be good and praiseworthy.'

As a matter of fact Beethoven's conduct was *not* all good and praiseworthy in these years. His morality of Power led him into quarrels with his truest friends, rudeness to his patrons and (if the conclusions of some doctors are to be trusted) into a lapse from sexual morality that later brought on him its retribution. Even in 1796 he wrote to his brother Johann: 'I hope that you will enjoy living in Vienna more and more. But do be on your guard against the whole tribe of bad women.' Had Beethoven already become the burnt child who dreads the fire?

His brothers had come to Vienna in 1795, after the debacle at Bonn. He had no false pride about acknowledging them in spite of his social successes, and helped both with money until they could earn their own livings, Karl as *Kassa-Officier* in the Staatsschuldenkasse and Johann as an apothecary.

Also it is just to say there was more wisdom in Beethoven's inconsiderateness towards Prince Lichnowsky than appeared on the surface. After the liveried servitude of the Bonn orchestra it was a giddy emancipation to be a free inmate of a palace, but even here there were rules. Wegeler relates that the prince's dinner hour was fixed at four o'clock. 'Now,' said Beethoven, 'it is desired that every day I shall be home at half-past three, put on better clothes, care for my beard, etc.—I can't stand that!'

Wegeler thought this mere waywardness. But Beethoven was right. The times and seasons of a creative artist do not follow the clock. If to Prince Lichnowsky and his suite punctuality seemed the keystone of their code, to posterity one work by Beethoven is more important than all the dinners they ever ate.

As the creative power in Beethoven strengthened, he hoped for a home of his own. He was always in love with some pretty girl or other, and had been so ever since Bonn days, as his men friends knew. But in 1795 his feelings for

41

Magdalena Willmann, a charming singer, were serious enough for him to propose marriage. She refused, because 'he was ugly and half crazy.' The disappointment did not prove lasting. The intended home simply became independent lodgings. Work went on as usual. Beethoven made his first public appearance in Vienna with his own piano Concerto in B flat major, Op. 19, at the Burgtheater (at a concert in aid of the widows of members of the Tonkünstler-Gesellschaft), and in 1796 he went on a concert tour to Prague and Berlin, which perhaps included Dresden and Leipzig. On 21st June Beethoven appeared at the meeting of the Berlin Singakademie. 'A chorale, the first three numbers of the mass (by Fasch, in sixteen parts) and the first six of the 119th Psalm were sung for him. Hereupon he seated himself at the pianoforte and played an improvisation on the theme of the final fugue.' It made an overpowering impression on the audience, who crowded round him weeping. He was disgusted. 'That is not what we artists wish—we want applause!' he told Bettina von Arnim years afterwards.

Beethoven, at the zenith of his powers as a pianist, gave his own first public concert in Vienna, 2nd April 1800, and projected extended and triumphant tours. A number of his compositions had been published. Among his best known works composed up till now were the Symphony No. 1 in C major; two piano Concertos (C major and B flat major); the three piano Trios, Op. 1; three piano Sonatas, Op. 2; two Sonatas for piano and violoncello, Op. 5; the piano Sonatas, Opp. 7, 10, 13, 14; the Sonatas for piano and violin, Op. 12; the string Trios, Opp. 3, 8, 9; his famous song, *Adelaide*; the scena *Ah! perfido*; and a bunch of smaller things. To his contemporaries these works seemed daring: to us they appear charming with occasional signs of the later man. They form a group fairly homogeneous in style, and for purposes of convenience critics have classed them into what they call Beethoven's first period. Lovely as they are, they would not, on their own merits, have given Beethoven supreme rank. Had he died at thirty, had he carried out his design of becoming a travelling virtuoso, he would never have fulfilled his greatness. Composition is a jealous art, requiring all a man's vitality. In the life of a virtuoso allegiance is divided. Beethoven might have become an earlier Liszt. He was saved from that fate by what appeared at the time his greatest disaster.

CHAPTER V

THE UNHAPPIEST OF GOD'S CREATURES

THE calendar may be a convention, but in the transition from one century to another there is something decisive that suggests crossing the Rubicon. Never was this more true than of the change from the eighteenth to the nineteenth century— a transition so marked that it might have been an isthmus between two worlds. Strangely—or perhaps not strangely, seeing how much Beethoven was an embodiment of his times —this transition synchronized with a great change in his own inner life.

Up to the end of the eighteenth century he had been the young man of genius, arrogant in his conscious power, riding his turbulent nature upon those winds of liberty, equality and fraternity that had blown away old classes and creeds in France, even if up to now his compositions had not been more than the beautiful consummations of eighteenth-century ideals. Looking at him in 1799, Beethoven's friends might well have felt that he had no anxieties and only success left to anticipate. Financially he was secure; Prince Lichnowsky had set aside a fixed sum of six hundred florins for him to draw against so long as he was without an official position worthy of him; his compositions brought him in a good income and more commissions than he could fulfil; his prestige as a solo pianist was at its zenith, and his wide circle of aristocratic patrons, pupils and intimate friends gave him the *entrée* to the best society in Vienna. His brother's severe illness had had a happy issue; Beethoven's own health, poor in the past, was now improving, and even his 'lacerated heart' of six months earlier had recovered from the Demoiselle Willmann's rejection.

Actually as 1799 passed into 1800 Beethoven crossed the Rubicon that sundered him for ever from his hoped-for career as a virtuoso, and divided his creative work from its 'first period.' Already for two years a horrible spectre had been lurking in his mind: the fear would not be beaten off; it was a disaster that advanced upon him as relentlessly as the Commandant's statue on Don Giovanni, and he was as powerless to avert it. He, Beethoven, whose hearing had been to him his 'noblest faculty,' was becoming deaf! It was a hideous, an unthinkable catastrophe. At first it was slight and passed for absent-mindedness. By 1800 it had so increased that Beethoven avoided all social gatherings from the sick fear of detection. In the summer of 1801 Beethoven realized there was no likelihood of cure and saw that his career as a pianist was probably ruined. It was a mental agony all the fiercer in that for the most part he suffered in silence. Only to Amenda and Wegeler did he give a glimmering of his torment, and to them not for two years. Writing to Amenda on 1st July 1801, he says:

How often would I like to have you here with me, for your B[eethoven] is leading a very unhappy life and is at variance with Nature and his Creator. Many times already I have cursed Him for exposing His creatures to the slightest hazard, so that the most beautiful blossom is thereby often crushed and destroyed. Let me tell you that my most prized possession, *my hearing*, has greatly deteriorated.

In this letter, in spite of his misery, the old haughty Beethoven still speaks; the Beethoven who refers to some of his friends as 'instruments on which I play when I please.'

Yet all the time, beneath this Lucifer-pride, a profound spiritual change was taking place. As his outer hearing

45

failed, his inner hearing quickened. He felt that he had something for which he must live, even if he never played a note in public again. Where once in his music he had gone to poetry for an inspiration, he now began to find direct access to those well-springs of eternity to which only the greatest may come. Some stages of this tremendous struggle can be glimpsed in two letters to Wegeler, written in the same year. On 29th June 1801 he writes:

I must confess that I lead a miserable life. For almost two years I have ceased to attend any social functions, just because I find it impossible to say to people: I am deaf. If I had any other profession I might be able to cope with my infirmity; but in my profession it is a terrible handicap. And if my enemies, of whom I have a fair number, were to hear about it, what would they say? . . . Already I have often cursed my Creator and my existence. *Plutarch* has shown me *the path of resignation*. If it is at all possible, I will bid defiance to my fate, though I feel that as long as I live there will be moments when I shall be God's most unhappy creature—I beg you not to say anything about my condition to anyone, not even to *Lorchen*.[1] . . . I live entirely in my music; and hardly have I completed one composition when I have already begun another. At my present rate of composing, I often produce three or four works at the same time.

Then on 16th November Beethoven wrote again to Wegeler:

I am now leading a slightly more pleasant life, for I am mixing more with my fellow creatures. You would find it hard to believe what an empty, sad life I have had for the last two years. My poor hearing haunted me everywhere like a ghost; and I avoided—all human society. I seemed to be a misanthrope and yet am far from being one. This change has been brought about by a dear charming girl who loves me and whom I love. After two years I am again enjoying a few blissful moments; and for the first time I feel that—marriage might bring me happiness. Unfortunately she is not of my class—and at the moment—I certainly could not marry. . . . Had it

---

[1] Eleonore von Breuning, who became the wife of Dr. Wegeler in March 1802.

not been for my deafness, I should have long ago travelled half the world over; and that I must do. . . . Do not imagine that I should be happy living with you at Bonn. In any case what is there to make me any happier? Even your anxiety would hurt me. Every moment I should see your face expressing pity and should only feel more unhappy. . . . Oh, if only I could be rid of it I would embrace the whole world[1]—My youth, yes, I feel it, is only just beginning, for was I not always a sickly fellow? For some time now my physical strength has been increasing more and more, and therefore my mental powers also. Every day brings me nearer to the goal which I feel but cannot describe. And it is only in that condition that your Beethoven can live. There must be no rest. . . . If only I can be partially liberated from my affliction, then—I will come to you as a complete and mature man, and renew our old feelings of friendship. You will find me as happy as I am fated to be on this earth, not unhappy—no, that I could not bear—I will seize Fate by the throat; it shall certainly not bend and crush me completely—Oh, it would be so lovely to live a thousand lives.

'So lovely to live.' When Beethoven cries out those words, one hears the same cry echoing from a century later when a poet puts it into the mouth of a woman. 'Why, Life is sweet,' says Pervaneh in Flecker's *Hassan*, and says it even beyond death, because she loves.

Beethoven gave no name to his lady. We have none for her now, but the probabilities point to a fascinating girl of seventeen, Giulietta Guicciardi, noble in birth, a cousin of the young Countesses Josephine and Therese von Brunswick, who were already Beethoven's pupils. Giulietta took lessons from him too. Though the last to come, she was the first in this lovely trilogy to capture his heart. Like Shakespeare's Juliet she kindled as swiftly to romance as she roused it in others; she may even have been the heroine of Beethoven's

[1] Note the connection of idea with the lines, 'Seid umschlungen, Millionen,' in the ninth Symphony.

famous love-letters, though the balance of evidence seems to place them six years farther on in his life. A possible claim can be made for Giulietta. The fact that Beethoven had originally dedicated the Rondo in G to her (was the initial intentional?), and then took it back to give to Countess Lichnowsky, giving Giulietta instead the so-called 'Moonlight' Sonata, proves nothing either way. He might even have felt the sonata more appropriate than the rondo if Thayer's contention is correct that the sonata was founded on Seume's poem *Die Beterin,* in which a young girl kneels in prayer before the high altar. Giulietta, being a minx, must have seemed the incarnation of artlessness! Again, though Beethoven's string Quartet in F major, Op. 18, no. 1, had been finished in its original form by the end of June 1799 (a date at which Giulietta *may* not yet have come to Vienna), it is at least worth remembering that Beethoven told Amenda the slow movement was founded upon the tomb scene in *Romeo and Juliet.* Giulietta=Juliet?

Whatever the course of Beethoven's love affair, during the winter of 1801 and the summer of 1802 fresh hope seems to have come to him. He changed his physician. The new one, Dr. Schmidt, ordered him to spare his hearing by living in country retirement at Heiligenstadt. It was then a charming village outside Vienna, with a view across meadows to the Danube and the far Carpathians. There Beethoven went into physical retreat while his spirit roamed into some of the happiest, brightest works of his life—perhaps as a refuge from hard, material realities. But the summer brought no improvement, and hope died within him. Also, a fresh blow. Giulietta's marriage to Count Gallenberg, a man in her own rank, was finally arranged. Given such a girl as Giulietta, nothing else could have been expected, but her behaviour hurt Beethoven bitterly. It was one more stone in a load of sorrow that brought him down near to the grave this autumn.

The Heiligenstadt Will

Whether he was so ill that he anticipated death, or whether he had not altogether mastered the temptation to suicide, no one will ever know; but on 6th October he wrote the 'Heiligenstadt Will'—a document designed for his brothers in what he felt to be the near event of his death. Every sentence vibrates with profound feeling:

O my fellow men, who consider me, or describe me as, unfriendly, peevish or even misanthropic, how greatly do you wrong me. For you do not know the secret reason why I appear to you to be so. Ever since my childhood my heart and soul have been imbued with the tender feeling of goodwill; and I have always been ready to per/ form even great actions. But just think, for the last six years I have been afflicted with an incurable complaint which has been made worse by incompetent doctors. From year to year my hopes of being cured have gradually been shattered and finally I have been forced to accept the prospect of a *permanent infirmity*. . . . Moreover my mis/ fortune pains me doubly, inasmuch as it leads to my being mis/ judged. For me there can be no relaxation in human society, no refined conversations, no mutual confidences. I must live quite alone and may creep into society only as often as sheer necessity demands; I must live like an outcast. . . .

I was on the point of putting an end to my life—The only thing that held me back was *my art*. For indeed it seemed to me impossible to leave this world before I had produced all the works that I felt the urge to compose; and thus I have dragged on this miserable existence. . . . *Patience*—that is the virtue, I am told, which I must now choose for my guide; and I now possess it—I hope that I shall persist in my resolve to endure to the end, until it pleases the inexor/ able Parcae to cut the thread; perhaps my condition will improve, perhaps not; at any rate I am now resigned—At the early age of 28 I was obliged to become a philosopher, though this was not easy; for indeed this is more difficult for an artist than for anyone else— Almighty God, who look down into my innermost soul, you see into my heart and you know that it is filled with love for humanity and a desire to do good.

After some charges to his brothers, he continues:

My wish is that you should have a better and more carefree existence than I have had. Urge your children to be *virtuous*, for virtue
alone can make a man happy. Money cannot do this. I speak from
experience. It was virtue that sustained me in my misery. It was
thanks to virtue and also to my art that I did not put an end to my
life by suicide—Farewell and love one another. . . . Joyfully I go to
meet Death—should it come before I have had an opportunity of
developing all my artistic gifts, then in spite of my hard fate it would
still come too soon, and no doubt I would like to postpone its
coming—Yet even so I should be content, for would it not free me
from a condition of continual suffering?

Four days later Beethoven, on the verge of leaving Heiligenstadt for Vienna, added the most heartbroken cry as postscript:

Heiligenstadt, October 10, 1802—Thus I take leave of you—and
what is more, rather sadly—yes, the hope I cherished—the hope I
brought with me here of being cured to a certain extent at any rate—
that hope I must now abandon completely. As the autumn leaves
fall and wither, likewise—that hope has faded for me. I am leaving
here—almost in the same condition as I arrived—Even that high
courage—which has often inspired me on fine summer days—has
vanished—Oh Providence—do but grant me one day *of pure joy*—
For so long now the inner echo of real joy has been unknown to me
—Oh when—oh when, Almighty God—shall I be able to hear and
feel this echo again in the temple of Nature and in contact with
humanity—Never?—No!—Oh, that would be too hard.

The disaster was as complete as any in a Greek tragedy, and
if biographers are right who believe that Beethoven's deafness
resulted from syphilis, then it also fulfilled the doctrine of
Nemesis. But there was in him something that transcended the
ethics of Aeschylus and Sophocles—something that set him
beside blind Homer and Virgil, whose high thoughts caught
and reflected 'the radiance of some mysterious and unrisen day.'
Like them, he could pass through tragedy to the greater
knowledge beyond, where birth and death, joy and sorrow,

are but different sides of the same golden coin of life minted by God in eternity.

Beethoven had walked the meadows of Heiligenstadt, and his mind had roamed the Elysian fields of music before he passed into the crisis of his black sorrow. It was a veritable going down into the valley of the shadow of death. But just before the path had gone down, he had seen, as sometimes happens in mountain regions, across the near gulf and intervening ranges, a radiant vision of distant mountains on the horizon — he had seen Joy. He has left us that vision in the passages of his D major Symphony which prefigure the Choral Symphony that was to come. He saw that vision because 'he always held his head high even when in pain,' as one of his biographers said of him.

Beethoven had entered the nineteenth century as the composer of the Symphony in C major. Toward the end of 1800 he had composed a ballet which must be considered in relation to his symphonic work, though few biographers have noticed all that is implied by *The Men* (or the Creations) *of Prometheus*. In it, as in his oratorio, *Christus am Ölberge* (Christ on the Mount of Olives), Beethoven occupied himself with the theme of a beneficent saviour of mankind. *Prometheus* was a turning-point in his career. His old style no longer contented him. Conventional religion Beethoven had none, but his mind was beginning to search into the deepest mysteries of the universe at the same time that he recognized the mission within himself which he must fulfil. The musician must be the liberator of mankind from sorrow. In those last weeks at Heiligenstadt Beethoven was brought down to the lowest point of his sorrow. It is in darkness, not daylight, that the stars are seen. In his blackest trouble Beethoven learned how to look straight into the face of God. The struggles, though now being fought upon an ascending plane, were not quickly over. Beethoven returned to Vienna for the winter and took up work with a rough energy and knock-about humour in which there was no happiness. Yet inwardly he must have known tremendous flashes of exaltation, for one of his grandest works, the *Eroica* Symphony, was now coming into being.

On 5th April 1803 Beethoven organized a concert of his own compositions at the Theater an der Wien. The programme contained the first and second Symphonies, the piano Concerto in C minor (soloist Beethoven) and the first performance of the oratorio *Christus am Ölberge*. The rehearsal was a penance. It began at 8 a.m.; by 2.30 every one was exhausted and angry. But for dear, kind Prince Lichnowsky (whom one grows to love as one sees him quietly watching over Beethoven like an undemanding providence) the day would have been a fiasco. He it was who thoughtfully provided baskets of bread and butter, meat and wine, fed the hungry men and persuaded them to try again. Even then the oratorio had not a great success. For once the crowd instinct was right: Beethoven had misjudged his style, as he himself admitted later. His treatment of the music for Christ was, he said, too modern; in other words, too secular and dramatic.

Whether the offer Beethoven received from Schikaneder (Mozart's old impresario) to compose an opera preceded or followed the début of the oratorio is not quite clear, but—funny as it seems—an idea got about that Beethoven would make a good operatic composer, because his oratorio had been too theatrical. However, the project fell through for the time, and Beethoven spent the summer at Baden and Unter-Döbling, hard at work on the *Eroica* Symphony. The first suggestion of a symphony on Napoleon had come from Bernadotte in 1798, while Napoleon was still First Consul. Beethoven admired him then, likening him to the great Roman consuls. Now he fused this ideal with his own belief in the musician as hero and benefactor of mankind. The result was a symphony of such importance that its discussion must be deferred till later, though one may note here that in it life was raised to a splendour and power hitherto unknown in music, and that the *Eroica* remained Beethoven's own favourite symphony even after the stupendous fifth and seventh had blazed out in their glory. But the *Eroica* did not please on a first hearing; it was too new, strange, difficult and original in its effects, said the critics. The faithful elect of wealthy amateurs stood by it, though. To his eternal honour Prince Lobkowitz bought the rights of performance not for one year—as was usual—but for several, and when Prince Louis Ferdinand of Prussia paid him a visit he entertained him with a performance.

The prince listened to it with tense attention which grew with every moment. At the close he proved his admiration by requesting the favour of an immediate repetition; and, after an hour's pause, as his stay was too limited to admit of another concert, a second. The impression made by the music was general, and its lofty contents were now recognized.

Lucky Louis Ferdinand!

This was apparently in 1804, a year in which Stephan von Breuning and Beethoven decided in May to share lodgings. Beethoven was already in an overstrung condition when the news was brought in by his pupil, Ries, that Napoleon had proclaimed himself emperor. A copy of the full score of the *Eroica* was on the table. Beethoven flashed up in anger, crying out: 'Is he then, too, nothing more than an ordinary human being? Now he too will trample on all the rights of man and indulge only his own ambition. He will exalt himself above all others, become a tyrant!' (Which is exactly what did happen.) 'Beethoven,' continues Ries, 'went to the table, took hold of the title-page by the top'—it contained the names 'Buonaparte' at the head and 'Luigi van

Beethoven' at the foot—'tore it in two and threw it on the floor,' thus sundering himself from Bonaparte for ever.

Anger always made Beethoven ill. He fell seriously ill now. Breuning nursed him devotedly. When after weeks the strain abated, both were so unstrung that one day early in July they quarrelled violently, and Beethoven departed to Baden and Döbling. In this affair Breuning, not Beethoven, came out as the hero, for he uttered no reproaches, though Beethoven must have been an appalling patient. One can see it from what Breuning said—and did not say—in his letter to Dr. Wegeler on 13th November:

He who has been my friend from youth is often largely to blame that I am compelled to neglect the absent ones. You cannot conceive, my dear Wegeler, what an indescribable, I might say, fearful, effect the gradual loss of hearing has had upon him. Think of the feeling of being unhappy in one of such violent temperament; in addition reservedness, mistrust, often towards his best friends, in many things want of decision. For the greater part, with only an occasional exception when he gives free vent to his feelings on the spur of the moment, intercourse with him is a real exertion, at which one can hardly trust to oneself. Worry and the care of him tried me rather severely. Now he is completely well again.

The quarrel was typical of the worst in Beethoven, the reconciliation was typical of the best. He was great enough to recognize he could have been wrong, and noble enough to humble himself to an apology. Some biographers think he blamed himself overmuch at times, but he knew better than they the depth of the hurt he had to heal. Beethoven hardly ever lost a friend.

It can also be said there was hardly ever a time when he was not in love. The bright star of this year was the Countess Josephine von Deym, who has already been mentioned as the sister of Therese von Brunswick and cousin of Giulietta Guicciardi. Josephine had been married against her will,

while yet in her teens, to a man twice her age. At the end
of 1803 he died, leaving her, an exquisite young widow, with
four children, fragile health, and financial worries with which
she was quite unable to deal. In the first months of her
widowhood, Therese (who loved Josephine passionately)
came to her and tried to help her in the care of the children,
and the summer of 1804 was spent in the country. By
accident or design Beethoven took up his quarters near by,
and saw much of the charming, exotic Josephine. No
one now can tell certainly the thoughts of their hearts, but
reading the facts from a woman's point of view, it would
seem that Beethoven was the real cause of the tension
which developed between Therese and Josephine. Both were
powerfully attracted to Beethoven; he in return was attracted
by the sisters, though Josephine (more accomplished in
matters of charm and finesse) held first place. Therese meanwhile had the double pain of feeling herself supplanted
in Josephine's love by Beethoven, and in Beethoven's by
Josephine. Things came to a breaking-point in this summer
of 1804.

I still feel all the bitterness, the pain and the despair that took
possession of me [wrote Therese] when after several attempts [to
live together] she told me for the last time that she could not keep
me with her, that I dragged her down, that I hindered her from
advancing and that, in her sick state, with four children to look
after, it was impossible for her to have the influence on me that
she would have liked. . . . I went away, and thought I was
separated from her for ever.

Josephine knew Therese was a formidable rival.

Therese, cast out from Josephine and Beethoven's little
world of two, flung herself into a love affair with a young
officer, 'Toni,' whose admiration and courtship apparently
offered some balm to her miserable heart. From November
1804 she carried on a passionate correspondence with Toni.

But her family disapproved of the match; a year later he was killed, and all that was left Therese was to write a fierce cry for vengeance on his slayers, the French. It did not ring quite true.

Meantime the summer of 1804 wore into autumn and the friendship between Josephine and Beethoven intensified. With winter it reached a bright glow. Through the correspondence between Therese and Charlotte (a younger sister) one can watch the successive stages. 'Beethoven is extraordinarily amiable; he comes every day and stays with Pepi [Josephine] for hours,' writes Charlotte on 20th November. A month later she thinks: 'This is becoming a little dangerous. . . . Beethoven is here almost every day.' In January poor Therese writes asking: 'But tell me, what is going to happen with Pepi and Beethoven. She must look out.'

The Brunswick family, though devoted to Beethoven as a friend, had no intention of allowing him to become Josephine's husband; they were of the nobility, he of the people, and Therese had her own reasons for wishing the affair ended. Interference—and possibly a recognition by Josephine of the untamed and untamable nature of Beethoven—cooled their intercourse into something near an estrangement. Neither of them suffered permanently. Only poor Therese reproached herself years afterwards and wrote in her journal (1847): 'Beethoven . . . he who was so very like her in spirit! . . . Josephine's friend in house and heart! They were born for each other, and had they been united, they would have been living now.'

Did Beethoven love Josephine greatly?

Certainly some of his most beautiful works belong to the period when Josephine was his confidante before all others. Early in 1804 he had been commissioned by Schikaneder to compose an opera for the Theater an der Wien. He chose for his libretto the theme of a wife's courage and constancy and her husband's rescue from death. It was a heroic story; the only one that ever really pleased him for an opera, his sturdy morals revolting from such plots as served Mozart in *Don Giovanni* and *Figaro*. Beethoven's opera was called *Fidelio*. Some writers have suggested Josephine as the model for its heroine, Leonora. If she was, then all I can say is that a woman who had not the grit to accept Beethoven or to refuse him could never have been a Leonora. Yet she warmed his imagination. Indeed he was never nearer writing true love music than in these years of the composition of *Fidelio* with its three overtures to *Leonora*; the Sonata in F minor, Op. 57 (the Appassionata); and the fourth Symphony in B flat major.

Work on *Fidelio* was extraordinarily exacting—even for that terrific worker Beethoven—and occupied him over two years. The first performance of the opera took place on 20th November 1805. It was an ironic circumstance that, *Fidelio* having been founded on a true incident in France under the Terror (transferred to Spain for diplomacy), French soldiers should have formed the major part of the audience at its first performance. Those French armies which always seemed marching into Beethoven's life, had just besieged and occupied Vienna. Bonaparte was at Schönbrunn, Murat in the palace of the Archduke Albert, General Hulin in that of Prince Lobkowitz.

Between the inherent faults of the libretto, the difficulties of Beethoven's music, the dramatic defects of the work, and the general dislocation caused by the French occupation, *Fidelio* was a failure. After three performances it was withdrawn.

Strenuous efforts were made by Beethoven's friends to get the defects remedied and *Fidelio* performed again. After a terrible evening at Prince Lichnowsky's, when the prince, princess and a select group of experts battled with Beethoven from 7 p.m. to 1 a.m. to persuade him to certain alterations, he gave in to their views, and Breuning was allowed to revise the libretto. 'Though the friends of Beethoven were fully prepared for the impending battle, they had never seen him in *that* excitement before,' says one of them. Imagination fairly trembles at the scene.

In spite of the improvements, and in spite of a new overture (*Leonora* No. 3), *Fidelio* had no real success when given again in the spring of 1806. Cabals sprang up and the hoped-for performances, on which Beethoven depended for his honorarium, stopped short at two.

'Nothing, perhaps, has caused Beethoven so much vexation as this work, the value of which will be appreciated only in the future,' wrote Breuning to the Wegelers. . . . 'He will recover from the set-back all the more slowly since the treatment which he has received has robbed him of a great deal of the pleasure in and love for the work.'

Beethoven himself called *Fidelio* his 'crown of martyrdom.' Yet, true to the law of parenthood, by which what has been suffered for in the attaining is loved, he loved *Fidelio* to the end of his life.

CHAPTER VI

LOVER AND LION

IT may be mere coincidence or it may be significant that Beethoven, Therese and Josephine all spent the winter of 1805–6 in a whirl of social gaiety. Therese, with her stormy, deep heart and richly gifted mind, had deliberately schooled herself into a brilliance and beauty capable of holding their own against the graces of Josephine. Josephine, on her side, was at the height of her natural fascination. The two young countesses at their mother's house of Ofen were like 'queens of wit and beauty' in the festivities arranged for the Grand Duke of Tuscany. The grand duke indeed was so taken by Therese that she might have become the grand duchess. Or so, at least, it is said. Beethoven, on his side, emerged from his self-imposed solitude and went freely into Viennese society. Why? Did he sometimes find Therese there? And what—or who—helped him to the final moral victory over his deafness? It was about this time he pencilled on a page of sketches for the Rasoumovsky quartets: 'Just as you are now plunging into the whirlpool of society—just so possible is it to compose *operas* in spite of social obstacles. Let your deafness no longer be a secret—even in art.' In those last words there is something that rings like the voice of Therese, the self-consecrated priestess to truth.

Beethoven at length had won the triumphant solution of his problem, and the great works he now poured out were full of an extraordinary splendour. Again and again in their glory the compositions dating from 1805 to 1812 make one think they have been touched by that spirit of which Christ spoke when He said: 'I am come that they may have life, and have it more abundantly.'

It was precisely during those years that Therese and Beethoven drew nearest to each other. With the exception of Eleonore von Breuning, she was the only woman of a nobility of character comparable to his own whom he loved, and she had learned charity of soul in the hard school of suffering.

Whether Therese was really the 'Immortal Beloved' of Beethoven's famous letter will never be sure, but a number of his responsible biographers believe that she was. The longer I survey the facts in the light of human experience, the more I am inclined to share their point of view.

This is not the place to discuss the complicated testimony of dates, nor the scraps of collateral and presumptive evidence. Those should be sought in the pages of Thayer, Romain Rolland, La Mara, Specht, etc. Suffice it to say here the letter was found after Beethoven's death in a secret drawer in his room, and the finders' first idea was that it had been intended for Giulietta Guicciardi. Later biographers considered Therese von Brunswick the heroine of the romance; still later inquirers suggested Therese Malfatti or Amalie Sebald. Few clues are certain. Beethoven was often careless over dates. So though he headed this letter 'Monday, 6th July,' and the years in which 6th July fell on a Monday were 1801, 1807 and 1812, he *may* have been a day out, which would change the year.[1] The letter itself is in three parts, written at different times during the twenty-four hours from 6th to

[1] Schindler thought it had been written in 1801 to Giulietta Guicciardi; Thayer favoured 1806 or 1807 and Therese von Brunswick. Romain Rolland considered the date settled as 1812 and championed Therese von Brunswick.

Therese von Brunswick

7th July. The following are extracts:

My angel, my all, my very self.—Only a few words today, and, what is more, written in pencil (and with your pencil)—I shan't be certain of my rooms here until tomorrow; what an unnecessary waste of time is all this—Why this profound sorrow, when necessity speaks—can our love endure without sacrifices, without our demanding everything from one another; can you alter the fact that you are not wholly mine, that I am not wholly yours?—Dear God, look at Nature in all her beauty and set your heart at rest about what must be—Love demands all, and rightly so, and thus it is *for me with you, for you with me*—But you forget so easily that I must live *for me and for you*; if we were completely united, you would feel this painful necessity just as little as I do. . . . You are suffering—Oh, where I am, you are with me—I will see to it that you and I, that I can live with you. What a life!!!! as it is now!!!! without you. . . . Even when I am in bed my thoughts rush to you, my eternally beloved, now and then joyfully, then again sadly, waiting to know whether Fate will hear our prayer—To face life I must live altogether with you or never see you. Yes, I am resolved to be a wanderer abroad until I can fly to your arms and say that I have found my true home with you and enfolded in your arms can let my soul be wafted to the realm of blessed spirits—alas, unfortunately it must be so—You will become composed, the more so as you know that I am faithful to you; no other woman can ever possess my heart—never—never—Oh God, why must one be separated from her who is so dear. Yet my life in V[ienna] at present is a miserable life—Your love has made me both the happiest and the unhappiest of mortals. . . . Be calm; for only by calmly considering our lives can we achieve our purpose to live together—Be calm—love me—Today—yesterday—what tearful longing for you—for you—you—my life—my all—all good wishes to you—Oh, do continue to love me—never misjudge your lover's most faithful heart.

    ever yours
    ever mine   L.
    ever ours

It is characteristic that this tells us spiritually so much, materially so little. To him there could be no nobility in passion unless it meant also a union of souls. The predominance of soul-states in the letter shows how greatly Beethoven felt lifted above the common world—and also how sure he was that the 'Immortal Beloved,' to whom he poured out his burning words, moved spiritually on the same plane as himself. That was true of Therese von Brunswick—*not* of the other women. Again, though clues of time and place have yielded little information, Beethoven's allusions to love demanding everything, to the pain the lovers would feel so little were they united, and to the 'humility of man towards man—it pains me,' are all understandable if they refer to the difference in rank between Beethoven and Countess Therese, for under the old cruel code of Austrian nobility marriage between an aristocrat and a plebeian meant social ostracism. Finally, one fact emerges crystal clear from the letter: Beethoven had spoken his love, and knew it was returned.

So, though the mystery remains unsolved, I like to think of the Countess Therese as the 'Immortal Beloved.' We do know that in the summer of 1806 Beethoven went to stay with her brother, Count Franz von Brunswick, at his country seat. Franz adored Beethoven. Friendship between the two men ripened to a fraternal fondness; they used the intimate *du* and addressed each other as 'brother.' Therese was there too. Thoughts of her and of marriage ran together in Beethoven's mind, lurking beneath the jocose phrases of his letter to Count Franz 'on a Mayday': 'Schuppanzigh has got married—*to somebody very like him,* I am told—what will their family be like????—Kiss your sister Therese and tell her that I fear that I shall have to become a great man without a monument of hers contributing to my greatness.'

Yes, a wonderful May, in which Beethoven began the composition of his Rasoumovsky quartets. Yet an ominous May, for then Beethoven's brother Karl married Therese

Love and Art Opposed

(Johanna) Reiss. Their son, born in September, was to be the second great sorrow of Beethoven's life. But in 1806 Beethoven was as near real happiness as at any time in his career. One fancies he and Therese were in the state of attracted antagonism which is an early stage of love. Later, whether in 1806 or 1807 does not matter, their souls rushed into a transcendent unity that seemed as if it must last for ever. It did not, and the cause of their separation can only be guessed. Beethoven was a great musician above and beyond all else—one who had heard the call of the stellar spaces and saw that greater spiritual life beyond the temporal which makes all things earthly seem distant. The legend of Saint Felix, to whom a century passed like a minute while he heard the song of the heavenly bird, is only a medieval symbol of a spiritual truth. Yet alongside this spiritual power, so strong that Therese likened Beethoven to an eagle looking at the sun, he vacillated in a way that drove his friends almost to despair. It may well be that at first he believed he and Therese could live together: and then later was undone by indecision. Fräulein Karoline Languider, an old friend of the Brunswick family, probably came near the truth when she said:

I do not believe that the *Schwärmerei* for Countess Julia Gallenberg-Guicciardi—though it may have been warm and wonderful, for she was a very beautiful, elegant woman of the world—ever took such possession of the heart of Beethoven as did the later love for Countess Therese Brunswick, which led to an engagement. That was decidedly his profoundest love, and that it did not result in marriage, it is said, was due to the—what shall I call it—real artistic temperament (*Natur*) of Beethoven, who, in spite of his great love, could not make up his mind to get married. It is said that Countess Therese took it greatly to heart.

Poor Therese! To have loved so long and faithfully, to have been ready to marry Beethoven with all his unrefined

63

habits, his uncertain health (living with him would have been like living with a gorilla, as a shrewd critic said), to have been willing to go into social exile for his sake—and then to find that Beethoven did not consider her worth any sacrifice on his part! Could anything have been more painful to a woman of her sensitivity and pride? If this be the true reading of her story, I do not wonder she considered that 'the misfortune of my whole life' was decided between 1807 and 1809. I think that by 1808 Therese had seen the hopelessness of it all. When Josephine asked her that summer to accompany her to Switzerland, she went. They visited Pestalozzi at Yverdon. His genius, his 'heavenly goodness,' the sight of his work for children came to Therese as a revelation at the moment of her extremity. From then onwards she dedicated herself to 'that work of education and social action, the magnificent creation of which—the love of poor and abandoned children, a sort of universal maternity—Hungary celebrated in 1928,' says M. Rolland. The love she had felt for Beethoven was so great that when he ceased to want it and she let it flow into the world, it was sufficient to bless hundreds of little children.

But if Beethoven and Therese saw the only service left they could do each other was to part, I think they exchanged tokens of an invisible companionship. Therese gave him her portrait, painted by Lampi, with the words on the back of the frame:

> To the Unique Genius
> To the Great Artist
> To the Good Man

> from T. B.

It hung always upon the wall of Beethoven's room in company with the picture of his grandfather.

Beethoven gave to Therese the Sonata in F sharp major,

Op. 78, composed and dedicated to her in 1809; a far more beautiful portrait than the painting.

Neither of them ever married. Therese lived to be eighty-six and died a canoness in a convent.

Beethoven, however, continued falling in and out of love. He was caught almost immediately by a girl in her teens—Therese, the niece of his doctor, Malfatti. This was apparently in 1810. It proved a humiliating affair. His infatuation for the young minx was absolutely foolish; her family were furious, and she, after playing with him, turned down his proposal of marriage. Therese Malfatti, without meaning it, revenged Therese von Brunswick.

How convenient, though flippant, it would be to reduce Beethoven's successive love affairs to a list of the ladies' names and dates—as for example:

> 1810. Therese Malfatti and Bettina Brentano.
>
> 1811. ⎫
> 1812. ⎭ Amalie Sebald.

But not all the names are known, and the charmers had less and less influence upon his work. Only to the end of his days he sighed to find 'her who shall strengthen me in virtue.' When temptation came his strong principles of purity were not always proof against an ignoble gratification of the world, the flesh and the devil—a gratification which he loathed in retrospect. When he sinned he was (like Lancelot) never 'the sleeker for it.'

Between 1805 and 1812 his compositions poured out in a glorious spate. Music was his true life. Hearing the piano Concerto in G major, the violin Concerto, the fourth Symphony, the three Rasumovsky Quartets and the third overture to *Leonora*, it is nothing to us whether he was then in love with Josephine or Therese. Nor when we hear the fifth and sixth Symphonies, the overture to *Coriolan* and the Mass in C (1807) do we care that in the spring of this year Beethoven applied unsuccessfully for the post of composer to the royal imperial court theatre. Still less are we interested in King Jerome Bonaparte's invitation to Beethoven to become his *Kapellmeister* at Cassel in 1808. We only remember that the Fantasia in C major, Op. 80, the cello Sonata, Op. 69, and the Trios, Op. 70, all belong to that year. Beethoven was rather attracted towards Cassel on account of the good salary offered, but he disliked the dissolute tone of Jerome's court. Besides, he had already connections with the Austrian imperial family through his pupil the Archduke Rudolph. The prospective theft of their Beethoven roused the Archduke Rudolph, Prince Lobkowitz and Prince Kinsky to guarantee him a salary of four thousand gulden, on condition he did not leave Austria without their permission. He remained with pleasure. Next year, 1809, Vienna was besieged by Napoleon; a heavy bombardment disturbed Haydn's last days on earth and drove Beethoven into the refuge of Karl van Beethoven's cellar with pillows tied over his ears. He wrote to Breitkopf & Härtel in July:

We have been suffering misery in a most concentrated form. Let me tell you that since May 4th I have produced very little coherent work, at most a fragment here and there. The whole course of events has in my case affected both body and soul. I cannot yet give myself up to the enjoyment of country life which is so indispensable to me. . . . What a destructive, disorderly life I see and hear around me, nothing but drums, cannons, and human misery in every form.

So once again the tramp of French armies had swelled from a low thunder on the horizon of Beethoven's life to a lashing tempest that beat down all resistance. No glamour about Napoleon now. Beethoven was furious and unafraid. 'If I were a general and knew as much about strategy as I, a composer, know about counterpoint, I'd give you fellows something to do,' he cried.

When listening to Beethoven's piano Concerto in E flat major, Op. 73, who would guess that this was the year in which he completed it—music wherein is embodied all the splendour, joy and power of the world—or that he wrote it in surroundings of Spartan rigour? In 1810 Bettina Brentano paid her famous visits to Beethoven and found him at the piano, in a room of extraordinary bareness and disorder.

She was a poet herself, already knew Goethe, and understood genius by intuition. Beethoven found himself able to talk to her as he had never done to his men friends, and she was a real link between him and Goethe—the sole man of his own lofty genius whom he believed would understand him.

This summer, happily, Beethoven went to the country as usual, Baden being the chosen spot. Next year, 1811, the depreciation of money resulting from the war reduced his salary to one thousand three hundred and sixty gulden. None the less, he spent August at Teplitz in the midst of a circle of brilliant folk on holiday, among them Varnhagen, Rahel Levin, Tiedge, Elise von der Recke and Amalie Sebald. This year and the next brought him the stupendous seventh Symphony, the deliciously happy eighth Symphony and the Olympian Trio in B flat major, Op. 97; 1812 being also the year of the ethereally lovely Sonata for piano and violin in G major, Op. 96, the 'little' B flat major Trio, the three Equali for four trombones, and smaller things.

By the singular habit which the royalties and statesmen of mid-Europe had of carrying on political consultations, disguised as 'cures,' at summer watering-places (a habit practised as late as 1914!), a great concentration of royalties took place at Teplitz in 1812. A very strategic spot from which to view Napoleon's campaign in Russia! Moving in and out of this august group were the lovely Amalie, Bettina Brentano (now Frau von Arnim), her husband and other celebrities. Beethoven and Goethe met here for the first time, and were disappointed in each other. Beethoven approached Goethe with a heart full of admiration. He told Rochlitz years later: 'How patient the great man was with me! . . . How happy he made me then! I would have gone to my death for him; yes, ten times.' His devotion, however, did not prevent Beethoven from rebuking the poet for what he considered his weak sensibility over music and his subservience to rank. He wrote to Breitkopf & Härtel: 'Goethe delights far too much in the court atmosphere, far more than is becoming to a poet. How can one really say very much about the ridiculous behaviour of virtuosi in this respect, when poets, who should be regarded as the leading teachers of the nation, can forget everything else when confronted with that glitter—' Beethoven had ideas of the moral responsibility of artists towards the world that would appear ridiculous to some poets of to-day.

Goethe on his side began by saying of Beethoven that:

A more self-contained, energetic, sincere artist I never saw. I can understand right well how singular must be his attitude towards the world.

But after he had seen more of him, Goethe's verdict was:

His talent amazed me; unfortunately he is an utterly untamed personality, not altogether in the wrong in holding the world to be detestable, but who does not make it any the more enjoyable either for himself or others by his attitude. He is very excusable, on the other hand, and much to be pitied, as his hearing is leaving him, which, perhaps, mars the musical part of his nature less than the social. He is of a laconic nature, and will become doubly so, because of this lack.

And all the time Beethoven was ill and very unhappy. To 1812—probably September—belongs this cry in his journal:

Submission, absolute submission to your fate, only this can give you the sacrifice . . . to the servitude—O hard struggle! Turn everything which remains to the planning of the long journey—

you must yourself find all that your most blessed wish can offer, you must force it to your will—keep always of the same mind.

Thou mayest be no longer a man, not for thyself, only for others, for thee there is no longer happiness except in thyself, in thy art— O God, give me strength to conquer myself, nothing must chain me to life. Thus everything connected with A. will go to destruction.

Words which carry with them the conviction that he had finally recognized he was debarred from marriage.

As if this inner struggle were not enough, an outer contest arose over Johann van Beethoven's liaison with Therese Obermeyer. This unprincipled young woman proved to be living with him at Linz, where he was now a thriving chemist. Beethoven rushed off at once, intent on severing the connection —animated no doubt by the old sense of responsibility towards his brothers and the memory of his mother. Heartily as he disliked his first sister-in-law, Karl's wife, he loathed the Obermeyer as thoroughly. After hateful scenes between the brothers, Johann married Therese, to the intense mortification of Ludwig. 'Troubles never come singly,' says the proverb: about the same time brother Karl fell dangerously ill. As usual, distress and anger made Ludwig himself ill. This, coupled with money worries due to Prince Kinsky's death (Kinsky had been one of the patrons who guaranteed Beethoven's salary), may explain the slackening in his output at this time. Necessity made him think of a journey to England, where Haydn had earned a modest fortune twenty years earlier. An acquaintance, Mälzel, inventor of the metronome and an orchestrion, was anxious to join him, but the project was postponed on account of Karl van Beethoven's illness, by which time Beethoven and Mälzel were both short of money. Mälzel ingeniously suggested that, as Wellington had won the Battle of Vittoria on 21st June 1813, Beethoven should write a battle piece to celebrate the event, which would

please the English greatly and bring in money. For once
Beethoven was tractable. He composed *Wellington's Victory*
(Battle Symphony), Op. 91, for the orchestrion, which
turned out so well, in his own estimation, that he scored it
for full orchestra. 'It is certain that one writes most beautifully
when one writes for the public, also that one writes rapidly,'
he scribbled dryly in his *Tagebuch*.

The symphony was produced at a grand concert in aid
of wounded Austrian and Bavarian soldiers, in the University
Hall, 8th December 1813. The programme opened with
the *première* of Beethoven's seventh Symphony; two marches
by Dussek and Pleyel followed; and *Wellington's Victory*
capped the occasion. Every one was wrought to a patriotic
fervour. Spohr, Schuppanzigh, Dragonetti, Romberg (bassoon), Meyerbeer and Salieri gave their services in the band.
Beethoven conducted. The thing had a *succès fou*. The
concert had to be repeated, and the Battle Symphony continued its triumphant career far into the next year. Vienna,
which had disparaged the *Eroica,* raved over its antithesis.
Beethoven knew this and declared the work to be folly; he
said he 'liked it only because with it he had thoroughly
thrashed the Viennese.' Irony put its final touch on the
situation when this work, which he had composed to bring
him in funds for an English tour, now paid so well that he
remained in Vienna. Mälzel, enraged, tried to pirate the
score, and a lawsuit developed which lasted till 1817.

Throughout the years 1813, 1814 and 1815 Beethoven was
immensely popular and prospered well enough to put by
eight thousand florins in bank shares. *Fidelio*, again revised,
was revived at the Kärnthnerthor theatre in May 1814, hailed
with enthusiasm and chosen for the opening of the season.
The Congress of Vienna (winter 1814-15) formed the climax
of this brilliant period. Among all the great, Beethoven was
a lion too. For the time being he was also brought into

something near a civilized existence by the endeavours of his good friends, the piano-maker Streicher and his wife, *née* Nanette Stein. What his previous condition had been in dirt and disorder beggars description. Nanette said he had not a whole shirt to his back—and one can believe it. But to be made a lion and a lamb at one and the same time is a distracting experience. Beethoven's compositions during these years were few.

On 18th June 1815 Napoleon, one hero of the *Eroica*, was defeated at Waterloo and went into exile. On 16th November 1815 a disaster befell Beethoven, the other hero of the symphony, which sent him into virtual exile from music for three years. Only the piano Sonata, Op. 101, a Fugue for string quintet and some small vocal works belong to them.

This disaster was the death of Karl van Beethoven and the legacy of his child as a ward.

I appoint my brother, Ludwig van Beethoven, guardian [wrote Karl in his will]. Inasmuch as this, my deeply loved brother, has often aided me with true brotherly love in the most magnanimous and noblest manner, I ask, in full confidence and trust in his noble heart, that he shall bestow the love and friendship which he often showed me upon my son Karl, and do all that is possible to promote the intellectual training and further welfare of my son. I know that he will not deny me this request.

And the dying man added a codicil:

Having learned that my brother, Hr. Ludwig van Beethoven, desires after my death to take wholly to himself my son Karl, and wholly to withdraw him from the supervision and training of his mother, and inasmuch as the best of harmony does not exist between my brother and my wife, I have found it necessary to add to my will that I by no means desire that my son be taken away from his mother, but that he shall always and so long as his future career permits, remain with his mother, to which end the guardianship of him is to be exercised by her as well as my brother. Only by unity can the object which I had in view in appointing my brother guardian of my son be attained, wherefore, for the welfare of my child, I recommend *compliance* to my wife, and more *moderation* to my brother.

God permit them to be harmonious for the sake of my child's welfare. This is the last wish of the dying husband and brother.

Thus Beethoven (as Specht ironically points out) had been appointed when a boy as the guardian of his father, and now became the guardian of a boy thirty-six years his junior! In each case there was good cause, as the brothers knew, and Johanna was not a woman to trust.

Beethoven had long objected to her as immoral. Immediately following on Karl's death, he took most determined action to remove little Karl, aged nine, from her influence. After legal processes lasting two months, he was awarded the custody of the child, and on 19th January 1816 he appeared as the legally appointed guardian of his nephew Karl, 'and vowed with solemn hand-grasp before the assembled council to perform his duties.'

Thus Beethoven crossed the second Rubicon of his life.

CHAPTER VII

THE GENERAL OF THE MUSICIANS

FROM 1816 to 1818 there was an almost complete break in Beethoven's creative work. What no good woman, no 'Immortal Beloved,' had ever done, Johanna the Bad and the small Karl accomplished—they brought Beethoven to earth, and kept him there, in an endless round of litigation, intrigue, agitation, anguish and anger. The mother constantly tried to get back her child; Beethoven was even more determined she should have no control, and beat her off fiercely. He was quite prepared to be generous over money matters and to allow her to see Karl at intervals, but where moral training was concerned he was adamant, for he loathed her lightness that could be bought (it was said) for twenty gulden, and he despised her bribery and lies. It is almost impossible for Anglo-Saxon countries to realize the extent to which intrigue was carried on in old Vienna. The system was as much a matter of course as *natchai* under the old Russian empire. Any one who cares to read such an independent account as that given by Lady Frances Shelley in her diary for 1816 will see how the upper world floated on intrigue, while the *demi-monde* and underworld wallowed in it. Anything was possible in a city and time where such a grim episode could happen as that of the Countess Erdödy, her two sons, one daughter and the tutor Brauchle, who was suspected of causing the boys' death and of driving the girl to attempted suicide. Thayer and Hevesy, who learned the story from the police reports, can only hint at it. Yet it is relevant here, because the Countess Erdödy was one of Beethoven's best friends up to the time when she was banished from Austria, and the years of the tragedy coincide with those of Beethoven's struggle against Johanna for Karl.

Beethoven was thus amply justified in his fears, if not in his methods with Karl. *The Magic Flute* had always been his favourite Mozart opera; he now fitted its circumstances to his own. Johanna was the wicked Queen of Night, he was the wise high priest Sarastro and Karl was Pamina, the child whom Sarastro would save from the mother's machinations. The allegory did not work out on all fours. In the opera Sarastro, as supreme arbiter, had no opposition to contend with save that of the Queen of Night, while Pamina was absolutely docile to the ordeals imposed on her. Beethoven, on the other hand, was compelled to go to law as the plaintiff and to fight the case right up through the courts for three years before he obtained sole rights over Karl. Meanwhile Karl, far from maidenly docility, was an unregenerate, deceitful little boy, who found himself in the unpleasant position of a wish-bone or cracker, which people are pulling at opposite ends. He may well have felt, as a schoolboy once reported Agag to have said when he was hewn in pieces: 'My punishment is greater than I can bear.'

On first receiving the sole care of Karl, Beethoven had put him into an excellent private school owned by Giannatasio del Rio. The loyalty and good sense of Giannatasio were severely tried, but remained staunch against the attacks of the Queen of Night, and he and Beethoven struck up a firm friendship. Giannatasio was a sensible man: Beethoven's ideas on education were wise and humane; he was anxious that Karl, whom he thought very gifted, should not be overworked as he himself had been. Unfortunately the experiment of a school domicile was not altogether successful and Beethoven decided to make a home for the boy himself. How incapable he was of doing such a thing may be gleaned from Fanny Giannatasio's journal. She, with her father, sister and Karl had been invited to visit Beethoven at Baden in September 1816.

Although our host had been informed of our coming, we soon noticed that no arrangement had been made for our entertainment. . . . When we came to his lodgings in the afternoon a walk was proposed; but our host would not go along, excusing himself, saying he had a great deal to do; but he promised to follow and join us, and did so. But when we came back in the evening there was not a sign of entertainment to be seen. B. muttered excuses and accusations against the persons who had been charged with the arrangements and helped us to settle ourselves. Oh, how interesting it was! to move a light sofa with his help. A rather large room, in which his piano stood, was cleared for us girls to use as a bedroom. . . . In the morning a very prosaic noise roused us out of our poetical mood! B. appeared soon with a scratched face, and complained that he had had a quarrel with his servant, who was going away. 'Look,' he said, 'how he has maltreated me!'

Fanny and her sister were the proverbial little pitchers with long ears. When the party presently went for a walk in the Helenenthal, the girls, strolling on ahead, overheard their father advising Beethoven to rescue himself from his difficulties by marrying. Beethoven's reply is significant beyond its immediate application. 'Five years ago,' he said, 'he had made the acquaintance of a person, union with whom he would have considered the greatest happiness of his life. It was not to be thought of, almost an impossibility, a chimera—nevertheless it is now as on the first day. . . . It had never reached a confession, but he could not get it out of his mind.'

It? She? Amalie Sebald? Beethoven had known her just five years. Proof too that Amalie was not the 'Immortal Beloved,' because almost the only sure thing about the famous letter is that it was written *following* a declaration of love.

Months slipped by and still the disturbance in Beethoven's life continued. The wretched child Karl was as guiltless

as Newton's dog Diamond of the loss he was inflicting on
the world, but Beethoven became practically non-creative
through worry and distress. He wrote letters, letters, letters:
letters on litigation, his ill-health, his domestic troubles. He
made pathetic efforts to gather practical information about
running a household. 'What ought one to give two servants
to eat at dinner and supper both as to quantity and quality?
How often ought one to give them roast meat? . . . How
much wine and beer?' were a few of the unaccustomed
questions he wrestled with. Friends tried to help him by
finding him servants. Good Zmeskall, as usual, was on
the spot and was rewarded by a letter that began: 'Dear Z.!
Your refusal to recommend the servants I have engaged I also
cannot recommend. . . . All my plans for my nephew have
collapsed on account of those wretched people.' To Giannatasio he wrote: 'Dear Friend! My household is almost exactly
like a shipwreck or tends to resemble one. In short, a soi-
disant expert in such matters has cheated me over these people.'

To Frau Nanette Streicher (his sheet-anchor against these
calamities) he wrote: 'Thank you for the interest you are taking
in me—Things are really better—although today I had to put
up with a good deal from N[anni]—But as a New Year wish
I threw half a dozen books at her head.' Then later: 'Yesterday
morning they [the servants] both resumed their devilish tricks.
I made short work of them and threw the heavy chair beside
my bed at B[aberl].'

Perhaps most striking of all is his letter to Zmeskall giving
him the dedication of the magnificent F minor string Quartet,
Op. 95, a letter in every way as characteristic as the Quartet:

16th December, 1816.

Well, dear Z., you are now receiving my friendly dedication. I
want it to be a precious memento of our friendship which has persisted here for so long; and I should like you to treat it as a proof of
my esteem and not to regard it as the end of what is now a long

drawn out thread (for you are one of the earliest friends I made in Vienna).

All good wishes. Keep away from rotten fortresses, for an attack from them is more deadly than one from well preserved ones.

Ever your friend

BEETHOVEN.

(N.B. If you have a moment to spare, please let me know the approximate cost at present of a livery, without a cloak, but with hat and boot money.) Wonderful changes have taken place in my establishment. The husband, thank God, has gone to the devil; but the wife, it seems, is all the more determined to settle down in my home.

How could a child be happy in such an atmosphere, and how could a man of Beethoven's absent-mindedness keep the boy in even a reasonable degree of physical cleanliness? Karl was miserable, and even became verminous at one time.

The story of those years would read like a knock-about farce, except that it was actually a searching tragedy. Beethoven had come to love Karl passionately. All his starved instinct of fatherhood, all his protective habits towards kith and kin, concentrated upon the child with an intensity near to the terrible intentness of insanity. A young mother sometimes goes through agonies of fear over the care of her first child until, as years advance, the increasing risks of life are less felt because custom has brought confidence. Beethoven took over his 'son' at an age when all the risks and responsibilities had to be faced simultaneously. Between his fears, his feeling of eternal isolation due to his deafness, and the constant heart-stabs which he endured at finding his exquisite love returned with tepid affection, Beethoven suffered tortures. That some of them were unnecessary and that Beethoven felt them more keenly than other men would have done in his position is simply to say that he was Beethoven—a matter neither he nor Karl could alter.

To pry out the secrets of a soul in pain is near to sacrilege. Yet by the light of the music which at length emerged from this purgatory, one understands that in his own suffering as an unloved father, Beethoven's thoughts turned to the Father-hood of God, as when in the old morality play of *Everyman,* God says: 'I perceive here in My Majesty how that My creatures be to Me unkind.'

Whatever historians may write of Beethoven's great Mass in D having originated from his desire to pay a tribute to the Archduke Rudolph on his enthronement as Archbishop of Olmütz in 1820, I feel convinced the work would never have been imagined if the words of the Mass had not chimed with Beethoven's mood. Where the belief in immortality (*et expecto resurrectionem mortuorum*) lies at the heart of Bach's B minor Mass, a sure knowledge of God as the all-loving Father (*Pater Omnipotens*) lies at the heart of Beethoven's *Missa Solennis* in D major. Sketched in the summer of 1818, two years did not suffice for the completion of the Mass. Two years might be enough for *Fidelio,* but the Mass required five.

To 1818 belong the piano Sonata in B flat major, Op. 106, and some small things. For a composer who had mainly to depend on his pen for his own and a boy's livelihood these lean years must have been a gnawing anxiety. They palliate, though they do not justify, his very unpleasant treatment of the Phil-harmonic Society of London, when he palmed off old overtures as new, haggled over prices and made unfounded accusations.

Meanwhile Karl's affairs continued to be a curse. Some-where at the end of 1818 the naughty child ran away to his mother. Beethoven wrote of this to the Archduke Rudolph: 'A terrible event took place a short time ago in my family circumstances, and for a time I was absolutely driven out of my mind.' At the end of March Beethoven surrendered his guardianship. By July he had to resume it, for Councillor von Tuscher, who had undertaken it, had more than enough in a short time. In 1819 the council deprived Beethoven of the guardianship and assigned Karl jointly to his mother and the official sequestrator. Beethoven fought the case, first against the council, then against the court of appeal, and on 8th April 1820 secured a final victory. He and Hofrat Peters were appointed co-guardians. The 'Queen of Night' appealed to the emperor without success. So at last came some peace for the harassed composer.

Nothing rouses a stronger sense of Beethoven's greatness than the nature of the music which he brought with him out of great tribulation. The piano Sonatas in E major, Op. 109 (1820), A flat major, Op. 110 (1821) and C minor, Op. 111 (1822); the stupendous *Missa Solennis*; the ninth Symphony, in D minor (1824), in which joy not only shall, but does, 'overtake us as a flood'—these were his works, full of blessing and consolation.

Though in a way the development of great men is always continuous, Beethoven's music shows clearly three successive phases or periods, divided from each other by the Rubicons of the two terrible griefs of his life. Thus the first period includes the time up to 1800 and the disaster of his deafness; the second that up to 1815 and the legacy of Karl; the third extends to Beethoven's death in 1827. In the first, Beethoven saw the *material world* from the *material standpoint*; in the second he saw the *material world* from the *spiritual standpoint*; in the third he saw the *spiritual world* from the *spiritual standpoint*.

The majority of mankind live in three dimensions. A minority, the saints and seers, attempt to live in four and make this practicable by reducing the lower dimensions to a minimum. Hermits, monks and fakirs deliberately divorce themselves from common life. Beethoven could do nothing of the kind, and in consequence was cruelly battered by the cross-currents of his existence.

Schindler, a young student who out of devotion to

Beethoven's music became a sort of famulus to the master, records that towards the end of August 1819 he and the musician Horsalka went to visit Beethoven at Mödling.

It was four o'clock in the afternoon. As we entered we learned that in the morning both servants had gone away, and that there had been a quarrel after midnight which had disturbed all the neighbours, because as a consequence of a long vigil both had gone to sleep and the food which had been prepared had become unpalatable. In the livingroom, behind a locked door, we heard the master singing parts of the fugue of the Credo—singing, howling, stamping. After we had been listening a long time to this almost awful scene . . . the door opened and Beethoven stood before us with distorted features, calculated to excite fear. He looked as if he had been in mortal combat with the whole host of contrapuntists, his everlasting enemies. His first utterances were confused, as if he had been disagreeably surprised at our having overheard him. Then he reached the day's happenings, and with obvious restraint he remarked: 'Pretty doings, these! Everybody has run away and I haven't had anything to eat since yesternoon.'

Here is another example of his unworldliness, which happened next year—1820. Beethoven, then staying at Baden, got up early and went out. Absentmindedly he walked on until evening; then, having lost his way and having had nothing to eat, he was seen looking in at the windows of the houses. The alarmed inhabitants called the local constable, who arrested him. 'I am Beethoven,' said the composer. 'Of course, why not! You're a tramp: *the* Beethoven doesn't look so,' was the reply, and he was locked up. The next stage of the story is that as the Commissioner of Police was enjoying himself with a little party in a tavern garden, a constable arrived saying: 'Mr. Commissioner, we have arrested somebody who gives us no peace. He keeps on yelling that he is Beethoven; but he's a ragamuffin, has an old coat and no hat . . . nothing to identify him by.' The Commissioner ordered the man to be kept under arrest till morning and retired to rest himself. At 11 p.m. he was waked by a policeman saying: 'The prisoner keeps demanding that Herzog, the musical director of Wiener Neustadt, shall be fetched to identify him.' At this the Commissioner was wise enough to get up, dress and fetch Herzog in the middle of the night. The instant Herzog saw the 'tramp' he exclaimed: 'That *is* Beethoven!' The comedy ended by Herzog entertaining Beethoven at his house and the Commissioner sending the guest home next morning in the magisterial state-coach!

In 1822 *Fidelio* was revived. Towards the end of the same year Beethoven received a request from a new patron, Prince Galitsin, to compose one, two or three string quartets, for which Galitsin would pay any sum that Beethoven liked to fix and he would accept the dedication gratefully.

Life has curious symmetries. As a lad Beethoven had been taken to play to Mozart. Now, in 1823, a young prodigy called Franz Liszt was brought to play to Beethoven. Like Mozart, the older man was sceptical. What won him, it is said, was Liszt's astonishing performance of preludes and fugues from Bach's *Well-Tempered Clavier,* transposing them into any key chosen by Beethoven. Playing the 'Forty-eight' had been Beethoven's own great feat as a boy.

During this same 1823 Beethoven was considerably occupied over getting together subscriptions for the publication of the *Missa Solennis.* Goethe was among those who did not subscribe. He ignored Beethoven's letter, just as he never noticed Schubert!

Beethoven was now going forward with the great ninth Symphony, his setting of Schiller's *Ode to Joy.* By February 1824 it was complete. On 7th May it was performed for the first time at a grand concert organized by Beethoven at the request of thirty of his friends. On the evening every one attended — except the imperial family. Even poor Zmeskall, now bedridden, was carried there in a sedan chair. For once the Viennese recognized an historic occasion.

They went wild with excitement, and it was in that tumult that Fräulein Unger, the singer, suddenly saw that Beethoven heard nothing, and gently turned him round to the audience. All his friends had co-operated to make the concert a success, yet the money results were poor. The composer was bitterly disappointed and did not hesitate to say he had been cheated. Few scenes in his life are more repellent than that in which, having invited Umlauf, Schuppanzigh and Schindler to dine with him at a restaurant, he abused them and the laws of hospitality by levelling the most insulting charges at them. Yet later his penitence was so genuine that —as usually happened—he won them back.

For years Beethoven had never been what one could call a 'well' man. Now he complained still more frequently of various maladies. But he had commenced the great E flat major string Quartet, Op. 127, in 1824, and by March 1825 it was ready. Somewhere about this time, Karl Holz the violinist had come into Beethoven's circle as an intimate—a friendship viewed askance by older friends, since Holz was a merry fellow, suspected of leading Beethoven into intemperate habits. The best denial of the charge is that during 1825 Beethoven composed the B flat major and A minor string Quartets, Opp. 130 and 132—both the works of a mental Titan.

Nephew Karl was now nineteen, and gadded about Vienna like the most accomplished young rake. It was said he knew every woman of bad repute in the town. Beethoven endured agonies of anxiety, from which sprang fresh volleys of reproaches. Karl riposted, even to the extent, it is believed, of striking his foster-father. Then in 1826, desperate from his debts and the whole miserable business, Karl did what many young Austrians were apt to do when in difficulties—he attempted suicide. For some time he had threatened; then one day at the end of July he gave the slip to those who would have saved him, went to the ruins of Rauhenstein near Vienna in the Helenenthal—a peculiarly mean choice of locality, for the Helenenthal was one of Beethoven's favourite spots—and shot himself in the head. He was not killed, only wounded, but to Beethoven the shock was indescribable: he was stricken to the heart. Suicide was a crime under the Austrian code. Thus, besides the wretched medical details, police intervention had to be dealt with. Beethoven was haunted by the fear of other secrets being disclosed, the secret of how Karl had stolen his books, and some worse crime unknown to this day. When Frau von Breuning heard the story from him, and asked if Karl were dead, 'No,' he replied, 'it was a glancing shot; he lives, and there is hope he will be saved. But the disgrace he has brought upon me! And I loved him so.'

Beethoven had once written in his journal: 'He who would reap tears should sow love.' He now became suddenly bowed and broken, as if he had grown very old . . . Beethoven who had always resisted suicide himself because 'no man has a right to take his own life so long as he can still accomplish one good action.'

By the last week of September Karl recovered sufficiently to be taken to the country to recuperate, prior to entering the army, which had now been decided on as his career. Johann van Beethoven, who had come to Vienna, invited his brother and Karl to return with him to his lately acquired estate at Gneixendorf. It seemed a good plan, so all three set off. Beethoven had completed the marvellous C sharp minor Quartet in July, just before Karl's attempted suicide, and had sketched the F major, Op. 135. At Gneixendorf he began to feel the shadows falling on himself, but looked for some respite yet. In December he wrote to Wegeler: 'I still hope to create a few great works and then like an old child to finish my earthly course somewhere among kind people.' He completed the F major Quartet, but otherwise the visit was wretched. He was unwell, full of self-reproach for Karl's debacle, terribly

83

apprehensive for Karl's future. He had but a modest fortune to leave the young man—seven out of the eight bonds of a thousand florins each which he had saved from the affluent times of the congress. He accordingly urged the prosperous Johann—who had made money out of army contracts—to will his property to Karl. Johann had no intention of doing anything of the kind, and fierce quarrels ensued. About 1st December they culminated in one so furious that Beethoven shook off the dust of the house from his shoes, refused to wait for a proper carriage—Johann did not lend him the closed coach—and, taking Karl with him, hastened back to Vienna in arctic weather. He arrived on 2nd December, ill from rage and exposure, and went straight to bed in his lodging at the Schwarzspanierhaus. No one seems to have taken the matter seriously, thinking perhaps it was a case of 'Wolf! wolf!' and Karl went off to play billiards instead of calling in a doctor. Finally Beethoven sent for Holz, who summoned Professor Wawruch—a doctor new to the case but the only one then available. Pneumonia seems to have been the malady at the moment. Beethoven was snatched back from that only to pass through four months of a mortal illness which baffled the physicians, but which modern diagnosis pronounces to have been cirrhosis of the liver.

They were months of dreary pain and physical squalor. The surgeons who tapped Beethoven five times for dropsy were careless and insanitary even by the standards of those days. His nurses allowed him to be devoured by vermin. Karl and Johann, who came to Vienna on hearing of his brother's illness and helped to look after him, were comfortless as kith and kin.

The New Year—1827—was ushered in by a violent quarrel between Beethoven and Karl—the last, for on 2nd January Karl went to join his regiment. The friends came out better. Stephan von Breuning, his wife and his son Gerhard (a charming child who had the good sense to bring Beethoven some insect powder), Schindler, Holz, Dr. Malfatti (now stiffly reconciled to his old friend), were among his visitors, and once Franz Schubert came, moved almost beyond speech by the sight of the dying master.

Beethoven lay there, quite unafraid of death, still planning his tenth symphony and pathetically resolved that whatever his own severe poverty, nothing should induce him to use a penny of the inheritance set apart for Karl. He still made grim jests, but he was terribly lonely, and turned to reading his old loves the classics. Such presents as friends made him—Handel's complete works, a case of wine, the picture of Haydn's birthplace—pleased him exceedingly. By February his funds were so low that he wrote letters to his London friends Stumpff, Moscheles and Smart asking them to use their influence with the Philharmonic Society for a benefit concert on his behalf. On 14th March no answer had arrived, so he wrote again to Moscheles:

What is to be the end of it all? And what is to become of me, if my illness persists for some time?—Truly my lot is a very hard one! However, I am resigned to accept whatever Fate may bring; and I only continue to pray that God in His divine wisdom may so order events that as long as I have to endure this living death I may be protected from want. This would give me sufficient strength to bear my lot, however hard and terrible it may prove to be, with a feeling of submission to the will of the Almighty.

From the time when he was a boy of fifteen Beethoven had learned not to fear death. Long ago he had learned to trust God. 'God has never deserted me. Somebody will be found to close my eyes,' he had written to Karl more than a year before his last illness.

His trust was not betrayed. On 18th March the help arrived. The Philharmonic Society, whose musical perceptions Beethoven had despised, here showed a prompt grasp of realities and an amazing kindness. Without waiting for a concert (which could come later) they had dispatched a gift of a hundred pounds! Beethoven received it with touching gratitude. 'My dear, kind Moscheles! I cannot put into words the emotion with which I read your letter of March 1st. The Philharmonic Society's generosity in almost antici‑ pating my appeal has touched my innermost soul,' dictated Beethoven. He was past help, but at least he had the joy of knowing it had come. The English money paid for his funeral.

His old friend Hummel, hearing of Beethoven's illness, hurried with his wife across Germany to his bedside. The act pleased Beethoven, though the sight of Hummel's married happiness made him very wistful. 'You are a lucky man, you have a wife who takes care of you—but poor me——' he sighed heavily.

The portrait of Therese von Brunswick was still with him, the miniature of Giulietta Guicciardi and the letter to the Immortal Beloved lay hidden in the secret drawer of his bureau. Not one woman who had meant anything in his life was there at its end. Only the score of *Fidelio,* the opera which enshrined his dream of a wife, lay in a corner beneath a pile of papers.

There had been a short time when, under Dr. Malfatti's treatment of iced punch, the patient's condition improved, but by the end of February all hope had gone. On 24th March Beethoven, long aloof from organized religion, con‑ sented to receive the last rites of the Church. He did so devoutly, thanking the priest for the comfort he had brought. After the latter had left, he said to Breuning and Schindler: 'Plaudite, amici, comoedia finita est.' His mind had gone back to his beloved classics and to the words of the dying Augustus, which were themselves an echo of the phrase used by Roman actors. Later in the day he lapsed into unconscious‑ ness. Occasionally he roused a little. Once he said: 'Strange, I feel as if up to now I had written no more than a few notes.'

Dear old Zmeskall, bedridden in his own lodging, was kept informed of affairs at the Schwarzspanierhaus. He wrote to another friend who, his heart told him, still loved Beethoven: 'Our beloved Beethoven is struggling with death. It is dropsy; five operations already. His nephew was in prison, now they have made a musketeer of him. The nephew's education has cost his uncle his peace of mind and his fortune.'

The letter was to Therese von Brunswick. Peace be on Zmeskall's memory for that kind act.

In ancient mythology, and in the Greece of the War of Liberation, a belief still held that when a hero died the heavens showed portents. Only three years before, as Byron lay dying at Missolonghi, an April thunderstorm had broken over the island. Night was coming on: the lightning lit up the dark outline of islands and lagoon. Soldiers and shepherds sheltering in their huts exclaimed: 'Byron is dead.' It was so.

Beethoven, the hero, similarly departed. It was late after-noon on 26th March; Frau van Beethoven (one of the sisters-in-law) and Hüttenbrenner, the friend of Schubert, were watching alone by the dying man. Soon after five 'there came a flash of lightning accompanied by a peal of thunder which garishly illuminated the death-chamber,' said Hütten-brenner. 'Beethoven opened his eyes, lifted his right hand and looked up for several seconds with his fist clenched and a very serious threatening expression. . . . When he let the raised hand sink to the bed, his eyes closed half-way. My right hand was under his head, my left rested on his breast. Not another breath, not a heart-beat more.'

Three days after, on 29th March, Beethoven was buried in the Währing cemetery. His friends and the common people made of the funeral a great farewell rite. The schools were closed. Twenty thousand people crowded the square in front of the Schwarzspanierhaus. The coffin, under a richly embroidered pall, lay in state in the courtyard of the house. Nine priests were there and all the musicians, singers, poets and actors of Vienna. They wore complete mourning, white roses were fastened by bands of crape to their sleeves and they carried draped torches. In the deep silence of the waiting multitude the sound of music—Beethoven's own Equali for All Souls' Day, now arranged for voices—rose through the still air with overpowering effect. When it ceased, the procession moved off to the church of the Minorites in the Alserstrasse. A stranger, seeing the enormous crowds, asked an old woman what it was all about. 'Do you not know?' she replied. 'They are burying the general of the musicians.' Hummel and Kreutzer walked among the pall-bearers, Schubert among the torchbearers. After the service, so imposing in its musical ritual, was over, the coffin was placed in a four-horse hearse, and the procession followed it slowly to Währing, where again a vast crowd waited. At the cemetery gates the actor Anschütz recited the funeral oration, written by Grillparzer. Then entering, and without further speech or music (for they were forbidden by Währing rules), the coffin was silently lowered into the grave. Three laurel wreaths were placed upon it by Hummel. Thus in silence, which Mozart called 'the most beautiful thing in music,' Beethoven was laid to rest.

Many years after, the Viennese prepared a musicians' Valhalla in their new Zentral Friedhof. Beethoven was translated thither, but the old design for his monument was retained. It is a slender obelisk rising from a base on which stands the one word BEETHOVEN; above is a lyre and at the summit a butterfly, with wings outspread, set in a circle—emblems of the liberated soul and of eternity.

BEETHOVEN'S PERSONALITY

CHAPTER VIII

BEETHOVEN THE MAN

'You make upon me the impression of a man who has several heads, several hearts and several souls,' said Haydn when Beethoven once asked him for a criticism of himself and his work.

That is a shrewd summing-up of Beethoven's nature and genius. In a lesser man these multiple elements would have split into the fragments of insanity: with Beethoven they were synthetized into a magnificently unified mind—a mind at peace with itself upon the heights.

A writer who should in words describe Beethoven as fully and truly as Beethoven in music depicted Napoleon, hero and symbol of glorious Liberty, would himself first have to be a Beethoven—and Beethoven was unique! To achieve a description faithful so far as it goes seems almost impossibly hard.

First impressions of a man are usually received from his appearance. Posterity has not been well served in this respect. The painters, etchers, sketchers and sculptors who 'took Beethoven's likeness' were a poor set, without a spark of that vital intuition which made Houdon's bust of Gluck incomparable. Klein's bust of Beethoven cannot be named in the same breath. The life-mask (1812) which probably served as Klein's starting-point is technically mechanical and unfaithful, because the weight of wet plaster slightly depressed the softer parts of the face and gave undue prominence to the bones. The death-mask, heartrendingly expressive though it is, shows Beethoven after the doctors had finished their ghoulish post-mortem examination to discover—among other things—why his brain was so musical and his ears were so deaf. Of portraits on the flat the eminent authorities Th. von Frimmel and the late W. Barclay Squire agree that among early pictures the engraving by J. Neidl from a drawing by Stainhauser (1801), a miniature by C. Horneman (1803) and a painting by W. J. Mähler (1804 or 1805) are the best, while among the later ones they single out Ferdinand Schimon's painting (1818 or 1819), quietly made while Beethoven was at work on the Credo of the *Missa Solemnis*, also J. C. Stieler's portrait of Beethoven holding that work (1820) and J. P. Lyser's little sketches of later date, showing how Beethoven 'used to leap and run rather than walk about the streets of Vienna.' The chalk drawing by Aug. von Klöber (dating perhaps from 1818) is also held in some esteem.

Aided by these representations, and by a number of written descriptions that have come down to us, it is possible to arrive at some idea of Beethoven's appearance.

He was, then, not more than five feet five inches in height —broadly made, vigorous, muscular, very quick in his movements (therefore impatient of slowness in others)—with a fine torso hidden away beneath his carelessly worn clothes. That fine torso indeed looks like having been the *raison d'être* for a modern statue by Max Klinger, which continental critics admire, but which to the uneducated English sense of humour almost inevitably suggests Beethoven sitting with a towel over his legs while he reasons earnestly with an eagle to persuade it to let him get into his bath. The towel tactfully conceals the fact that in life Beethoven's legs were short in proportion to his body. His hands were broad and red, with short fingers and bitten nails, hands ineffably clumsy in the commonplaces of existence such as food, dressing, trinkets, crockery, glass. But on the keyboard these clumsy hands were divinely different—capable of producing a *cantabile* tone that moved people to tears by its beauty.

Beethoven's head was large, his forehead (perhaps his sole handsome feature) broad and noble. A story goes that at some party a lady exclaimed: 'What a noble brow he has!' to which Beethoven promptly replied: 'Salute it then, madam,' and offered it her to kiss. (No doubt she was pretty!)

His nose was 'square (*viereckig*=four-cornered) like that of a lion.' In that simile the observer has left us a marvellous impression of Beethoven's strength and sensitivity. The mouth too was broad, strong, sensitive, with a slightly protruding lower lip and a chin divided by a deep cleft that became more conspicuous as he grew older. His teeth were even and white. His hair, very thick and black, turned steel-grey in 1816; it stood out straight in tumbled masses, not because of coarseness—on the contrary it was very fine—but probably because of some extra charge of electricity in his constitution. At the time of his death his hair had turned white, just as his complexion, swarthy in youth, red in middle age, became a sickly brown in his last months. Like Gluck, Haydn and Mozart, he had suffered from smallpox and showed the marks on his skin.

Those eyes of his—what can one say that will give an idea of their terrifying power? Even across a century they excite and frighten. Black eyes, said one observer; bluish-grey, said another; brown, thought a third. Myself, I think that, like those of some other men with a dash of genius, they literally changed colour with their owner's changing emotions. Probably the foundation colour was a sort of flecked hazel-grey, though M. Rolland hazards blue-grey as the real colour. Under strong feeling such eyes might easily look black; indeed, Beethoven's eyes did dilate in an extraordinary way when in a *raptus*; yet in moods of contentment they might just as well seem bluish-grey with the iris calm and clear. In any case they were short-sighted and Beethoven wore glasses till about 1817, when his sight lengthened. Were they beautiful eyes? Dr. Müller (1820) said yes: 'Beautiful, speaking eyes, sometimes gracious and tender, sometimes roving, menacing and terrible.' But in anger they must have kindled to such glinting sparks of fury as might scatter from a devil's eyes. In later life their habitual expression was stern, with an upward gaze—'nach oben'—which Klöber tried to reproduce in his portrait. It was typical of the opposites in his character that he was careful or careless of his appearance with equal equanimity. As a schoolboy he had been negligent, with no distaste for dirt. On settling in Vienna he turned over a new leaf, dressed carefully, bought black silk stockings, took dancing lessons, sported a cravat made for him by Eleonore von Breuning and wrote (November 1793) begging her to give him 'another waistcoat of angora wool knitted by you, my beloved friend. Do forgive your friend's presumption, which is prompted solely by his great preference for everything worked by your hands.'

For a number of years he remained reasonably careful of his appearance—or perhaps it is truer to say he went through regular phases of carelessness when he was at work on some great composition, and carefulness when he was not. Every morning he had a wash all over. When very absorbed in thought, he continued pouring water over his hands for ages (so nice for the ceilings below!), and also at times in the heat of composing he would empty a jug of cold water over his head, a very Beethovenish version of the proverbial wet towel. Shaving was a comprehensive business; he had to shave almost up to his eyes. Apropos of this his pupil Ries told an absurd story, which Thayer quotes. Ries had just returned from a prolonged visit to Silesia and went to see Beethoven.

The master 'was just about to shave, and had lathered himself up to the eyes . . . he jumped up, embraced me cordially and, behold! he had transferred the soap from his left cheek to my right so completely that there was nothing left of it on him. Didn't we laugh!'

One usually reads of Beethoven in his later years as wearing light trousers and an old blue or green coat, with a low top-hat crammed on to the back of his head. He had a best coat of fine brown cloth though, with mother-of-pearl buttons. In his last years everything, even clothes, somehow gets tied up in the tangle of grotesque comedy and heartrending pathos that constituted his contact with the world. I feel as if I could cry when I read Beethoven's letter to Karl: 'I would have managed for two years with the one frock-coat. Admittedly I have the bad habit of putting on a worn out coat at home. But that gentleman Karl, faugh, the shame of it, and why should he do it? Well, because Herr L. v. B[eethove]n's money-bag is there solely for that purpose.' Yet when Karl had needed clothes, Beethoven had written sending money, telling his 'dear son' that 'a little more or less than 21 gulden seems to me the best amount. . . . But indeed for the sake of *one* gulden per ell it is not worth while not to take the best cloth. Choose, or perhaps get someone to choose for you, the best of the two costing about 21 gulden.'

In speech Beethoven's voice was loud and harsh, with the lack of modulation often noticeable in the wholly deaf; his singing voice was raucous; his laughter loud, with something almost frightening about it. Some observers say that from his face it was impossible to judge what he felt. Much of his own knowledge of the world was gleaned through his eyes, for after he could no longer hear what people said, their questions had to be written down in the book he carried for this purpose. Usually he spoke his answers, but sometimes he wrote them down, so that these conversation books became an extraordinarily valuable record of his daily life. Nothing brings home to one more pitifully than these books the isolation in which Beethoven passed over a quarter of a century—unless indeed it be the entries which he made for no eyes but his own, since his deafness denied him the solace of human sympathy tenderly spoken in free intercourse.

'God help me, Thou seest me abandoned by all men, for I do not wish to do wrong, hear my supplication, only for the future to be with my Karl, since the possibility shows itself nowhere, oh, harsh fate, oh, cruel destiny, no, no, my unhappy condition will never end.'

Beethoven's handwriting is not easy to read, but it conveys an overwhelming impression of his personality. As a young Hungarian girl once said: 'Beethoven's handwriting is like an elemental force.' That is true, his letters have lines and curves such as Michelangelo might have traced. But in Beethoven's musical manuscripts the writing is still more a revelation of himself, because it changes with the developments of his genius. One may follow these changes through the manuscripts preserved in the Beethovenhaus at Bonn. In early manhood the general character of the writing is bold, legible, orderly and distinctive. Later, in the 'Moonlight' Sonata, the tremendous urgency of the inspiration is reflected in the manuscript; the notes look as if driven forward on to the paper by a whirlwind. In the last period the writing is less complete in the formation of the signs but infinitely grander in their suggestions; there is something about it hard to express except by the word apocalyptic.

Beethoven had a desultory education, and he was no mathematician, but he knew French, Latin and Italian after a fashion, while the range of his interests, and the quality of mind he brought to bear on them, rightly placed him beside the great intellectuals in an age when intellect was functioning at its keenest. He was acquainted with Persian, Egyptian and Hindu philosophy. A quarter of a century after his death Giulietta Guicciardi, when speaking to Thayer, specially recalled Beethoven's nobility, refined feeling and culture. That would be easily believed from the books in his library, even were they the sole testimony that remained to us. They included Kant's *Theory of the Heavens,* the Bible in French and Latin, the Apocrypha, La Fontaine's *Fables,* Thomas à Kempis, Goethe, Schiller's and Klopstock's complete works, Shakespeare's plays, Plutarch's *Lives,* Cicero's *Epistolae*— also twenty volumes of Campe's *Tales for Children,* an entry which gives one an odd lump in the throat, because Beethoven must have got them for Karl. The classical authors were those whom Beethoven knew and loved when a boy. As a young man he had first learned resignation from Plutarch in the stormy crises of his life; when death approached he turned again to the classics he loved so well. Little Gerhard von Breuning, Stephan's son, running in and out of Beethoven's sick-room, knew this and brought his school-book with pictures of classical antiquities because he thought it might please the dying man. It did. What a charming boy! Beethoven called him Trouser Button, because he clung so to him, and Gerhard with his eager heart gave Beethoven an affection such as Karl had never felt. If Gerhard had been Karl . . .

Poetry was indissolubly woven into the nature of Beethoven's musical thought, and one can hardly separate the two. He read poetry constantly. In his earlier days Klopstock's poems were his delight; later Goethe and Schiller, with Ossian and Homer were his favourites. He told Rochlitz: 'He [Goethe] has killed Klopstock for me. Aha! You smile that I should have read Klopstock! I gave myself up to him many years —when I took my walks and at other times. Ah well! I did not always understand him. He is so restless; and he always

begins too far away, from on high down; always *maestoso*, D
flat major! . . . But why should he always want to die?
That will come soon enough. . . . But Goethe—he lives
and wants us all to live with him. That is the reason he
can be set to music.

Beethoven was a man of intense vitality. He should have
been a healthy one. Yet while his work went on from strength
to strength his physical health was seldom good and failed
lamentably in the last years. No doubt it was partly his own
fault, for though abstemious by the code of the day (he 'only'
drank one bottle of wine at a meal!), he still took more than
was wise for him with his family history. In the same way,
though frugal over food (fish being the delicacy he most liked),
he took his meals so irregularly that one imagines he was
chronically over or under fed. Worst of all were the medicines
he swallowed. The Austrian doctors prescribed 'cures' of a
kind more likely to kill according to modern ideas. One gets
a glimpse into such affairs from a letter Beethoven wrote to the
Countess Erdödy. It is dated Heiligenstadt, 19th June 1817:

MY BELOVED SUFFERING FRIEND, MY DEAREST COUNTESS! Of
late I have been tossed about far too much and overwhelmed with
far too many cares. Then after feeling constantly unwell since
October 6, 1816 I developed on October 15th a violent feverish
cold, so that I had to stay in bed for a very long time; and only after
several months was I allowed to go out even for a short while.
Until now the after effects of this illness *could not be dispelled*. I changed
my doctors, because my own doctor, a wily Italian, had powerful
secondary motives where I was concerned and lacked both honesty
and intelligence. That was in April, 1817. Well, from April 15th
until May 4th I had to take six powders daily and six bowls of tea.
That treatment lasted until May 4th. After that I had to take
another kind of powder, also six times daily; and I had to rub myself three times a day with a volatile ointment. Then I had to come
here where I am taking baths. Since yesterday I have been taking
another medicine, namely, a tincture, of which I have to swallow

12 spoonfuls daily—Every day I hope to see the end of this distressing condition. Although my health has improved a little, yet it will be a long time apparently before I am completely cured.

Of his last illness the medical details are so melancholy that one fairly moans over them. He suffered as much from the treatments as the maladies. In the first month alone he was made to swallow seventy-five bottles of physic, without counting powders. . . . Left to himself, Beethoven's own ideas of hygiene were often sensible. In the matter of lodgings, he insisted that the rooms must be light and airy, not overlooked, with a pleasant view and within easy reach of the country. Most careful. Any one who knows Vienna knows that rooms looking into an inner courtyard are less healthy. Where the careless side of Beethoven's nature showed was in recklessly renting several lodgings at the same time. If he liked the rooms, furnishing them was a secondary affair. His bed was of military hardness. Practically all accounts agree on the poverty and scarcity of his furniture and on the frightful confusion of manuscripts, old meals, old clothes, old anything else, layers of dust, and floor with many places wet. To visit him was an adventure. Major-General Kyd discovered as much when Dr. Bertolini, at Kyd's urgent request, took him to call on Beethoven in September 1816. They found the great man shaving; he looked frightful, his face disfigured by razor cuts, bits of paper and soap. The major-general sat down; the chair immediately crashed under him. (No doubt it had seen service as a missile against a servant!) Kyd naturally supposed Beethoven was in poverty. He offered him two hundred ducats (a hundred pounds) to compose a symphony which he undertook to have performed by the Philharmonic Society in London. Unfortunately Kyd wanted the symphony to be in the style of Beethoven's earlier, rather than his later, ones. Kyd's chance of the symphony crashed like the chair. Beethoven was angry, deeply affronted as an artist. . . . Next day when he saw Kyd in the street, he told Simrock: 'There's the man whom I threw downstairs yesterday!'

Yes, certainly, to visit Beethoven was an adventure.

His personal habits heightened the nightmare. He used to spit out of the window when he remembered, but often enough into the mirror as a substitute. His public manners were so primitive that people usually avoided his table at a restaurant—what must they have been at home! Yet in the midst of his home-slum conditions were to be found his valuables, in the shape of several pianos and the quartet of precious pedigree Italian instruments (a Joseph Guarnerius violin, a Nicholas Amati violin, a Vincenzo Ruggieri viola and an Andreas Guarnerius violoncello) given to him by Prince Lichnowsky. The pianos are reported as looking in a perilous condition. Inkpots had been overturned into their interiors (which is easy to understand), and some of them were without legs (which is difficult to explain). One biographer hazards the guess that Beethoven liked to work lying on the floor! It seems to me arguable that, as he changed his lodgings frequently, the pianos were better carried up and down stairs without their legs. Specht sees in this passion for moving an instance of the same instinct that produced Beethoven's numerous sets of variations, and his fondness for puns; an instinct for bringing the last ounce of development out of some small root. An acute view of the variations and puns; but I am not so sure about the residences. There neighbours must be taken into account. The deaf Beethoven could not realize how much his noises disturbed other people; also he was nervously ready to be disturbed himself. Two stories from his later life illustrate this. Having spent some time at Baden in 1822 with enjoyment, he wished to return to the same rooms next year. The landlord refused, but finally relented on the condition that Beethoven replaced the window shutters which had been removed. Beethoven agreed—and was a good deal amused to learn then that the landlord was killing two birds with one stone, for Beethoven had a habit of writing notes on the shutters, which the landlord had sold as autographs to admiring visitors!

The other story belongs to the year 1824, when Beethoven took rooms on the first floor of a house in Penzing. All promised well; only an old couple inhabited the parterre. But the house was near the bridge over the river Wien: people crossing it stopped to gaze at Beethoven's windows. He probably did look odd, and at no time more so than when dressing. Czerny, who as a child first saw Beethoven about 1803, logically mistook him for Robinson Crusoe, Beethoven being attired in a hairy suit, and with a growth of beard that almost matched the bush of his hair. When he shaved by the window or stood there in his nightshirt he was perfectly unselfconscious; he could not understand why he attracted notice. 'What are those damned boys hooting at?' he asked. Rochlitz, in the year 1822, described Beethoven as giving the impression of 'a very able man reared on a desert island and suddenly brought fresh into the world.' So it was that at Penzing the sophisticated act of pulling the curtains did not appeal to him. Off he went to Baden, and for the rest of the summer paid for both sets of rooms and his flat in Vienna. Unreasonable? Yes, by ordinary standards. But who shall say what obscure laws govern the creation of great art works? The early morning was one of Beethoven's best times for ideas—just as it was with Virgil—and Beethoven had in a tremendous degree the instinct which shields any creative work from observation until it is complete. Outside comments, made too soon, paralyse the growth of a poem or composition.

Beethoven's relations towards his fellow-creatures were a bundle of contradictions. For mankind in general he entertained the loftiest fraternity. This had begun in the generous liberating spirit of the Revolution; it continued under the stimulus of Goethe and Schiller, and was completed by his own nobility. But where individuals were involved, detachment vanished and Beethoven became intensely human and impulsive.

Family loyalty he held sacred. His veneration for his grandfather has been already described. For his father there was always a stern, sheltering silence. To his life's end Beethoven never allowed any one to disparage Johann in his hearing. For his mother there was always tender love and tender memory. Towards his brothers Beethoven acknowledged the blood-tie by repeated acts of financial assistance (highly acceptable to them) and by torrents of advice (non-acceptable), but he felt under no obligations to them, and still less so to their wives. Johann, who incurred his special wrath, he persistently named his pseudo-brother; Johann's wife and her illegitimate daughter he called *Fettlümmerl* and *Bastard*, and Karl's wife was of course 'The Queen of Night.' Such nicknames do not increase family happiness. Thayer excepted, most biographers have represented Beethoven as receiving all the provocation; actually he gave a good fighting account of himself. If brother Johann borrowed money from him, he later borrowed from Johann and was highly unwilling to repay. If his brothers, under cover of helping him with his business affairs, purloined and sold to publishers his early pieces, which he did not intend to publish, he redressed the balance by butting in over their matrimonial affairs, and when Johann sent him a card inscribed 'Johann van Beethoven, Landowner,' he returned the compliment by a card with the words 'Ludwig van Beethoven, Brainowner.' Beethoven was indeed remarkably well able to look after his affairs, so long as his emotions were not too deeply involved. An American music publisher once assured me that, on the evidence of

Beethoven's correspondence with his publishers, Beethoven was a first-class business man. He was capable of singular expedients to meet singular emergencies. The episode of the pirated string Quintet, Op. 29, is an instance. It seems that Breitkopf & Härtel at Leipzig were to publish the work in 1802. Simultaneously and mysteriously an edition issued from the house of Artaria in Vienna—Artaria by sharp prac- tice having obtained a copy of the score from Count Friess, to have it copied hurriedly and surreptitiously. The edition was full of mistakes. Beethoven was furious about the whole thing. However, he requested Artaria to send all the printed copies to Ries, that they might be corrected. 'At the same time,' says Ries, 'he instructed me to use ink on the wretched paper and as coarsely as possible; also to cross out several lines so that it would be impossible to make use of a single copy or sell it. The scratching-out was particularly in the scherzo.' One can imagine the gusto of young Ries over the job.

The matter was eventually settled, but not without a terrific amount of rushing about. Beethoven and brother Karl, who rallied to his assistance, both left racy accounts. Beethoven wrote to Breitkopf & Härtel: 'My *poor brother* has so much business to transact and yet *has done everything he possibly could* to rescue you and me. When doing so he lost *in the general con- fusion* a faithful dog, which he called his favourite. He deserves to be thanked by you in person, as I have already done on my own account'—the thanks being due for a signed agreement extracted from Artaria to withhold his edition from sale till Breitkopf & Härtel's had been in circulation in Vienna for fourteen days.

Beethoven had some ground for his resentment against publishers, yet even for those times his feelings were extreme and his language strongly explosive when he wrote to Holz in August 1825: 'It is all the same to me what hellhound licks or gnaws away my brain, since admittedly it must be so; but let us hope the answer will not be delayed for too long. That hell-hound at L[eipzig] can wait and in the meantime enjoy in Auerbach's cellar the company of Mephistopheles (the editor of the L[eipziger] Musikal[ische] Zeitung). Beelzebub, chief of the devils, will shortly seize the latter by the ears.'

To be frank, Beethoven too was not above reproach. His strong natural probity warped when money had to be wrung out of his compositions to support Karl. On Karl he centred everything: his love for him was the sum total of his nature, yet by its intensity and possessiveness it defeated itself.

Every year increased the heartbreak for Beethoven. Reading his letters to Karl, their poignant humanity leaps out of the pages as agonized as if they had been written yesterday. Of course they are all wrong for the result they were intended to produce, but a hundred years ago people still believed in the efficacy of moral precepts, reminders and reproaches. Here is an example of the precepts, a letter written from Baden in 1825:

DEAR SON!

The old woman has just turned up. So don't worry, work hard at your books and get up early in the morning. By doing so you could even manage to do several things for me which might crop up—It is certainly very desirable for a youth who is almost nineteen to combine the duties pertaining to his own education and advance-ment with those he owes to his benefactor and supporter—Why, I certainly fulfilled in every way my duties to my parents—

> In great haste,
> your faithful father.

Here is a specimen of the reproaches—Karl having concealed the fact that he had got money from some unknown person:

Spoilt as you are it would not do you any harm to cultivate *at last simplicity and truth*. For my heart has suffered too much from your deceitful behaviour to me; and it is hard to forget it. Even if I were willing to pull the whole burden like a yoked ox and without murmuring, yet your behaviour, if it is directed against others in the same way, can never attract to you people who will love you—God is my witness that my sole dream is to get away completely from you and from that wretched brother and that horrible family who have been thrust upon me. May God grant my wishes. For I *can* no longer trust *you*—

Unfortunately your father
or, better still, not your father.

Karl's point of view remains to us in a record of a conversation between him and his uncle in 1826.

'You consider it insolence,' says Karl, 'if after you have upbraided me for hours undeservedly, that this time at least I cannot turn from my bitter feeling of pain to jocularity,' and much more in the same strain. Yet even in his natural resentment at being treated like a child, Karl's posing and vanity peep out, and as one reaches the point at which the fear of Karl's suicide dawned on Beethoven, one's heart is wholly with the foster father when he wrote:

MY BELOVED SON!

Stop, no further—Only come to my arms, you won't hear a single hard word. For God's sake, do not abandon yourself to misery. You will be welcomed here as affectionately as ever. We will lovingly discuss what has to be considered and what must be done for the future. On my word of honour you will hear no reproaches. . . . But do come—come to the faithful heart of

your father
BEETHOVEN.

Come home as soon as you receive this note. Si vous ne viendres pas vous me túerès surement. . . . For God's sake, do come home again today. If not, who knows what danger may confront you? Hurry, hurry.

If love and anxiety kill, Karl did ultimately bring Beethoven to his grave.

Beethoven's love affairs, numerous, romantic and mysterious though they be, are incidental by comparison—a set of variations on the single theme of a search for the ideal wife. Like a white Don Juan he always sought and never found. One of his biographers—Specht, I think—shrewdly remarks that all his love affairs were in reality with the same woman—the ideal being, she whom he had imagined in his youth and sighed for till the end. Perhaps she did not exist, but had she done so, Beethoven could never have found her. He had not the great understanding, loving-and-giving heart requisite for a true-love marriage.

Yet in the corrupt Vienna of that day, where most married women of fashion took a lover as a matter of custom, Beethoven kept his honour sternly. He wrote to Marie Bigot and her husband in 1807: 'It is one of my chief principles *never to be in any other relationship than that of friendship with the wife of another man. For I should not wish by forming any other kind of relationship to fill my heart with distrust of that woman who some day will perhaps share my fate*—and thus by my own action to destroy the loveliest and purest relationship.'

Herein lay one secret of Beethoven's marvellous circle of friends. Men and women alike trusted him morally. What friends they were! The Breuning family and Wegeler, like Good Deeds in *Everyman,* went with him to his life's end. Then there was that fine old loud-voiced aristocrat Prince Lichnowsky, and his delicate wife, who was a second mother to Beethoven.

Prince Lobkowitz has already been mentioned. His friendship survived even insults. At one of the general rehearsals for *Fidelio* in 1805 the third bassoon[1] was absent. Lobkowitz tried lightly to pacify Beethoven by saying that as two bassoons were present 'the absence of the third could make no great difference.' This infuriated Beethoven, who vented his wrath

[1] Presumably the contrabassoon.

on the way home by shouting 'Lobkowitzian ass' into the door of the Lobkowitz palace!

Among other friends were the Archduke Rudolph, who could play Beethoven's music so well, the generous Prince Kinsky, Count Franz von Brunswick, whom Beethoven called 'brother,' Zmeskall, and then the unceasing stream of young men who admired and served Beethoven, chief among them Ferdinand Ries, Schindler, Holz. These men saw more of the rough side of Beethoven's nature than his women friends, with whom he was often astonishingly intuitive, especially in time of sorrow. Every one knows the story of his playing to Baroness Ertmann, and probably saving her reason, when she was overwhelmed with grief by the death of her child. Less well known and not less touching is the story that relates how, when Madame Brentano was laid up ill for long weeks, he used to come regularly, seat himself at a pianoforte in her ante-room without a word and improvise; after he had finished 'telling her everything and bringing comfort' in his language, he would go as he had come, without taking notice of another person.

These friendships with women were a remarkable feature in his character, for though he was seldom without some romantic attachment, he could and did carry on fine, frank friendships with a number of gifted women that for lack of a better name must be called Platonic. The Countess Erdödy and Nanette Streicher have been mentioned already. Others were the pianists Marie Bigot and Marie Pachler-Koschak, and the Baroness Dorothea von Ertmann, an amateur so musical that he called her his 'dear Dorothea Cecilia.' Women, it is said, played his piano works better than men at that time—at least they appear to have grasped what he wanted more quickly, though one finds it hard to believe any woman could have played the Sonata Op. 111 to his satisfaction.

But man or woman, friendship with Beethoven was no

sinecure. The strong peasant vein of suspicion running through his nature had been increased by his deafness, and his experience of Viennese intrigue made it worse. Friends might suddenly find themselves smitten with a thunderbolt of Beethoven's anger. The following letters were addressed to the same person, whose identity is uncertain. The first is written in the third person in the original German—a sign of contempt:

Don't come to me any more! You are a false dog, and may the hangman do away with all false dogs.

Dear little Ignaz of my heart![1]

You are an honest fellow and I now realize that you were right. So come to me this afternoon. You will find Schuppanzigh here too and we shall both blow you up, cudgel you and shake you so that you will have a thoroughly good time.

Kisses from your Beethoven, also called dumpling.[2]

It is to be hoped he entertained Hummel more enjoyably than those friends whom he once invited to a meal cooked by himself. Genius has a foible of priding itself on second-string accomplishments, as Browning knew when he wrote:

> None but would forgo his proper dowry,—
> Does he paint? he fain would write a poem,—
> Does he write? he fain would paint a picture.

(Though it is a shame to wrest those lines from their lovely context.)

Well, Beethoven had become sufficiently Viennese to regard food and cookery as an art, and when his guests arrived he greeted them in the guise of a cook, a nightcap on his head, a white apron tied round him and a ladle in his hand. After

---

[1] *Herzensnazerl.*

[2] *Mehlschöberl,* said to be Viennese dialect for a sort of soup dumpling.

a long wait the meal appeared—the soup dish-water, with a little grease, the beef leather, the vegetables a nondescript paste. The master, it is related, beamed with satisfaction; he never noticed that his guests starved!

To be a special crony of Beethoven's was to attract nicknames from him as steel pins go to a magnet. They sometimes pricked, but the devoted Zmeskall seemed to thrive on them. Beethoven's letters to him are full of knockabout humour—as, for instance, when he asked for some more pens:

> The Honourable Herr von Z. must hurry up a bit with the plucking of his quills (amongst which there are probably a few foreign ones). We hope that they are not too firmly stuck into you—As soon as you do all that we wish, we shall be with the greatest respect wholly your
>
> BEETHOVEN.

His whole intercourse with Zmeskall, until just before the end, was like a succession of his scherzos enacted in life. That humour was no light play of wit (like the French) nor kindly fun (like the English), but a tremendous force that leaped out, struck and buffeted, laughed like the waves under a flashing wind and high sun. Beethoven hurled his puns, hit or miss; he loved a bad pun better than none at all, and sometimes went beyond discretion, as when he made play with the name of Holz and 'Holz vom Kreuze Christi,' the wood of the Cross. Sometimes his humour became a bear's rough-and-tumble, though not quite so much out of hand as it appeared. In a letter to Breitkopf & Härtel in 1812 he writes: 'So in Saxony the saying runs "as rude as a musician". And indeed it might well be applied to me, for incidentally I told you in jest a few home truths.' Yes, Beethoven was very well able to fend for himself when he spared time and thought to do so, and one is inclined to impute some of his comparative freedom from enemies to this salutary knowledge among his compatriots.

His immunity from political molestation was, however, due to other causes. Politics were his favourite subject. He discoursed on them freely in public, criticized the Austrian Government, the aristocracy and the police to his heart's content.

'The police paid no attention to his utterances,' says Thayer, 'either because they looked upon him as a harmless fantastic or had an overwhelming respect for his artistic genius.' Yet here again Beethoven had a shrewd side, for he said: 'There is nothing smaller than our great folk, but I make an exception of the archdukes,' and as a political forecast, few things more neatly hit the mark than his letter to Simrock where he says:

We are having very hot weather here; and the Viennese are afraid that soon they will not be able to get any more *ice cream*. For, as the winter was so mild, ice is scarce. Here various *important* people have been locked up; it is said that a revolution was about to break out—But I believe that so long as an Austrian can get his *brown ale* and his *little sausages,* he is not likely to revolt.

CHAPTER IX

BEETHOVEN THE MUSICIAN

To Beethoven's friends the man who walked and talked with them in the streets of Vienna was the real man, a bundle of consistent inconsistencies, with an appeal to their loyalty that was simultaneously royal and lost-child-like.

To Beethoven himself it appeared that he realized his true being only in music and in the intercourse with nature which was for him an entrance into the unseen world.

One turns with something like relief from the troubled half-truths of his outer existence to the radiant truths of his inner life. Here were no inconsistencies, only an unswerving dedication of himself to an ideal of music which, for height, purity and grandeur resembled that of an inspired prophet. First glimpsed when he was a boy, he travelled towards the ever-growing splendour up to the moment when death opened for him the unknown doors into full light.

Before studying him as a composer, it is well to consider him as an executant, on the principle of proceeding from the less to the greater.

Beethoven, then, had learned to play the piano, organ, violin and viola, and he was a conductor, though an eccentric one. The organ he abandoned when still young, because the heavy vibrations affected his nerves. The conducting abandoned him when he became deaf. The violin was never his real *métier*. He roared with laughter at the legend of having charmed flies and spiders as a child, and told Schindler his scrapings were far more likely to have driven them away. Probably his viola playing was no better. But though Beethoven might not be a fine string player, he understood the soul of string instruments and was quick to appreciate the distinctions in style between the numerous violinists who performed his works. No one could suppose for a moment that he had the same player in view when he composed the 'Kreutzer' Sonata and the Sonata in G major, Op. 96, for violin and piano. Indeed he had not, for the dashing Bridge-tower was the first to play the 'Kreutzer' and Op. 96 was designed for the lofty, classic, calmly beautiful style of Rode.

As with the violin, so with all other instruments in the orchestra; Beethoven took pains to inform himself exactly of what they could and could not do. If he sometimes demanded so much from them that orchestral players laughed at his passages and declared them impossible (as, for example, the famous double bass passage in the trio of the fifth Symphony), it was because he formed his opinion on the capacity of exceptional players. Instinctively he knew that the 'excep-tional' of one century becomes the 'standard' of the next in matters of executive technique.

So it must be remembered that Beethoven was intimate with the playing of such remarkable artists as Kreutzer, Clement, Rode, Schuppanzigh (violinists), Weiss (viola), Bernhard Romberg (cello), Dragonetti (double bass), Anton Reicha (flute), Ramm (oboe), Anton Romberg (bassoon), Punto (horn). Not that all of them were ready to learn from Beethoven. Bernhard Romberg once asked Spohr how he could play such *barockes Zeug* (absurd stuff) as Beethoven's Quartets, Op. 18; he is also said to have thrown the first Rasumovsky Quartet on the floor and trampled on it.

But while Beethoven was ready to learn from all these players, he stood second to none himself as a pianist. In youth his playing had rather too much of organ style about it; in age he was too vehement and (because of his deafness) inaccurate. A fantasia from him was enough to put a piano out of action, and once, in a rage, he broke six strings with the first chord. But when he was in his prime, say in the years 1796 to 1801, to hear him must have been the most memorable experience of a lifetime. Small, smooth-groomed playing never appealed to him, though he could imitate it elegantly when he liked. On the contrary, he loved a big, grand style, bordering on the orchestral, with a resultant diversity of tone-colouring then new, and a *cantilena* said to have been 'stirring,' full-toned and sustained like organ notes; the tones ran together in long, unbroken melodic lines, 'like the drawing of a violin bow.' Ah! if one could but hear Beethoven's playing, instead of piecing together these written accounts. Tomaschek, who head him in 1798 and called him 'the giant among pianoforte players,' said that Beethoven's playing is extremely 'brilliant, but has less delicacy [than that of Wölfl], and occasionally he is guilty of indistinctness'—which looks as if Beethoven made considerable use of the penumbra of after-sounds obtainable through the pedal. Cherubini thought him rough as a player. He was also a variable one —sometimes confused and freakish, at others brilliant, intellectual, full of characteristic expression, capable of producing the most extraordinary emotional effect upon his hearers. Czerny says that no one equalled Beethoven in the rapidity of his scales, double trills, skips, etc., and mentions that he used both pedals far more frequently than is indicated in his works. The school of Carl Philipp Emanuel Bach was the foundation of his technique. He attached great importance to the correct position of the fingers, and his own were very powerful, though not long. When playing, his demeanour was 'masterfully quiet, noble and beautiful, without the slightest grimace— only bent forward low, as his deafness grew upon him.'

It was like him that for music he would bend that proud head which pain could not bow.

Beethoven was a king of musicians and he knew it with the directness of great dignity. When Frederick William of Prussia sent him a ring and a friend said something about his accepting it because it came from a king, Beethoven replied quite simply: 'I too am a king.'

Being a king, he had little patience with pretenders, though towards pupils—the humble and meek—he was endlessly patient. There was a streak of the pretender in Ignaz Pleyel, Haydn's former pupil and rival. Czerny relates that Pleyel had come from Paris bringing his newest quartets, and he and they were fêted at a big party at Prince Lobkowitz's. Beethoven was present. After the programme ended, he was asked to play. Bad-tempered about it, he walked to the piano, picked up on the way the second violin part of one of Pleyel's quartets, threw it on the desk upside down and began to improvise. Czerny continues:

He had never been heard to improvise more brilliantly, with more originality and splendour than on this evening, but through the entire improvisation there ran through the middle voices like a thread or *cantus firmus* the notes, in themselves utterly insignificant, which he found on the accidentally opened page of the quartet, upon which he built up the most daring melodies and harmonies in the most brilliant concerto style. Old Pleyel could show his amazement only by kissing his hands.

There was also an occasion when the renowned Abt Vogler and Beethoven extemporized to each other. What a subject for Browning to put into poetry! As it was, Gänsbacher, the man to whom we owe the account, preferred Vogler's learned fuguing to Beethoven's 'abundance of the most beautiful thoughts.'

To-day it is the fashion to deprecate extemporization, academic musicians regarding it as a spurious approach to composition. Really? A method which served in the production of such music as that of Gluck, Haydn and Beethoven cannot be seriously wrong. Besides, although Beethoven never attended a conservatorium, his voluntary academic training had been so rigorous that he could have got a Mus. Doc. at a university any day. There is another argument. Beethoven was acknowledged on all sides as supreme in extemporization long before his written compositions had shown the magnitude of his genius. This offers a personal parallel to Romain Rolland's theory about the tendencies of a nation becoming audible in its music long before the events happen. It was so with Beethoven. He first found access to his ideal and to true self-expression through extemporization; from that he advanced to the earliest full written personal expression in his piano music; and finally reached unfettered eloquence in all forms of music.

It is enthralling to trace the successive stages of his genius. In early years he certainly learned much that was never taught him—effects impressed on his sensitive nature by the music of other composers. Mozart was the predominant influence. Beethoven felt it so strongly that he realized the danger and for a time avoided hearing Mozart's operas, lest they should destroy his individuality.

That Mozart affected him powerfully is not surprising, for Mozart was a revelation of perfection such as music had never known before. He has been called 'the composers' composer.' Beethoven loved Mozart, and 'that which I love educates me,' as a modern composer has well said. Those magic touches of Mozart, simple yet miraculous, moved Beethoven to the core of his being. That we know—quite apart from the evidence of his music—by the story which Madame Cramer preserved of her husband. John Cramer and Beethoven were walking in the Augarten, listening to a performance of Mozart's piano Concerto in C minor (K. 491). (Cramer, it is worth remembering, was the only pianist whom Beethoven praised.) As the concerto neared its end Beethoven suddenly stood still, drew Cramer's attention to the lovely motive which is first introduced towards the close and exclaimed: 'Cramer, Cramer, we shall never be able to do anything like that!' and then surrendered himself entirely to the music, swaying to and fro and marking the rhythm in extreme delight. The *love* of Mozart remained throughout his life, though the danger of a swamped individuality passed. It may be fancy—yet I think not—that I seem to hear behind the ceremonial music of even so late a work as Beethoven's overture, *Die Weihe des Hauses* (*The Dedication of the House*, 1822), the solemn tones and fugal dignity of Mozart's *Zauberflöte.* It was Beethoven's favourite Mozart opera.

Other influences that entered his early life are not so recog-nizable. M. Cucuel remarks thematic *rapports*—rather far-fetched perhaps—between Grétry's operas, *Le Tableau parlant, Richard Cœur de Lion, Le Jugement de Midas* and *La Rosière de Salency,* given at Bonn when Beethoven was there, and Beethoven's own Sonatas, Opp. 7, 13, 24, 27 and 31, no. 2, the *Albumblatt für Elise,* the Scene by the Brook in the Pastoral Symphony, the opening to the Waldstein Sonata, and the overture to *King Stephen.* Cucuel also asserts similarity between the theme of Joy, ninth Symphony, the final chorus of *Fidelio* and the final chorus of the *Deserter* by Monsigny. Other writers have alluded to certain harmonic and thematic devices imbibed from a study of Carl Philipp Emanuel Bach's music. Beethoven certainly valued his work, for as late as 1809 he wrote to Breitkopf that 'I have only a few samples of Emanuel Bach's compositions for the clavier; and yet some of them should certainly be in the possession of every true artist.'

Beethoven also valued Clementi, 'the father of the piano-forte.' How much of his work was known to Beethoven during early years is hard to determine, but M. Prod'homme, following Teodor de Wyzewa, thinks Neefe made him play Clementi's Opp. 5, 6, 8 and 14, and that 'the expression, so novel, which Clementi gave to his thoughts, must have pleased the pupil of Neefe.' It is sure, however, not conjectural, that Beethoven's compositions show traces of Clementi's methods, though the two men never met till 1804 and did not make friends till 1807, when, 'by a little management and without committing myself, I have at last made a conquest of the haughty beauty, Beethoven,' wrote Clementi to Collard.

I am disposed to believe that Beethoven's mental relations with the music of Handel, Gluck and J. S. Bach have not been sufficiently considered. He certainly became acquainted with works by all three composers at Bonn. In vocal writing his style is much nearer to Handel and Gluck than to Mozart, for it has the same curious unplastic effect as Handel's arias—an effect comparable to a frieze in bas-relief, as against the fully rounded style of Mozart's operatic writing. Young ears are receptive, and Beethoven had a glowing admiration for Handel. Towards the end of his life he raised Handel to the supreme place in his regard. 'Whom do you consider the greatest composer that ever lived?' asked Stumpff. 'Handel; to him I bow the knee,' said Beethoven instantly, and bent one knee to the floor. At that time he knew only the scores of *The Messiah* and *Alexander's Feast*. Two years later Stumpff gladdened Beethoven's last days by a present of Handel's complete works. With Gluck we are on less certain ground, but Beethoven heard his operas at Bonn, and Czerny refers to his playing of the scores of Handel and Gluck as unique, 'in that he introduced a full-voicedness and a spirit which gave these works a new shape.' The correspondence in feeling between a portion of Gluck's music for the scene in the Elysian Fields in his opera *Orfeo* and Beethoven's Scene by the Brook in his Pastoral Symphony merits more than casual thought. There is the same sort of glowing serenity and unbroken beauty—even the birds appear in both.

Beethoven

In Beethoven's time John Sebastian Bach had not come into his own. Nevertheless I feel convinced that Beethoven knew more of his music than is generally supposed. Neefe had seen to that when he grounded him on the *Well-tempered Clavier*. The direct references to J. S. Bach in Beethoven's letters are illuminating. To Hofmeister in 1801 he says: 'Your desire to publish *the works of Sebastian Bach* is something that really warms my heart which beats sincerely for the sublime and magnificent art of that first father of harmony. . . . Enter my name as a subscriber to the works of *Johann Sebastian Bach*, and also the name of *Prince Lichnowsky*.' To Breitkopf in the same year, he calls Bach 'the immortal god of harmony' and offers to publish a work for the benefit of Bach's daughter, now in poverty.

Again in 1803: 'Thank you very much for the fine works of *Sebastian Bach*. I will *treasure and study* them—If there is to be a sequel, do let me have it too.'

Then in 1810: 'I should like to have all the works of Carl Philipp Emanuel Bach, . . . and also a Mass composed by J. Sebastian Bach [the Mass in B minor] in which there is said to be the following Crucifixus with a basso ostinato [quoted]. Again you are said to have the best copy of Bach's Temperiertes Klavier. Please have it sent to me as well.'

Finally, from 1822 to 1825, Beethoven projected an overture on the musical motive of Bach's name:

B A C H

Bach himself had employed the theme in his *Art of Fugue,* and Beethoven perhaps planned his overture as a tribute. Alas! it was never written, though sketches lie scattered about among those for the last quartets.

So much, then, for direct references to Bach. The indirect

---

[1] In German B natural is called H.

ones are even more interesting, for they show J. S. Bach constantly in the background of Beethoven's æsthetic code. At least, so it seems to me, though I must shoulder responsibility for the idea. I believe, then, that Beethoven's strong feeling for key-character and key-colour was derived from J. S. Bach, as exemplified in his *Well-tempered Clavier*. Neefe, Beethoven's best teacher during boyhood's days (therefore during the most impressionable time), had come to Bonn steeped in the tradition of J. S. Bach at Leipzig. In turn he steeped his pupil in the wonderful forty-eight preludes and fugues of the *Well-tempered Clavier,* wherein Bach had enshrined his finest instincts and convictions with regard to key and scale. Bach was predominantly a contrapuntal composer, Beethoven predominantly of the new harmonic style, but key was the basis of that new style, and in the '48' Bach established key in a security that lasted for nearly two hundred years. Beethoven's mastery of key relations and contrasts has never been equalled by any other composer. I believe it was Johann Sebastian Bach who put that key into his hands, if I may be forgiven the bad pun.

Few sayings of Beethoven on the æsthetics of music have come down to us. Happily a talk he had with August Kanne, a poet-musician, has been preserved. Kanne contended that it made no difference to a composition whether it stood in the original key or was transposed. Beethoven was positive that keys had definite inner significance. 'He defended his position on logical grounds, claiming that each key is associated with certain moods, and that no piece of music should be transposed.' From other records we know that Beethoven associated D flat major with solemnity and death; B flat minor for him was a 'black' key.

Without pushing the correspondence too far—which would reduce the feeling between Bach and Beethoven from the spirit to the letter—I think their similarity of view over key characteristics can be tested by any one who cares to compare their compositions. Take Bach's two Preludes and Fugues in C sharp minor and then place beside them Beethoven's Quartet in C sharp minor, Op. 131. Or compare Bach's Fugue in E major, Book II (which Samuel Wesley called 'The Saints in Glory'), with Beethoven's Sonata for piano in E major, Op. 109. Look at the F major Fugue, Book I, and then turn to the *andante* from Beethoven's first Symphony, or consider the character of Bach's two G major Preludes and Fugues and note the sense one experiences of breathing the same atmosphere in Beethoven's two Sonatas in G major for piano and violin.

Beethoven's debt to Bach was unacknowledged because unconscious. His acknowledgments to Haydn were withheld, maybe, for the same reason, though I find it hard to believe he did not know that Haydn's bold strokes of enharmonic modulation were the startingpoint for his own, or that the famous trumpet calls in his overtures, *Leonora* No. 2 and No. 3, had their prototype in the unaccompanied trumpet solo in Haydn's Military Symphony. Whatever Beethoven chose to tell the world, his music proves again and again that in reality Haydn's influence upon him was stronger and far more lasting than that of Mozart.

With smaller composers Beethoven was perfectly aware of his debt, as for instance with old Aloys Förster, from whom he learned the true art of writing quartets. His debt to Paer was more cynically acknowledged when he went to hear the latter's opera *Achilles*. After repeated exclamations of praise, Beethoven exclaimed: 'I must compose that!' 'That' was the much admired Funeral March! Beethoven did exactly what he said—the first result was the Funeral March in his Sonata in A flat major for piano, Op. 26; the second, his Funeral March in the *Eroica* Symphony.

Of the outward times and seasons of Beethoven's work, we know that he spent the winters in Vienna, completing and scoring the music for which the inspirations had come to him during his summer and autumn sojourns in the country. His Viennese day was something like this. Rose very early, worked all the morning with breakfast somewhere, dinner some time after noon (if he remembered to eat it), then for a walk round the ramparts of Vienna, and to friends or the theatre in the evening. The routine naturally varied when he had rehearsals to attend or pupils to teach, but roughly it represented the winter norm.

In summer all was changed. Beethoven would rise at dawn to spend long days, and even nights, in the open air. Later he gave up night rambling and in his last autumn (1826) came in at midday for dinner and a rest before going out again till sunset.

Gluck was fond of composing in the open air. If I recollect rightly his biographers describe him as placing his clavier in a meadow, putting a bottle of champagne on it, and then proceeding to compose. But with Beethoven nature was a passion, for which the best parallel can be found in Words-worth. The poet, however, gleaned and gave out less than Beethoven, with whom it was as if in a special way he felt himself part of the great spiritual life of the universe. In old mythology and folk-lore there have been men who understood the speech of birds, the voice of waters, and could see the unseen things. Beethoven loved until he too something saw and understood.

Neate, the English pianist to whom Beethoven took a warm liking, testified that he had never met a man who so enjoyed nature, or who took such intense delight in flowers, in the clouds, in everything—nature was like food to him, he seemed really to live in it.

That is true. Beethoven did live in it because when with nature he was most himself, and to be 'most himself' meant for him, as for Mozart, to be most a musician. Though the letter in which Mozart is supposed to explain the way in which he composed has long been shown to be spurious and can hardly be accepted as an authentic account of his methods, it does none the less carry conviction as to its substance by its uncanny knowledge of the processes of musical creation:

When I am, as it were, completely myself, entirely alone, and of good cheer—say, travelling in a carriage or walking after a good meal, or during the night when I cannot sleep; it is on such occasions that my ideas flow best and most abundantly. *Whence* and *how* they come, I know not; nor can I force them. Those ideas that please me I retain in memory, and am accustomed, as I have been told, to hum them to myself. If I continue in this way, it soon occurs to me how I may turn them to account, so as to make a good dish of it, that is to say, agreeably to the rules of counterpoint, to the peculiarities of the various instruments. All this fires my soul, and, provided I am not disturbed, my subject enlarges itself, becomes methodized and defined, and the whole, though it be long, stands almost complete and finished in my mind, so that I can survey it, like a fine picture or a beautiful statue, at a glance. Nor do I hear in my imagination the parts *successively*, but I hear them, as it were, simultaneously (*gleich alles zusammen*). What a delight this is I cannot tell! All this inventing, this producing, takes place in a pleasing, lively dream. Still the actual hearing of the *tout ensemble* is after all the best.

(If any one wants to contend that it is impossible for a piece of music to be heard all at once, since music depends on its progress through Time, let them remember that Time is comprehended in Eternity.)

Now hear Beethoven to Breitkopf (in 1812):

If only Heaven will give me patience until I have gone abroad, then I shall be in a position to find in myself my true calling, which is the sole possible good for a man and especially for an artist.—If only I can be patient. But if all else is denied to me, I can once more find comfort in nature and immediately too in my heavenly art, the only true divine gift of Heaven.

Inspiration

He told Louis Schlösser in 1823:

I carry my thoughts about me for a long time, before I write them down. Meanwhile my memory is so tenacious that I am sure never to forget, not even in years, a theme that has once occurred to me. I change many things, discard and try again until I am satisfied. Then, however, there begins in my head the development in every direction and, insomuch as I know exactly what I want, the fundamental idea never deserts me—it arises before me, grows— I see and hear the picture in all its extent and dimensions stand before my mind like a cast, and there remains for me nothing but the labour of writing it down, which is quickly accomplished when I have the time, for I sometimes take up other work, but never to the confusion of one with the other.

This tallies exactly with what Beethoven had told Wegeler many years previously, that 'hardly have I completed one composition when I have already begun another. At my present rate of composing, I often produce three or four works at the same time.' His sketch-books prove this.

Beethoven continued to Schlösser:

You will ask where my ideas come from. I cannot say for certain. They come uncalled, sometimes independently, sometimes in association with other things. It seems to me that I could wrest them from Nature herself with my own hands, as I go walking in the woods. They come to me in the silence of the night or in the early morning, stirred into being by moods which the poet would translate into words, but which I put into sounds; and these go through my head ringing and singing and storming until at last I have them before me as notes.

These accounts of Beethoven's creative process are profoundly interesting. With him, as with the author of the letter attributed to Mozart, the first condition for good composition was to be 'most himself'—a happy state found most readily in the open air or at night. But whereas the method described in that letter implies the shaping of initial ideas into a completed whole before anything is written down, there is reason to think that Beethoven glimpsed the completed whole first, and his endless sketches were his repeated attempts to catch the true likeness of what he already knew in his soul to be the reality. Musicologists have spent enormous labour in demonstrating from Beethoven's sketch-books how laboriously he built up his compositions, altering again and again almost to the scriptural seventy times seven. Even warm-hearted Sir George Grove went so far as to say: 'One is prompted to believe not that he [Beethoven] had the idea first and then expressed it, but that it often came in the process of finding the expression.'

Mr. Ernest Newman, in his brilliant study of *The Unconscious Beethoven,* saw through that fallacy, just as he penetrated behind the sketches to their cause. Of the sketches for the *Eroica* Symphony he says:

Here, more than anywhere else, do we get that curious feeling that in his greatest works Beethoven was 'possessed'—the mere human instrument through which a vast musical design realized itself in all its marvellous logic . . . We have the conviction that his mind did not proceed from the particular to the whole, but began, in some curious way, with the whole and then worked back to the particular . . . The long and painful search for the themes was simply an effort, not to find workable atoms out of which he could construct a musical edifice according to the conventions of symphonic form, but to reduce an already existing nebula, in which that edifice was implicit, to the atom, and then, by the orderly arrangement of these atoms, to make the implicit explicit.

That carries conviction. Furthermore, I should like to suggest that a distinctive feature of ideas which float up from the unconscious into consciousness is their evanescence, an evanescence comparable to that of the rainbow. One minute they are so bright, it seems impossible they could perish; the next they have faded and may never be seen again. Beethoven's habit of sketching sprang from such a feeling. He began it in boyhood, and there was no hour of the twenty-four when he had not a sketch-book at hand. He told the Archduke Rudolph in 1815 of 'the bad habit I formed in childhood of feeling obliged to write down my first ideas immediately, apart from the fact that they certainly have often come to nothing', and in another letter (1823) he advises him that 'when sitting at the pianoforte you should jot down your ideas in the form of sketches. For this purpose you should have a small table beside the pianoforte. In this way not only is one's imagination stimulated but one learns also to pin down immediately the most remote ideas.' How to *fix* ideas. In that sentence Beethoven explains the fundamental purpose of his sketches, and the apparent, but not real, discrepancy between his sketches and his statement that he never forgot any theme that had once occurred to him. The first sketch, tiny though it might be, was sufficient to anchor the meta-physical idea to the regions of material consciousness. Further, a close study of the processes by which Beethoven achieved his compositions strongly confirms the impression which many of his greatest works make of existing beyond the confines of this earth. In the first movement of the Choral Symphony, in the last quartets, and in the piano Sonatas Opp. 109 and 111 the location is definitely outside ordinary experience.

How was it, one asks, that Beethoven had access to this world of greater knowledge which has been known only to the few—to an Isaiah, a Socrates, Paul, Virgil, Dante— and which Christ came to reveal? It came, I think—and I say it very humbly—from Beethoven's understanding of God. Organized religion and ritual meant very little to him; God meant everything. He was profoundly religious in his aware-ness of God's reality, and his relation to that reality shaped his whole life. Every tree seemed to him to say: 'Holy, holy . . .'

On his desk stood constantly some sentences which he had written out and framed. They were his creed.

I am that which is.
I am all that is, that was, and that shall be.
No mortal man hath lifted my veil.
He is alone by Himself, and to Him alone do all things owe their being.

There is a precious manuscript page in the library of the Royal College of Music on which Beethoven copied some passages, drawn apparently from the sacred books of the East—the Upanishads, perhaps.

God is immaterial; as He is invisible, He can therefore have no form. But from what we are able to perceive in His works we conclude that He is eternal, almighty, omniscient and omnipresent. The mighty one, He alone is free from all desire or passion. There is no greater than He, Brahm; His mind is self-existent. He, the Almighty, is present in every part of space. His omniscience is self-inspired, and His conception includes every other. Of His all-embracing attributes the greatest is omniscience. For it there is no threefold kind of being—it is independent of everything—O God! Thou art the true, eternal, blessed, unchangeable light of all time and space. Thy wisdom apprehends thousands and still thousands of laws, and yet Thou ever actest of Thy free will, and to Thy honour. Thou wast before all that we worship. To Thee is due praise and adoration. Thou alone art the true, Blessed (Bhagavan), Thou the best of all laws, the image of all wisdom, present throughout the whole world, Thou attainest all things. Sun, Ether, Brahm.[1]

(Beethoven crossed out these last three words.)

Hymn

Spirit of spirits, who, spreading Thyself through all space and endless time, art raised high above all limits of upward struggling thought, from riot didst Thou command beautiful order to arise.

---

[1] Translation by J. S. Shedlock.

Before the $\begin{Bmatrix} \text{worlds} \\ \text{heavens} \end{Bmatrix}$ were, Thou wast, and before systems rolled below and above us. Before the earth swam in heavenly ether, Thou alone wast, until through Thy secret love that which was not sprang into being, and gratefully sang praises to Thee. What moved Thee to manifest Thy power and boundless goodness? What brilliant light directed Thy power? Wisdom beyond measure! How was it first manifested? Oh! direct my mind! Oh! raise it up from this grievous depth.[1]

Alongside of these religious utterances must be read two accounts which have come down to us of Beethoven's own words on the relation between religion and music. One is contained in a letter from Bettina von Arnim to Goethe, recounting her first talk with Beethoven:

He himself said: 'When I open my eyes I must sigh, for what I see is contrary to my religion, and I must despise the world which does not know that music is a higher revelation than all wisdom and philosophy. . . . Well I know that God is nearer to me than to other artists; I associate with Him without fear; I have always recognized and understood Him and have no fear for my music— it can meet no evil fate. Those who understand it must be freed by it from all the miseries which the others drag about with them selves. . . . Music, verily, is the mediator between intellectual and sensuous life. . . . Speak to Goethe about me; tell him to hear my symphonies and he will say that I am right in saying that music is the one incorporeal entrance into the higher world of knowledge which comprehends mankind but which mankind cannot com prehend. . . . We do not know what knowledge brings us. . . . Every real creation of art is independent, more powerful than the artist himself and returns to the divine through its manifestation. It is one with man only in this, that it bears testimony to the mediation of the divine in him.'

Beethoven truly speaks in these words. Bettina, clever as she was, could never have invented the thoughts they express,

[1] Translation by J. S. Shedlock.

because such ideas are not to be reached by mere cleverness. The same argument applies to J. A. Stumpff's report of what Beethoven said about composition; the *ideas* are unmistakably Beethoven's, though the words have taken on a certain grandiloquence in Stumpff's transcription.

Here they are:

When at eventide I contemplate in wonderment the firmament and the host of luminous bodies which we call worlds and suns, eternally revolving within its boundaries, my spirit soars beyond these stars many millions of miles away towards the fountain whence all created work springs and whence all new creation must still flow. . . . What is to reach the heart must come from above: if it does not come thence, it will be nothing but notes—body without spirit. . . . The spirit must rise up from the earth. . . . Only by hard, persistent labour through such powers as are bestowed on a man can the work of art be made worthy of the Creator and Preserver of everlasting Nature!

If it is possible for any great genius to explain the mysterious source and goal of his music, Beethoven does so here.

An exquisite poet, Alice Meynell, once sang of a daisy:

> Thou little veil for so great mystery,
> When shall I penetrate all things and thee,
> And then look back?

and she ended her sonnet on the question:

> O daisy mine, what will it be to look
> From God's side even of such a simple thing?

Beethoven *had* penetrated the veil and he looked back, in so far as any musician has ever done so, at the universe from God's side.

BEETHOVEN'S MUSIC

CHAPTER X

WORKS FOR PIANO ALONE

SETTING aside the doubtful Cressener Cantata, we know
on Beethoven's own authority that his first compositions were
a set of Variations on a March by Dressler and three Sonatas
for clavier dedicated to the Elector Maximilian Friedrich.
Thus the boy attacked at once two musical forms he was to
make especially his own.

It is also significant that these Dressler Variations and the
Sonatas were for clavier. Paul Bekker, one of the most
Beethoven-minded of critics, says: 'Beethoven's work is based
on the piano: therein lie its roots and there it first bore perfect
fruit.' Without quite supporting Bekker (for Beethoven's
work certainly rested on a broader basis), one must still
reckon the piano as among the most important influences of
his first period. What could be more natural? Beethoven,
though no iconoclast, was always on the side of modernity
and progress. The piano was *par excellence* the modern
instrument of that day. It came to the fore in Bonn during
the seventeen-eighties and it actually got its sixth octave of
compass during Beethoven's first decade in Vienna. The
powerful tone qualities offered him an adequate vehicle for
his boldest harmonic and melodic designs, and, being himself
a magnificent pianist, he expanded the scope of piano music
till it is hard to apportion the debt between instrument and
player. Later his deafness divorced in him the executant
from the composer, a disaster which proved, as Bekker says,

'the historic origin of the present-day distinction between productive and reproductive musical activity.' By the time Beethoven was fifty-three he had explored and exhausted practically every possibility of the piano.

There is one further matter of general application to be considered before surveying the music itself: Beethoven's faculty of prevision. What Mr. Newman said of single movements is, I believe, equally true of Beethoven's life-work: his 'vague general sense of the totality of the movement gradually condensed this into a vital structural material, and finally re-wrought this into a whole that was the first indefinite conception made perfectly definite.'

Even as a child Beethoven saw far off the things that were to be later.

> From the hid battlements of Eternity,
> Those shaken mists a space unsettle, then
> Round the half-glimpsed turrets slowly wash again.

Prevision is a faculty quite distinct from that of revision by which a composer either rewrites a work out of his mature experience, or else brings forward old material to serve new purposes. Beethoven had both capacities in an extraordinary degree, and held them in amazing equipoise. They are recognizable even in his first work.

The nine Variations on Dressler's March in C minor were composed in 1782 and published at Mannheim in the same year. On their own merits they are neat, discreet music, superior to the theme on which they are spun. But for us (who from the distance of more than a century can see Beethoven's career in the map-like manner enjoyed by the Intelligences in Hardy's *Dynasts*) the real excitement is that the Dressler Variations are a kind of child's sketch for the mighty thirty-two Variations on an original theme composed by Beethoven in 1806. Original theme? Yes, in that it is wholly Beethoven's;

but all the same it is like the ghost of Dressler's March, trans-
formed into a chaconne and translated to an Olympian
grandeur.

TEMA (Dressler)
Maestoso

TEMA (Beethoven)
Allegretto

Note how magnificently the bass marches with Beethoven;
with Dressler it simply goose-steps. Beethoven's basses are
worth a study in themselves. Continuing the comparison
between the two works one sees they run a not dissimilar
course, allowing for the infinitely grander scale and richer

decoration of the later work. At the end they diverge. In the short early Variations Beethoven modulates to C major for the last variation, thus making it an apotheosis of the old *tierce de Picardie* (the major chord which by ancient custom closed all works in a minor key), while in the thirty-two Variations he places a group of C major variations in the middle, flanking them by minor sections before and after in an organized design that approximated to aria form.

The three Max Friedrich Sonatas for clavier belong to nearly the same date (1782-3) as the Dressler Variations and are much more interesting. The first, in E flat major, cautiously follows the old type of binary (not triune) sonata form for its first movement; but already Beethoven showed his instinct for the psychologically sensitive spot in sonata form, viz., the return to the principal key after the development. In later works his imagination and inspiration often rose to their highest at this point. In this boyish movement he was not content to slide back by the routine reversal of the outward journey, so preceded the return by some arpeggios that queerly forecast his figure for the finale of his 'Moonlight' Sonata. The second Sonata, in F minor, is a still more remarkable presentiment of a later work—his *Sonate Pathétique* of 1799. One opens with a short, pathetic *larghetto*, the other with a *grave*, preparing an *allegro* in which the slow section recurs with strong emotional effect. There is even kinship of phrase between the two *allegros*. The other movements of the F minor, well contrasted as to material, are wonderfully 'in the picture.' 'A knowledge of suffering, appalling in a twelve-year-old boy, trembles through the quiet *andante*, and rages through the excited, urgent, *unisono* passages of the *presto*,' says Bekker.

The third Sonata, in D major, is rather Haydn-like in its tunefulness.

Compared with these sonatas Beethoven's other keyboard compositions for the next few years are unexciting, though several have some significance for students. For example, the two Preludes modulating through all keys show Beethoven as an elementary experimenter in the science of key relationship and contrast, where later his power was amazing. The Prelude in F minor is simply a handy little piece for clavier or organ with which to fill a gap.

The Rondo in A major is clean, neat and tuneful, with just one modulation which—simple as it seems—is, I think, Beethoven's earliest example of a pivot modulation, i.e. a

note or notes approached as belonging to one key and quitted as in another, the music being *swung* over on a pivot. The device may mean nothing with a commonplace composer, but in the hands of Beethoven and Schubert it can be magical. Therefore one looks with reverence at the little change here from A minor to C major, catching in it the first glimpse of things to be—for example, the superb passage in the Kyrie of the *Missa Solennis* where (as Professor Tovey says) the 'Christe eleison dies away on an incomplete minor chord which, by a method of modulation typical in Beethoven's works, becomes part of the original major tonic chord of the Kyrie.'

The remaining works for piano during Beethoven's Bonn period were a Rondo, a Concerto in E flat major, a Minuet (not published till 1805), a Sonatina written for Wegeler, and twenty-four Variations on Righini's Arietta *Venni Amore* (1790). These Variations show many authentic Beethoven-isms and, besides being valuable as a portrait of Beethoven the pianist in his last year or two at Bonn, they figured in his famous contest with Sterkel, and later at Vienna. Dr. Ernest Walker, in his admirable study of Beethoven, describes these Variations as of unusual technical difficulty and mentions their forecasts of much later music. A Concerto for piano in D major, for long attributed to Beethoven, is now known to be by J. J. Rösler.

Beethoven's first years in Vienna were not productive of much piano music. For one thing, he was seriously exploring chamber music, and for another, he was doggedly studying counterpoint. From 1792 till 1795 he apparently composed only two sets of variations, one on a theme by Dittersdorf and another for piano duet on a theme by Waldstein, and a couple of sonatinas. But in reality he had three works of first-class value on the stocks—his Sonatas for piano, Op. 2, dedicated to Haydn. Whether they dated from Bonn, or whether he began them in Vienna and incorporated with them some old material from his piano quartets of 1785, is unknown. The three sonatas made their appearance in 1795, the earliest peaks in that magnificent series of thirty-two sonatas which runs parallel to Beethoven's symphonies like a mountain chain in music and is not less glorious, though on a different scale.

Sonatas, Op. 2

Haydn and Mozart had been masterly in their treatment of sonata form. They had also coloured their music with feeling, sometimes even with emotion, and Haydn often composed to some little story in his mind. But where they were masterly, Beethoven was the master. His nature was charged with that excessiveness which Masefield remarks in Shakespeare. When Masefield says: 'The mind of the man was in the kingdom of vision, hearing a new speech and seeing what worldly beings do not see, the rush of the powers and the fury of elemental passions,' it might be of Beethoven, not of Lear or his creator, that he speaks. Beethoven's sonatas and symphonies, with their boundless variety, force, life, character and emotion, inevitably suggest a comparison with Shakespeare. Time and circumstance combined to give Shakespeare and England to each other at the period when the English language and drama were at their greatest. Beethoven came to music at the moment when its world-language and the superb medium of cyclic form were for the first time complete in essentials. 'His early works,' said Parry, 'were in conformity with the style and structural principles of his predecessors; but he began, at least in piano works, to build at once upon the topmost stone of their edifice. His earliest sonatas (Op. 2) are on the scale of their symphonies.' Quite true. Beethoven took over cyclic form[1] fresh from Haydn and Mozart, and from Clementi the new piano style, broad and almost orchestral; but the emotional content, the 'poetic idea' as Beethoven himself called it, was his own. 'I generally have some picture in my mind when composing,' he said.

[1] Here, and throughout this book, the term 'cyclic form' is used in the same sense as in the volume on *The Viennese Period* by Sir Henry Hadow in the Oxford History of Music, namely, to denote the entities of symphony, sonata, concerto, quartet, etc., formed by their characteristic and organized group of movements.

But his 'pictures' were very different things from the placidly held images that served Haydn. Beethoven saw his pictures with the terrific clearness of a spectator at a drama, and experienced them with the intensity of all the participants put together.

This intense reality was apparent from the first. Structurally there is little in the Sonata No. 1, in F minor, that might not have been done by Haydn or Mozart, but in feeling the difference is immense. The phrases of the first movement are clinched, the relentless rat-tatting chords of the finale ring through the dark F minor mood like military commands on the rush of a gale at night. The *adagio*, the most Mozart-like and least original, was taken over from one of Beethoven's Bonn piano quartets. The minuet and trio, though Haydn-like, are Beethovenish too at the point where the return of the tonic key in the trio is prefaced by a delicious passage in sixths that swells to *fortissimo* and sinks almost to nothing.

The Sonata in A major, No. 2, is generally considered the finest of the group in Op. 2. Its special features are the 'new aspect' Beethoven puts upon the limits of the first sections, the noble D major *largo appassionato*—which Dr. Walker describes as 'perhaps the earliest example of a slow movement charged with really deep, earnest feeling'—and the unmistakable Beethoven touch in the scherzo. Haydn and Mozart were perfectly acquainted with the scherzo as a form—Haydn, in fact, had established its presence in the cyclic scheme. But until Beethoven no one divined its real nature and functions.

The C major Sonata, Op. 2, No. 3, is extremely brilliant as piano writing. There is a cadenza just before the coda of the first movement and the finale is quite formidably difficult, with strings of rapid staccato chords of the sixth in the right hand. The second subject of the first movement, by the way, is said to come from the Bonn quartets.

The Sonata in E flat major, Op. 7, is yet more considerable.

Composed about 1796, it is dedicated to Beethoven's pupil, the Countess Babette von Keglevics, a young lady not generally considered handsome, with whom Beethoven is believed to have been in love. The energy and grace of the first move-ment, the emotional eloquence of the *largo con gran espressione,* the trio with its mysterious 'moonlight'-like triplets, and the caressing theme of the rondo—soft as the arms of the loved one—all corroborate the name *Die Verliebte* (*The Maiden in Love*) by which the Sonata was known in Beethoven's lifetime.

The next piano sonatas were begun in 1796, according to Nottebohm, and finished in 1798. There were three under the one number, Op. 10, of which those in C minor and F major are distinguished by melodic charm and stylistic resource, but are otherwise not very significant. The D major Sonata, last in the group, is a superb work. 'The individuality of style is absolute and unchallenged, the structure of all the movements is mature and flawless,' is Dr. Walker's summing-up. The slow movement is the famous *largo e mesto* in D minor, a magnificent poem of melancholy which makes one understand how Beethoven could move a whole audience to tears when he extemporized. He said of it himself that it 'expressed a melancholic state of mind, that it portrayed every subtle shade, every phase of melancholy.' The cluster of crushed seconds grinding upon each other in the final chords of bars 84 and 85 are perhaps the most famous example in Beethoven's piano music of his instinct for intensifying a harmonic situation. Crushed seconds have grown so ordinary in modern music that when a clever composer wants to produce an exceptional effect he does it by a common chord! But these legions of seconds are mean-ingless compared to those which Beethoven calculated and placed so perfectly with regard to their context and to psychological truth.

Beethoven

The *Sonate Pathétique* in C minor, Op. 13, composed about 1798, has already been mentioned as the fulfilment of Beethoven's own prophetic little sonata of 1783. Dussek too anticipated the *Pathétique*. It has been pointed out that his Sonata in C minor 'contains some startling likenesses to that work.' Dussek's Sonata dates from about 1793. Question: (1) Did the famous Dussek get his structural plan from the work of the young and obscure composer Beethoven? (2) Were both men indebted to some now forgotten original? (3) Were they independently inspired?

In poetic content Beethoven's *Pathétique* is tragedy as the young feel it, with the glamour, urgency, even exaltation, of a *Romeo and Juliet*. And few southern love-scenes could be more softly glowing than Beethoven's slow movement with its almost unbelievable melodic loveliness and velvety tone.

The next two Sonatas, in E major and G major, Op. 14, are happy things, that may be contemporaneous with the *Pathétique,* though published only in 1799. Speaking of them many years later, Beethoven said to Schindler: 'When I wrote my sonatas people were more poetic and such indications [of the music's meaning] were superfluous. At that time . . . every one saw that the two Sonatas, Op. 14, represented a struggle between two opposing principles, an argument between two persons.'

Just as Beethoven's pathetic phase in piano music had closed with Op. 13, so his 'first period' works for piano ended with the Sonata in B flat major, Op. 22, composed in 1800. It was on a grand scale throughout—as often happened when he was in the mood of his initial key—and the four movements displayed cyclic form at its 'full moon.' Beethoven was really pleased with it himself. 'Hat sich gewaschen,' was his phrase—an idiom that Professor Tovey translates by analogy as 'takes the cake.' In England we do not talk of sonatas that 'wash themselves,' though—come to think of it—to say that a sonata could stand London laundering would be a remarkable testimonial of immortality.

After achieving the fulfilment of everything the eighteenth century believed a sonata should be, most men would have rested on their laurels. Not so Beethoven. There was more than a dash of Bonaparte and Alexander about him. He felt the desire for fresh worlds to conquer. Besides, the Romantic Movement in German literature had just been born. Whether Beethoven was concretely acquainted with its ideals and output, or whether he felt them through that curious telepathy of genius by which artists become aware of ideas elsewhere, I do not know, but his next Sonata, A flat major, Op. 26, was a marked departure towards romanticism. From then onwards, through most of the sixteen sonatas of his middle period, it seems as if he were intent on enriching classic sonata form with the romantic elements in music—those same elements which in literature found their expression through lyric and ballad poetry. 'The imagination and the reason must both be satisfied, but above all things the imagination,' as Parry said. To unify two apparently opposite principles without the loss of any essential good in either was a task after Beethoven's own heart.

The A flat Sonata, the first of his new period, composed in 1800–1, shows signs of being a hybrid. An *andante con variazioni* takes the place of the customary *allegro* of cyclic form; then follows a scherzo, *molto allegro,* going like the wind, instead of the usual *adagio*; then an intensely sombre slow movement, the *Marcia funebre sulla morte d'un Eroe,* and then a rushing finale. Thus the order and character of the movements is new and thoroughly romantic. The material, on the other hand, casts back towards the past. Czerny rather implies that this sonata was written to score off Cramer (then in Vienna), who had made a sensation with his Sonata in A flat 3/4 time, dedicated to Haydn, and Beethoven purposely put a reminiscence of the

Clementi-Cramer passage work into the finale. A desire to eclipse Paer is also said to account for the inclusion of the Funeral March. These anecdotes may explain the presence of the older stylistic elements, but they do not explain the romantic plan of the Sonata as a whole. By placing the scherzo second in his group of movements, Beethoven showed that even at this early date he had no hesitation in sacrificing convention to æsthetic demands. He clearly thought the scherzo would upset his poetic plan if it followed the Funeral March.

The two Sonatas of Op. 27, in E flat major and C sharp minor, and the Sonata in D major, Op. 28, all belong to the year 1801. They are wonderful successes. Each of those in Op. 27 is designated as *Sonata quasi una Fantasia,* and designed to be played without a break between the movements. The order of the movements is dictated by their poetic content; they have the glamour that hangs over a magnificent extemporization, yet their æsthetic structure is masterly. The name 'Moonlight,' by which the C sharp minor is known, was not of Beethoven's bestowing, but it is at least a token of the enchantment cast by the music. The first movement, *adagio,* with its mist of slow-moving triplets and its melody slowly rising from 'monotone on a prevalent rhythmic figure,' is as impressionistic as anything in Debussy. The figure ♩♪ | ♩. as used by Beethoven is full of mystery.

There is nothing mysterious about the D major Sonata, Op. 28, to which the Hamburg publisher Cranz gave the name *Pastoral.* It is a felicitous work, more or less of a reversion to classic order, and the *andante* is said by Czerny to have been long a favourite with Beethoven.

The period between Op. 28 and the Sonatas of Op. 31 is the place assigned by Czerny to Beethoven's remark to Krumpholz: 'I am by no means satisfied with my works hitherto, and I intend to make a fresh start from to-day.'

If so, then the year was 1802, exactly the crisis of the conflict in Beethoven's own nature. I cannot honestly say I find anything new in the G major Sonata, Op. 31, No. 1, though Beethoven seems extremely preoccupied in it by experiments with odd syncopations, embellishments and dynamics. But the D minor Sonata, Op. 31, No. 2, is altogether magnificent from start to finish.

Beethoven's introduction of instrumental recitative into the first movement is a masterstroke; the *adagio* is as beautiful as profound; the finale is so wistful, sensitive and pliant that one only discovers afterwards with sheer amazement that with the exception of one quaver quite near the beginning Beethoven has maintained an unbroken rhythm of semiquavers right through a movement of 399 bars. It was just such a bit of wizardry as Beethoven liked to perform for his own satisfaction. It is also an example of his power to lift an idea out of the region of material phenomena into another world, for the suggestion of the regular rhythm of the first phrase came to him, according to Czerny, from seeing a horse gallop past his windows at Heiligenstadt.

The third Sonata in the group, the E flat major, is always a great favourite—perhaps because it so gracefully gives something of the best of two worlds—the new and the old—of music. For example the opening chords:

are a wonderful soft call to attention—as if the Evening Star tapped on the casement. The Scherzo is finely spirited and pure Beethoven. But the third movement, *Menuetto,* is a clean throw-back to a very early type of harmonic organization. The finale is another, and more varied, experiment in persistent rhythms.

The two Sonatas in G minor and G major, Op. 49, are sonatinas in all but name; though they were not published till 1805, they were written some years earlier—the G minor in

1798 and the G major in 1796. There is evidence that the sonata version of the *tempo di menuetto* in No. 2 is the original of the theme used for the minuet of the Septet (1800).

With the Sonata in C major, Op. 53, composed in 1803–4, dedicated to Count Waldstein, Bekker is right in saying that 'a hitherto unknown world of sound was revealed.' It is a glorious work, demanding an interpreter whose head and heart are as great as his technique is perfect. The splendour of the first movement, the depth of wisdom and feeling packed into the short *molto adagio,* and the final rondo which seems poised in the sunny realms of air—these things are unforgettable. Originally the Sonata had another slow movement which Beethoven withdrew on account of its length, but I think perhaps he turned against it also on account of a joke which Prince Lichnowsky played upon him with this *andante,* before the Sonata was ready. Whatever his reasons, Beethoven was right. The *andante* survives as the *Andante favori* in F, and its substitute in the Sonata is a fine example of Beethoven's power of retrospect and prospect, of seeing a thing from both sides. Here he approached it from the *allegro* as the slow movement and quitted it as the introduction to the rondo—a pivot movement in fact, yet complete with its own noble character.

The short Sonata in F major, Op. 54, also composed in 1804, is a pleasant valley between two heights, but none the less interesting because, to push my metaphor further, its materials seem to belong to the same geological formation as the peaks of the *Waldstein* and *Appassionata.* Beethoven reverts here to an early two-movement type of sonata. The first movement, named by him *In tempo d'un Menuetto,* has an opening subject that smacks strongly of Scotch folk-song, and its melody has obvious links with the famous second subject of the *appassionata*; a similarity which gives one to think. The second movement, an *allegretto,* is described by Professor Tovey as a 'perpetuum mobile in two-part polyphony on a single theme, with short archaic (melodic) exposition, but extensive development and coda; running at a uniform pace which nothing can stop.' He also points out that this movement is the only instance (except the early two Preludes in all the major keys) where Beethoven works round the 'whole circle of fifths.' In watching the graceful running semiquaver passages I find great pleasure in seeing how much they have in common with the finale of the *Waldstein*. Indeed I sometimes think that Op. 54 is made out of the excess of material for which Beethoven had no room in Opp. 53 and 57.

In the same year the Sonata in F minor, Op. 57, named by Cranz the *Appassionata*, was sketched, and finished in 1806. It touches the very depths and heights. Beethoven's imaginative and constructive power are seen functioning at their highest. 'Here the human soul asked mighty questions of its God and had its reply,' as Parry said. Precisely what Beethoven himself meant is easier to feel from the music than to understand from his own reference to it. He had been asked to explain the meaning of the Sonata in D minor and the *Appassionata*. His reply was: 'Read Shakespeare's *Tempest*.'

At first sight the connection is not very evident, though here and there one can glimpse something. But after thinking things over I have come to wonder whether the meaning may not be more philosophical than dramatic. *The Tempest* is the play where certain commentators believe Shakespeare made concealed allusions to esoteric wisdom, of which they think he had become an initiate. Beethoven was attracted by esoteric thought; witness his later study of Egyptian and Indian religious writings. Nor in this was he singular. Schiller had laid aside poetry for ten years to study philosophy. Haydn and Mozart were earnest Freemasons. *The Magic Flute*, Beethoven's favourite Mozart opera, was one long exposition of esoteric truths through a muddled symbolism. Therefore it would not be strange if Beethoven had been attracted by the symbolic vein in *The Tempest*. His reference to Shakespeare may even be taken as a faint shadow of evidence for the first subject of the *Appassionata* having been deliberately adapted from the tune *On the Banks of Allan Water*. Scotch, Welsh and Irish folk-tunes were well known in Vienna at that time. Haydn and others had arranged them by the dozen for British publishers. Beethoven took a turn at the game himself a few years later. So there is reason to believe he knew the tune of *Allan Water*, and I should not find it hard to believe that he linked it with Shakespeare in his mind because it too was British. One must not push these speculations far, however, because composition works along lines in a man's mind that can never be quite explained in words, since it is an act that transcends words. Whatever Beethoven's precise meaning in the *Appassionata*, the intention is unmistakable: it is an overwhelming tragedy.

From 1804 to 1809 there was an almost complete gap in Beethoven's output for piano alone. Then in 1809 came another period of sonata writing—the Sonata in F sharp major, Op. 78, the Sonata in G major, Op. 79, and in 1809–10 the Sonata in E flat major, Op. 81A, named by Beethoven *Das Lebewohl*. With these it is convenient to bracket the Fantasia, Op. 77, also composed in 1809, my reasons being that Czerny considered it a typical example of a Beethoven extemporization, and that Beethoven seems to have regarded it as a companion piece to the Sonata, Op. 78. He dedicated the one to Count von Brunswick and the other to Countess Therese von Brunswick, the brother and sister who were so devotedly attached to him. The Fantasia is curious, but interesting: the Sonata is one of the most subtly lovely things Beethoven ever wrote. The four opening bars of *adagio cantabile* are like a curtain drawn back to reveal the tender grace and playfulness smiling out from the *allegro*. No wonder Beethoven prized this Sonata. He thought it infinitely

superior to the 'Moonlight.' His choice of key—F sharp major
—is unusual. In two movements he conveyed the essentials
of a much larger work. That first movement gives the feeling
of both a quick and slow movement; the second, as Bekker
has pointed out, is a combination of rondo and scherzo—a
form which Beethoven employed occasionally when at the
height of his powers.

The Sonata in G major, *alla tedesca,* following it, is straightforward, bright and intentionally easy. 'Sonate facile ou
sonatina' was Beethoven's own label.

The *Lebewohl* Sonata is a return to Beethoven's grand
manner. It is also the sole example of declared programme
music in his sonatas, and was composed for his friend and
pupil, the Archduke Rudolph, when the latter was compelled
to leave Vienna before the advance of Napoleon's army. It
is a work on a noble scale; the ideas of departure, absence and
return are woven poetically into a powerful musical structure *qua*
music, and the treatment of the piano is broad and brilliant. Can
Beethoven have got his original suggestion for the programme
from J. S. Bach's *Capriccio on the Departure of a Beloved Brother*?

The Sonata in E minor, Op. 90, dedicated to Count
Moritz von Lichnowsky, is the last of Beethoven's second-
period works for piano. Its two movements glow with the
lyricism and colour of romance. Indeed Beethoven intended
to depict a romance. 'Amidst peals of laughter,' said
Schindler, 'he told the Count [Lichnowsky] that he had tried
to set his courtship of his wife to music, observing also that
if the count wanted a superscription he might write over the
first movement "Struggle between head and heart," and over
the second "Conversation with the loved one."' The point
was that Count Lichnowsky had married a plebeian—a
singer as good as she was charming. Beethoven evidently
followed the romance with amused interest; he always had
a soft spot in his heart for a love affair.

The E minor Sonata was followed about a year later, in 1816, by the Sonata in A major, Op. 101, earliest in the great five of the third period. By now Beethoven had completed his coloration of cyclic form with lyric hues and grace: his mind turned towards a harder task—nothing less than the conquest of the highly specialized province of contrapuntal music for harmonic form and expression. The two most intellectual forms in music—the fugue and the sonata—were to be brought into unity, for his new ethical message exceeded the capacities of lyric form. Furthermore he had been advancing in chamber music and in symphonic knowledge, and he had a new sort of thematic development which consisted of extensive evolution from compact material. His last five sonatas possess the breadth and majesty of symphonic thought and the intimacy and unworldliness of chamber music. He felt them intensely himself. For the first time in Op. 101 he gave his directions for expression in German. Also without relinquishing the lyric elements he here began to introduce contrapuntalism in the form of canon and fugato. The whole Sonata is wonderfully unified.

The Sonata in B flat major, Op. 106 (1817–19), generally known as the *Hammerklavier*, is even more closely unified. Beethoven brought his whole equipment to bear on the task and even reverted to a device known to composers of the early eighteenth century, which he had employed himself in his string Quartet in G major, Op. 18, and was to employ again in his Sonata, Op. 110—the device of thematic kinship (or thematic metamorphosis) between the movements.

Op. 106 is a terrifying Sonata—technically of immense

difficulty, exhaustingly long, and mentally the toughest thing he ever wrote, except perhaps the Quartet in B flat major, Op. 130. The contrapuntal devices and the intellectual power Beethoven put forth overwhelm one like the statements of an astronomer about the universe. Bekker considers the work a symphonic concert sonata on the old four-movement scheme. Maybe, but its gigantic form is also a Brocken shadow thrown by the distant, smaller being of modern music. After more than a century Beethoven's *Hammerklavier* Sonata and his Quartet, Op. 130, are just becoming fully intelligible.

Following the terrific *Hammerklavier,* the Sonata in E major, Op. 109 (1820), and the Sonata in A flat major, Op. 110 (1821), seem like havens of the islands of the blest. Not that Beethoven had abandoned his purpose of conquering fugue for the sonata—rather he had achieved it. The marvellous intellectual texture of these sonatas, the heavenly relevance of all their details, are there for every one who cares to study them, but it is their surpassing beauty which always shines out in our memories when their names are mentioned.

The Sonata in C minor, Op. 111, came a year later—in 1822. It was as if Beethoven had felt with Browning:

> I was ever a fighter, so—one fight more,
> The best and the last!

Yet the fight had long been foreseen. The theme of the first movement had been sketched twenty years before. When the conflict came, it was fought out with the very elements as protagonists; no human terms give an idea of its magnitude. Nor can words describe the serenity and light of the arietta that follows—a set of variations upon what one may call a theme of light and peace everlasting.

Beethoven lived four years more, to complete the *Missa Solennis*, the ninth Symphony and the last quartets, but he never wrote another sonata. Like Ulysses, it had been his

> To strive, to seek, to find, and not to yield.

Turning from the sonatas to survey Beethoven's miscellaneous pieces, one becomes aware of another chain of specialized works, running parallel with the sonatas—the twenty-one sets of variations for solo and the two sets for piano duet. Variation form interested Beethoven only less than sonata form. Though he usually reached his highest powers when the variations made part of a sonata or symphony, a few of the twenty-one separate sets are of significance in relation to his general development. Such things as the Variations on *God Save the King* and *Rule, Britannia* mean little more now than that Beethoven was scoring off Abt Vogler, or that sentiment was pro-British in Vienna during the Napoleonic wars. But the Dressler and Righini Variations meant something in Beethoven's early life, and the two sets of Variations composed during his summer at Heiligenstadt in 1802 are documents of real value. Beethoven's own verdict was:

I have composed two sets of variations, one consisting of eight variations and the other of thirty. Both sets are worked out in quite a *new manner. . . . Each theme is treated in its own way and in a different way from the other one.* Usually I have to wait for other people to tell me when I have new ideas, because I never know this myself. But this time—I myself can assure you that in both these works the *method is quite new so far as I am concerned.*

In view of what Beethoven did a year later in his *Eroica* Symphony these variations are of great importance, and deserve an attention they have not received. Op. 34 is usually remembered—when people remember it at all—as the set where Beethoven modulated to a different key for each variation. Which is very interesting, and seems a link with his early modulating Preludes. But speaking personally my imagination is more fired by the forecast of the Funeral March in the *Eroica* which I think I see in the C minor Variation V. So too with the fifteen Variations with Fugue in E flat major,

Op. 35, which enter the *Eroica* sphere. Their theme is the very one from Beethoven's own ballet *Prometheus* which he employed later for the finale of the *Eroica,* and the canonic and fugal devices, the treatment of the piano and the powerful intellectual progress of the music are a presage of his third-period style.

The thirty-two Variations in C minor (1806) are far better known to-day, and are a sort of landmark, though Beethoven's own exclamation on hearing them was: 'That nonsense by me? O Beethoven, what an ass you were!'

Compared with the sonatas and variations Beethoven's other works for piano—the Rondos, short dances, Polonaise for the Empress of Russia, etc.—are not more than little asteroids in a solar system of music—yes, even the *Rondò a capriccio* known as *Rage over a Lost Penny.*

An exception must be made in favour of the three collections of bagatelles, small pieces which, even if they are without the genuine lyrical quality that came into piano music with the next generation (Schubert, Schumann, Chopin, Mendelssohn), are nevertheless miniatures in which *motifs* of the lighter symphonic kind were set by Beethoven into logical, self-contained little frames of form. The seven Bagatelles, Op. 33, are of early date and least value. Perhaps written for Beethoven's pupils, they require nevertheless players well grounded in technique and interpretation. Of the far later eleven Bagatelles, Op. 119, Nos. 7 to 11 inclusive are known to have been composed for Friedrich Starcke's *Wiener Pianoforteschule* (piano method). The technique is deliberately simple. Beethoven apparently regarded these pieces as 'pot boilers,' but *grâce à Dieu* they turned out lovely little things, showing their filiation among the great works—the Mass in D major and the Sonata in E major, Op. 109, which were then occupying Beethoven's mind. The six Bagatelles, Op. 126, sketched earlier, were worked out after the ninth Symphony was

Variations and Bagatelles

practically complete. Nottebohm thinks they were designed
as a homogeneous series. Beethoven certainly called them
Kleinigkeiten, but considered they were probably the best things
of the kind he had ever written.

The year after he completed his last sonata, he produced
a work which was his last word in the series of solo variations
—an outer and greater planet!

One may regard these thirty-three Variations on a Waltz
by Diabelli as a sort of companion piece to Bach's *Kunst der
Fuge,* in that Beethoven here put forth his full power and
learning to demonstrate a form and his mastership. The
monumental work originated in a not very noble request
from Diabelli the publisher for a variation apiece from thirty-
three composers of the day on a waltz which he had composed.
Beethoven was among the invitees. He declined, called
Diabelli's tune a *Schusterfleck* (cobbler's patch) and in a sort
of savage pride—one Beethoven outweighing thirty-two other
composers—wrote thirty-three Variations himself. It was—
and is—an amazing display of virtuosity. There are moods
when one almost wishes it had been an impossibility, but it
was a marvellous last word!

CHAPTER XI

ORCHESTRAL MUSIC

SIR HUBERT PARRY, a strong man who loved strength in others, once wrote of Beethoven: 'The more difficult the problem suggested by the thought which is embodied in the subject, the greater the result. The full richness of his nature is not called out to the strongest point till there is something preternaturally formidable to be mastered.'

That is true. Beethoven's greatest works are his response to the greatest demands. Conversely, his occasional pieces are of subordinate value. Those within the sphere of orchestral music may be reviewed at once to clear the ground.

The *Ritterballet*, composed at Bonn *c.* 1791, is the earliest authentic orchestral work by Beethoven we possess—a whimsical turn of fate, for the ballet was done as a bit of ghosting for Count Waldstein. Its eight numbers are straightforward affairs largely concerned with tonic and dominant harmonies expressed through lilting tunes or square rhythms. The *Deutscher Gesang* (German song), No. 2, was evidently the one which pleased Beethoven best, for he repeated it as the middle section of the Coda, No. 8. The melody has a marked likeness to the *vivace* of the little Sonata for piano in G major, Op. 79—a link which excited me when I found it, for that Sonata is the very one where the first movement is the *presto alla tedesca*—the German waltz.

The history of *Wellington's Victory, or the Battle of Vittoria,* Op. 91, composed in 1813, has been given in Chapter VI. Æsthetically the work is no more a symphony—though often called the 'Battle Symphony'—than an old poster is an old-

BEETHOVEN'S BIRTHPLACE, BONN *(Beethovenhaus, Bonn)*

BEETHOVEN AT THE AGE OF THIRTY-ONE
(Neidl's engraving after Stainhauser's portrait, reproduced by kind permission of the Austrian National Library)

LYSER'S SKETCHES OF BEETHOVEN

REPRODUCTION OF A PAGE OF BEETHOVEN'S MS.—
THE 'MOONLIGHT' SONATA

BEETHOVEN'S 'CREED'

(facsimile of MS. in Beethoven's own handwriting, reproduced by kind permission from the collection in the Royal College of Music)

BEETHOVEN'S HOUSE IN HEILIGENSTADT *(photo: Max Jacoby)*

BEETHOVEN, BY FERDINAND WALDMÜLLER, 1823
(reproduced by kind permission of the Archiv für Kunst und Geschichte, Berlin)

PORTRAIT OF BEETHOVEN BY SCHIMON *(Beethovenhaus, Bonn)*

master picture. Its glaring faults are probably due to the fact that Beethoven wrote it to be performed on an orchestrion. Mozart could do one of his finest works—the Fantasia in F minor—for a musical clock, because his impulse was to compensate defects in others by his own inexhaustible wealth. But not so Beethoven. He knew the orchestrion was inferior; with an almost childish delight he gave it music to match on a programme sketched by Mälzel. The opposing armies are represented by two groups of wind instruments: the remainder of the orchestra is as strongly 'garrisoned' as possible. The tune *Rule Britannia* is the 'motif' of the British; *Malbrouck* that of the French—a tune we know better under the name 'We won't go home till morning'! When the battle is joined, copious cannon shots 'enrich' the score, and after a Storm March, where the English drums make a most horrible din, *Malbrouck* wavers chromatically into a tremolo and dissolves. A triumphant march leads to *God Save the King,* treated first as a hymn of thanksgiving and later as the subject for a fugue. . . . Beethoven, like Haydn, had a warm admiration for this tune, but to English ears his fugue is almost ribald.

Anyhow, there is the Battle Symphony. Bekker makes the apologetic comment that 'it is a copy-book example of a primitive form of programme music . . . a realistic representation of outward events . . . he [Beethoven] could not compose quickly . . . he had no time to sort and arrange his material. . . . The Battle Symphony is an example of his work in its crude state.'

Up to a point that is true, but I think the real distinction between the Battle Symphony and Beethoven's others is not one of *time,* but of *kind.* Beethoven usually had some picture, or programme—the poetic idea—in his mind when he composed. It was the *starting-point* for his music, from which his ideas could travel, expand, radiate. With composers of the Richard Strauss type, the programme is the *arriving-point,* upon which the music converges in a kind of 'ensmalled' effort at precision. Nobody could miss the message of Beethoven's *Eroica* Symphony through not knowing the exact story. But one must watch the themes and literary tags in Strauss's Alpine and Domestic Symphonies as a cat watches a mouse if one is to catch their purport. The Battle Symphony was Beethoven's prime excursion into crude programme music; its sole remaining merit is that it conveys his story without the aid of many words. Such realism and the idealism of the *Eroica* are worlds apart. The Pastoral Symphony, lying midway between, gives us the best insight into both, and furnishes the best statement of Beethoven's own theories. 'Pastoral Symphony, or a recollection of a country life. More an expression of feeling than a painting.' Note his word *recollection.* He had used its equivalent in the title of the *Eroica* Symphony 'composed to celebrate the memory (*sovvenire*) of a great man.'

The *Namensfeier* (Name-Day) Overture, Op. 115, composed in 1815, was Beethoven's offering to the Austrian emperor. He wrote proudly on the title page 'made into poetry by Ludwig van Beethoven.' L. van B. not being a very good poet, to judge from the poem he wrote to Bettina Brentano, we may accept his estimate, though perhaps not quite as he meant it.

Of the Marches for military band, the dances (dozens of them) for small orchestra, only a few are remembered, for example the *Gratulations Menuett* (1822). One, a little *Contredanse* in E flat major, is linked with his ballet *The Creations of Prometheus,* and it in turn is linked with the Variations for piano, Op. 35, and all of them with the *Eroica* Symphony, through this one theme. Whether the *Contredanse* or *Prometheus* represents the original is unknown, but assuming that Thayer's vague evidence in favour of *Prometheus* is right, here are the four appearances in successive years. Personally, however, I believe the *Contredanse* to be the earliest because the bass appears in a weaker form: (1) As the finale of the ballet *Prometheus*, 1800–1; (2) as *Contredanse*, 1800–1; (3) as theme for piano Variations, 1802; (4) as theme for finale of *Eroica* Symphony, 1803.

BASS OF THEME

THE PROMETHEUS THEME

One more scrap of history is the similarity (noted by Shedlock) between this and the theme in the first movement of Clementi's Sonata in G minor, Op. 7, No. 3.

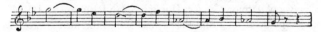

Technically Beethoven valued his theme for the excellent features it offered for development—the dual personalities of the melody and the bass providing at once two characters of importance. But beyond this, I am convinced the *Prometheus* theme became to Beethoven a symbol of creative power and divine completion. When a composer of his calibre introduces a new theme at the end of a big work, he obviously intends that theme as the crown of the whole, and the end is precisely the point at which this theme appears in *Prometheus*.

Ballet approached opera as a serious art-form at Vienna in 1800, and its prestige was enhanced by Salvatore Vigano, a dancer and producer of classical taste and skill. Wishing to compliment the empress, Vigano designed a ballet. Beethoven was commissioned to compose the music. The scenario was so peculiar that I suspect Beethoven put a compelling hand over Vigano's draft. Thayer surmises that the recent immense success of *Die Schöpfung* (*The Creation*) by Haydn may have influenced the choice of subject. Knowing Beethoven's propensity for 'going one better' than any celebrity, a topical origin for his *ballo serio, Die Geschöpfe des Prometheus* (the Creations—or Creatures—of Prometheus) seems highly likely. And if so, it would explain the double edge in the famous conversation between Beethoven and Haydn, quoted in Chapter IV.

The original book of the ballet has been lost, but a summary remains in a theatre-bill. Prometheus 'is a lofty spirit, who found the men of his day in a state of ignorance and civilized them by giving them the arts and sciences. Starting from this idea, the present ballet shows us two statues brought to life and made susceptible to all the passions of human life by the power of harmony.' Act II is 'placed in Parnassus and shows the apotheosis of Prometheus, who brings the men created by him to be instructed by Apollo and the Muses, thus endowing them with the blessings of culture.'

Vigano was no doubt responsible for the plan by which a mythical personage creates two figures, brings them to life and transports them to the delights of Parnassus—a scenario as near Adam and Eve and the Garden of Eden as he dare come. The obvious thing would have been to make the mythical personage Zeus or Apollo. But no—and this is where I believe Beethoven comes in—Prometheus, the fire-bringer, was selected. Stranger still, his Prometheus has next to nothing in common with that of Æschylus. Queerest of all, though no one has remarked the fact, Beethoven has here fused three myths—Prometheus, the heroic benefactor of mankind, Orpheus the musician endowed with godlike power by his art, and Pygmalion, the sculptor whose statue came to life—put briefly, three persons in one. Further, this beneficent being confers on mankind such services as Beethoven himself claimed to render. 'Music should strike fire from a man.' 'Music is a higher revelation than all wisdom and philosophy, it is the wine of a new procreation, and I am Bacchus who presses out this glorious wine for men and makes them drunk with the spirit,' as Beethoven said later, knowing he was the fire-bringer and lord of this Olympian vintage. What had begun as a topical skit on *The Creation* ended by becoming a turning-point in his career. The Grand Mogul merged into Prometheus the hero of peace.

Into his music for the ballet Beethoven put the best that was then in him. The overture is finer and bolder than anything in his first Symphony, and even anticipates passages in his overture to *Leonora,* No. 3. The introduction to Act I gives me an elusive feeling that Haydn's 'Chaos' with its sharp dynamic contrasts may have served Beethoven for model, and in many of the dances that follow—three in Act I and thirteen in Act II—there is a dewy freshness that suggests *The Creation,* though others are stiff and others again are typically Beethovenish. No. 5 is remarkable for woodwind solos, a harp accompaniment (almost the only time when he used it) and a cello cadenza leading to a long cello solo. No. 14 contains a long solo for basset-horn—again a rare appearance — and everywhere Beethoven makes more use of solo instruments than is customary with him.

The Pastorale (No. 10) is delicious. The famous Prometheus theme appears with the finale, proceeds as a rondo, and ends in the conventional triumphant flourish and fanfare—a move/ ment 315 bars long. Altogether a most important work, which must be reckoned with both on its own merits and in relation to the *Eroica*.

If the piano was the basis of Beethoven's style, the symphony was its core. The natural bias of his mind was towards cyclic form and the orchestra—a fact which gave him supreme command over symphonic writing, but cost him bitter struggles when confronted with vocal forms. Judged as a group his symphonies are the greatest the world has known. In them he developed the main design to a significance and the details to a relevance never before imagined.

There are nine symphonies. The so/called 'Jena' Symphony, discovered in 1909 by Prof. Fritz Stein, is not by Beethoven but by Friedrich Witt (1770–1837), Court *Kapellmeister* at Würz/ burg. The attribution to Beethoven arose from the fact that the second violin part was marked 'par Louis van Beethoven' —the kind of mistake that is not uncommon in eighteenth/ century instrumental music.

The series of Beethoven's genuine symphonies begins with the one in C major, Op. 21. There is no certainty about its date, but sketches scattered among counterpoint exercises suggest that Beethoven began it when studying under Al/ brechtsberger and that what he then intended for the first movement is now the finale. By 1800 the Symphony was complete, and had its first performance on 2nd April, being thus about a year ahead of *Prometheus*. Sir George Grove notes resemblances between the first movement of the one and the overture of the other. Both start on a discord leading out of the key to arouse attention by tonal ambiguity before settling down to the main key—a device Beethoven developed with consummate art in some of his later works:

SYMPHONY NO. 1

OVERTURE TO 'PROMETHEUS'

Still, the Symphony was bold enough for a very young man, and brought him censure from pedants. The short, slow introduction leads to an *allegro con brio* which is brisk, but not strikingly original. The slow movement, *andante cantabile con moto,* is of the type affected by Haydn in some of his later symphonies—elegant, polished, eschewing emotions that could disturb the cultivated charm. Beethoven's fugato passages are introduced much as men of the world then introduced Latin quotations into their talk to show their good breeding. The soft drum passage of dotted notes is the most Beethovenish thing in the movement.

The minuet and trio, however, have not the spirit of the old dance but of the new scherzo—modelled maybe a little bit on Haydn's scherzos. Berlioz described this movement as of 'a freshness, an agility and a grace exquisite—the one veritable novelty of the symphony.'

The finale was once frowned on by the learned for the comic

fooling of the violins with their false starts and for the triviality of the subjects, but nowadays it is great fun and always fetches an audience. How jolly to hear Beethoven being frivolous!

A couple of years later came the Symphony in D major, Op. 36, by which time, poor soul, he was in no state for frivolity, though longing ardently for happiness. I have already described in Chapter V the circumstances under which Beethoven composed the D major Symphony, finding a refuge in its Elysian beauty from the tragedy in his heart. It is a greater work than the first Symphony in every way save that of balanced design. Beethoven here expanded the constructive scheme of the eighteenth-century symphony to something larger than the strains which it had been built to carry. As a result he had much trouble with his architecture—it is said he rewrote the Symphony three times. The work is a hybrid. But how lovable! Think of that long, fine introduction—*adagio molto*—larger than anything designed by Haydn (though not so close-knit as Beethoven's later work), with its prophetic vision of the ninth Symphony in the phrase

The *allegro con brio*, with its crisp *gruppetti* in the first subject and its fiery string passages, belongs partly to the old world, yet is touched by Beethoven's own power.

Second Symphony

The slow movement—*larghetto*—is a long dream of beauty where Beethoven lavishes his unmatched skill on displaying, developing and adorning his lovely subjects. Generally speaking, when experimenting at this period upon a fusion of sonata form with lyricism, he poured lyricism into the weightier form; here he reversed the process, and wrote his lyric movement in sonata form.

The scherzo is the most significant part of the Symphony, with its characteristic explosions of energy and the remarkable forecast of the ninth Symphony in the trio.

The explosive element appears again in the finale, also another forecast of the ninth Symphony.

The D major Symphony has never been among the favourites, but it had to be written before the *Eroica* became possible, because Beethoven found his strength over it, just as he had begun to find his 'mission' in *Prometheus*.

The *Eroica* Symphony, Op. 55, was composed in the year 1803. It was his own favourite. The revolution it marked was so great that the distinguished critic, Dr. H. C. Colles, divides Beethoven's career simply into *pre-* and *post-Eroica*.

The history of the Symphony, from Bernadotte's first suggestion of a work on Napoleon to the moment when Beethoven tore off the dedication, has been sketched in Chapter V. To-day the only remaining sign of Bonaparte on the title page is the sentence: 'Sinfonia Eroica, composta per festeggiare il sovvenire d'un grand' uomo.'

In every way the Symphony is heroic. The themes, texture and treatment are superb, and though the movements are extremely long, their proportions are so fine that not one bar could be spared. They follow the order usual in a four-movement symphony: (1) an *allegro*, (2) slow movement, (3) scherzo and trio, (4) finale; but their poetic contents so transform the scheme that the Symphony presents one of the profoundest problems in music. What Beethoven did was this : he wrote a glorious opening *allegro* and followed it with a funeral march for the slow movement. Thus by the middle of the Symphony the hero had vanished from the scene. Yet Beethoven still went on, following the funeral march with a shimmering, resilient scherzo, and that in turn by a set of variations on the dance theme from *Prometheus*. Thus the Symphony divides, as it were, into two halves—the first noble and broad, weighted with majesty, courage and grief; the second altogether lighter, brighter, more imponderable.

What did Beethoven mean by it? Bekker thinks quite plainly he did not mean anything and says it was a mistake to introduce the scherzo after the march, interrupting the even development of the work towards its climax. He points out that later in the ninth Symphony and the *Hammerklavier* Sonata in B flat major, Op. 106, Beethoven avoided this anti-climax by placing the scherzo before the slow movement, and suggests that 'if we could make up our minds to perform the *Eroica* scherzo before the funeral march we should be giving it its proper place, a place which Beethoven did not dare assign to it at that time.'

Now I can imagine Beethoven as a young man taking over cyclic form with an acquiescence in its order, akin to that with which he accepted the positions of subject, answer and countersubject in a fugue; but that he should not *dare* . . . Heavens! I like the idea of any one daring to say that to him, and I like to think of his annihilating reply.

On the other hand many people attempt to explain the scherzo as it stands. Here are some of their theories:

Scheme of the 'Eroica'

(*a*) By this movement Beethoven typified an uprush of the un-dying creative energy of the world—light after darkness—spring after winter—and so on, with much high-sounding philosophy.

(*b*) Scherzo supposed to be founded on a soldier's song.

(*c*) A scene in the camp.

(*d*) A crowd, full of excitement, awaits the hero: he arrives and addresses them in the trio.

(*e*) The effect is 'chiefly that of portraying the fickle crowd who soon forget their hero, and chatter and bustle cheerfully about their business or pleasure as before.'

(*f*) Funeral games around the grave of the warrior, such as those in the Iliad.

This last is from Berlioz, who had great sensitivity.

Then, who are the heroes celebrated? Most musicians agree that Beethoven intended Napoleon in the first and second movements, a conclusion confirmed by reliable evidence, though some of Beethoven's friends started an idea that General Abercrombie was the hero. Further, there is a strong feeling that, in depicting Bonaparte, Beethoven unconsciously portrayed himself. That is true. But why should Beethoven have selected for his first theme in the first movement a subject which comes almost note for note from Mozart's early opera *Bastien and Bastienne*? Of course it may have been a coincidence, but as Beethoven almost certainly knew *Bastien and Bastienne,* and as he possessed a good memory, the coincidence theory is the least probable. For the finale Beethoven took his own *Prometheus* theme, and certainly identified himself with that hero.

Beethoven. Opening of *Eroica*

Allegro con brio

Mozart. Overture to *Bastien and Bastienne*

To summarize, there are then three problems to be solved:

(1) Did Beethoven mean anything, or did he not, by the order of the movements?

(2) What is the explanation of the dual nature of the Symphony?

(3) What is the intention behind each movement?

Well, every one must take the *Eroica* in his own way. I do not insist on mine, but as it contains some points which have not been touched on before, so far as I know, I will state them.

At first I inclined to think Beethoven had placed the scherzo third simply because that was its customary place. But when I examined his earlier works, I found one which disposed of that theory, for the very composition where he placed the scherzo second was the Sonata in A flat major, Op. 26, composed in 1801—*which has the funeral march as its third movement*. What Beethoven did in 1801, he could certainly have done in 1803. The deduction is that his poetical plan for the *Eroica* required the movements to follow the order in which they now stand. I am therefore convinced he-meant exactly what he did, and did not defer to any conventions. That being so, what was his plan? I believe Beethoven's beloved Plutarch supplies the answer. Plutarch's famous biographies, the *Parallel Lives,* are written in pairs, each pair consisting of a Greek warrior, statesman or orator, set side by side with a noted Roman counterpart—thus Alexander and Cæsar, Lycurgus and Numa, etc.

This arrangement would at once explain the duality and parallelism in the *Eroica* Symphony. I am disposed to believe that in the two opening movements Beethoven expressed everything that belonged to the glory, heroism and state of the hero in the material, contemporary world. Even Mozart's theme as the first subject may have been an intentional packing into the first movement of all that Beethoven held heroic, since Mozart was his earliest hero, and the greatest man he had known in music. For the last two movements—the parallel life—I like to think Beethoven removed everything into that ancient world which he looked upon as so much nobler than his own times—and took his music up on to its highest plane. Perhaps it is wild surmise, but the legend of Orion is the one I would guess for the scherzo; Orion, the great hunter, the hero of superhuman beauty, who, when slain, was translated to the skies, still to be seen there, with the shimmering stars of his belt and sword, and Sirius, his dog, leaping at his heel. The scherzo sparkles starrily; the horns in the trio might well be those of the hunter. Yet better than any legend is the true constellation itself, for in Orion are some of the mightiest mysteries of the universe.

Beethoven loved the stars. They stood for glorious nobility of thought. The E major slow movement of his second Rasoumovsky Quartet is known to have been inspired by a starry night. Into his diary for 1820 he copied Kant's saying: 'The moral law in us, and the starry sky above us.' Is it hard, then, to believe that the stars shine in his *Eroica*?

If the ideas seem too fanciful which I have suggested as starting-points for the *Eroica* scherzo and finale, I will ask readers to consider very seriously a memorandum which Beethoven made in 1818, about two symphonies he thought of writing. After noting his ideas for the earlier movements of the second, he says: 'The orchestral violins, etc., to be increased tenfold in the last movement. Or the adagio to be in some way repeated in the last movements, in which case the vocal parts would enter gradually. *In the adagio the text of a Greek myth—or Cantique Ecclésiastique—in the allegro a Bacchus festival.*' (The italics are mine.)

Thus the question whether Beethoven could ever have

taken a Greek myth for the 'poetic idea' of a movement is answered out of his own mouth. And the allusion to Bacchus strengthens the probability of his connections with Plutarch, for Plutarch is believed to have been an initiate of the mysteries of Dionysus (Bacchus)—an order to which Beethoven mentally attached himself, if his words, 'I am Bacchus', mean anything. After all, such thoughts were very natural: music and wine had been dominantly associated with his family for three generations.

But in the *Eroica* finale it is not Bacchus, but Prometheus, whom Beethoven celebrates in a magnificent series of variations. The warrior victories of the first movement have ended in conquest and death—life has receded to the skies. Then Prometheus-Beethoven, the fire-bringer, the creator, brings a new and better life back into the earth. From the two dry sticks of the theme as shown at the beginning Beethoven gradually develops beauty that becomes life, and towards the end reaches a vision of love and loveliness so divine that when Gounod wished to find a theme to typify the Redeemer he took this.[1] The finale is what Beethoven intended—an overwhelming demonstration of the power of the musician and the beneficence of music. The Pope's staff that blossomed is crabbed compared with this evocation of beautiful life from that dry theme. Walt Whitman's words ring out in memory as the right response:

After the seas are all crossed,
After the great captains and engineers have accomplished their work,
After the noble inventors,
Finally shall come the poet worthy that name,
The true son of God shall come singing his songs!

The *Eroica* Symphony is one of Beethoven's supreme works; it is one of the supreme treasures of the world. It remains to us as

A spiritual woven signal for all nations, emblem of man, elate above death.

---

[1] Gounod's appropriation of the theme is not without piquancy, for to Mendelssohn he called Beethoven *un polisson*.

Few things yield a more intense delight than a close study of Beethoven's scores, but it is better to hear the *Eroica* even once than to read all the analyses. Yet the more closely Beethoven's symphonies are analysed, the more beauty they reveal. Take the matter of proportion alone. The first movement of the *Eroica* approaches a miracle. Beethoven lays out the exposition, development and recapitulation on a scale never before attempted, and then enlarges the coda (which with Haydn had been a tiny tail on a movement) into a fourth section of importance equal with those preceding it and reflecting the development section, much as the recapitulation had reflected the exposition. The first subject has already been quoted. The second subject or group of ideas, is intimate, almost beseeching, in feeling and timbre, yet like the first subject, more harmonic than melodic.

In the development Beethoven compensates for the harmonic predominance by one of his loveliest melodies. I have already spoken of his instinct for the passage leading into the return of the principal key as the vital spot in sonata form. Even in such a small movement as the minuet of the A major Quartet, Op. 18, he withdraws into C sharp minor before the return, holds us there just long enough in another world to glimpse its loveliness and then whisks us back across a silent bar into the formal A major. That C sharp minor melody is an embryo of the divinely beautiful device of the great episode in the development of the *Eroica*, which assumes the importance of an integral theme. Beethoven's appreciation of the need for perspective in music and his power of producing it are amazing, and never more so than in the *Eroica*. According to academic rule, the development section in sonata form should not contain new material, but merely discuss what has already been postulated. Furthermore, themes with a harmonic, not melodic, nature are considered most suitable for development. Beethoven knew that in music melody is the thing most of the soul.

In the great episode of the *Eroica* first movement Beethoven uses his beautiful melody in distant keys and its orchestration, divided between woodwind and cellos, lightly held together by the other strings, is indescribably sympathetic. The moment of actual return to the first subject is one of his most astounding strokes. The orchestra is hushed almost to nothing. Against a tremolo in the violins held on dominant harmony, the horn enters with the first theme in the tonic E flat.

By academic precedent it was all wrong; psychologically it was gloriously right and immensely daring. Even to-day the effect is outstanding. Another point to note in this superb movement is the coda. Beethoven approaches it with two of those tremendous steps he used at moments of supreme crisis.

He knew, as no other composer before or since, the terrific *separating* effect of a step of one degree in harmony and the wonderful *joining* effect of a step of one degree in melody. His E minor episode in the development had been distant from E flat major, but the titanic descent of a tone to the D flat major chord, followed by the further descent to C major, gives one a feeling like the descent of three great, terraced rock faces. Some of Beethoven's most wonderful strokes are achieved by his knowledge of harmonic massifs. Conversely, out of his knowledge of the function of the step of one degree in melody, many of his finest tunes are made; the great one in the ninth Symphony is the supreme example.

The second movement of the *Eroica*, the funeral march in C minor, is so famous that it hardly requires description. The poet Coleridge once remarked it was like a funeral procession in deep purple. That conveys a true impression, and the C major section in the middle is like consolation from heaven. Hitherto no composer had reached such an overwhelming intensity of emotion in a symphony.

The scherzo, apart from any questions of 'programme,' is notable as the first of Beethoven's large orchestral scherzos— a wonderful thing to shine out on the world.

The finale also is remarkable. Beethoven here combines the finest elements of variation form and fugue, so that the most human feeling and firmest intellect are equally available to him. Moreover, as I have already explained, the Pro-metheus theme which he uses is practically double. In the long span of the movement between the fiery introduction and the coda that balances it at the other end, Beethoven exhibits the bass first in a series of fugal, intellectually cumulative variations, and then the real theme, where the tender, melodic, emotional personality assumes control. Both characters having been introduced, Beethoven develops them with magnificent mastery and interplay, during which process each one becomes more and more its full, true self till the fugal subject rises to its climax of brilliance in a kind of *stretto* above a dominant pedal on B flat, stands at pause for a moment on a great chord, and then falls to silence before the divine aspect of the melodic theme which now reaches its apotheosis in a long section, *poco andante*—one of the most eloquently beautiful things even Beethoven ever wrote. The finale is indeed what I believe Beethoven intended it to be—a great creative act.

More than two years elapsed before Beethoven completed his next Symphony, No. 4, in B flat major, Op. 60. Here he returned to the form—though not the spirit—of the symphony as Haydn knew it. The slow introduction leading to a bright *allegro*, a *cantabile* slow movement, a minuet and trio, a dancing finale—all are here, but suffused with colours, felicities, emotions, beyond anything in Haydn. Yet I think Beethoven was not unmindful of Haydn's introduction to the E flat 'Drum Roll' Symphony, perhaps even the 'Chaos' prelude in the *Creation,* when he composed the marvellous introduction to the B flat Symphony. Mysterious, shadowy, immense, it would not be hard to find in it Beethoven's vision of the earth without form, and the Spirit of God moving on the face of the waters. But Beethoven gave no programme and we only know that the first *allegro* is the sole one by Beethoven which grows out of the material of the introduction.

Neither is anything known of the circumstances under which he composed the Symphony. The evidence of dates, and certain cross-correspondences in the music, show that it occupied his thoughts during the same period as *Fidelio* (notably the overture *Leonora* No. 3), the violin Concerto and the first Rasumovsky Quartet.

The *adagio* of the fourth Symphony is so touchingly beautiful that few listeners realize it is also a supreme technical achievement. Two apparently opposite ideas are shown in it as being really parts of one surpassingly lovely whole. Kretzschmar is of the opinion (says Mr. Edwin Evans, senior, in his study of Beethoven's symphonies) that if the difficulty of the task which Beethoven here set himself were fully realized, with the necessary consequence of his wonderful solution of it being appreciated, the inclination would be to regard this work as the finest sample among all Beethoven's symphonies of delicate and tactful treatment.

The main theme is a magnificent example of Beethoven's *cantabile* conjunct melodies, and the rhythmic figure of the accompaniment produces an effect which, when properly played, unites with one's own heart-beats. Berlioz always felt this movement intensely. He says:

One is seized, from the first bars, with an emotion that by the end becomes shattering in its intensity! . . . the impression produced is like that one experiences on reading the touching episode of

Francesca da Rimini in the *Divina Commedia,* of which Virgil could not hear the recital without sobbing and weeping, and which, at the last verse, made Dante fall as if dead.

But in Beethoven's *adagio* there is no tragedy; only the extreme beauty and happiness bring one near to tears. If there be a heart-ache it is engendered by the sense of exile in ourselves.

For the minuet the emotional tension is reduced, the music broken up by cross rhythms and sudden changes, and the trio with its wistful charm is most lovable. The finale is in effect, though not in name, a *perpetuum mobile,* where the instruments swirl and flash in an endless ring, into the centre of which each in turn runs out to do a little solo and then retires in favour of the next. The moment when the bassoon does his is an inimitable bit of clowning.

Beethoven's original intention had been to follow the *Eroica,* not by this happy B flat Symphony, but by one in C minor which eventually became his fifth—and the world's favourite. It had been begun in 1805; then laid aside, to be completed in 1807 or early in 1808. The first subject is among the most dramatic things in music, and the whole movement is extraordinarily terse and close-knit.

'So pocht das Schicksal an die Pforte' (So Fate knocks at the door), said Beethoven. Remembering his resolve in 1801: 'I will take Fate by the throat; it shall not wholly overcome me,' one is justified in believing the C minor Symphony to be a record of his tremendous inner strife and victory. At any rate much of it was written at Heiligenstadt—the spot where his old battle had reached its climax.

The second movement, a theme and variations, *andante con moto* in A flat major, on an extended, somewhat free plan, has a purposeful progress that suggests a song of mankind marching towards freedom. But there is also a touch of coldness about its grace. Beethoven chiselled it much before he satisfied himself. Many sketched variants of the theme exist.

The scherzo is the most remarkable in existence. While adhering to the usual scheme of a scherzo and trio Beethoven infused such uncanny power into the music that, as Berlioz said, it causes 'the inexplicable emotion that one experiences under the magnetic gaze of certain individuals.' The notes, phrases, harmonies are perfectly within the range of normal usage, yet everything has a terrifying aspect of strangeness, akin to that which sometimes overwhelms one at twilight or on waking in the night. Beethoven's mere common chord of C minor in arpeggio becomes a shadowy menace. . . . The trio, with the huge lumbering of the double basses, is monstrous, portentous; the long bridge passage between the end of the scherzo and the finale holds one immobile with expectancy. Parry pointed out that the fifteen bars where nothing is going on but an insignificant chord continuously held by low strings and a *pianissimo* rhythmic beat of a drum would be meaningless taken out of its context, but that as Beethoven has used it, it is infinitely more impressive than the greatest noise ever made by Meyerbeer. When the passage opens out, by a great, sudden-surging *crescendo*, into the triumphant C major finale, the effect is amazing.

No wonder this C minor Symphony troubled some of Beethoven's contemporaries: they resented being forced to share these violent emotions. Goethe growled and grumbled to the young Mendelssohn: 'How big it is—quite wild! enough to bring the house about one's ears!' and Lesueur cried to the young Berlioz: 'Ouf! Let me get out; I must have air. It's incredible! Marvellous! It has so upset and bewildered me that when I wanted to put on my hat, *I couldn't find my head.'*

Symphony No. 6, in F major, Op. 68, bears the name Beethoven himself gave it—'The Pastoral,' and followed hard on the C minor in 1807-8. It too was composed in the Heiligenstadt district, but because it mirrors the outer scene, and not the inner world of the soul, Beethoven seems here to be a little less on the common ground of humanity. But how lovable it is all the same! with the fresh-springing tunes of the first movement, the second movement—the Scene by the Brook—with its murmuring phrases and the bird calls, put in (as he said) as a joke; the *allegro*, the Peasants' Festival with its delicious portrait of the country band; the storm which, though not very terrible nowadays as a noise, must always give a strange thrill at the opening where, in the sudden *tremolo* of the basses very softly on D flat and the little patter of quavers in the second violins, Beethoven has caught the very feeling of that queer moment before a storm breaks, when the first drops fall and the leaves show their white undersides. And then, when the tempest has passed, the final scale upwards of the flute leads into the shepherds' hymn of gratitude and thanksgiving which completes the work.

The naturalistic features have been much discussed, but the Pastoral Symphony is not the only work in which such things appear. Beethoven's setting of Herder's *Gesang der Nachtigall,* composed in 1813, opens with a perfect suggestion of the song of a nightingale, and Sir George Grove notes a sketch for the storm in the introduction to Act I of *Prometheus.*

Four years passed without another symphony. Then, in 1812, came two—the 'grand Symphony,' No. 7, in A major, Op. 92, 'one of my most important,' said Beethoven, completed in May, and the 'little one,' No. 8, in F major, Op. 93, dated October 1812.

No one will dispute Beethoven's statement that the A major Symphony is one of his best works. Wagner has called it the 'apotheosis of the dance,' but this conveys no idea of the grandeur of the introduction (*poco sostenuto*) which is more largely planned than any of its predecessors, and subtly forecasts, by its modulations, the key scheme of the entire work. The *vivace* into which it leads is gloriously rhythmic—Dr. Ernest Walker says its persistent rhythmic spring can hardly be paralleled elsewhere—and the orchestration is brilliant. For the slow movement Beethoven makes the innovation of a movement that is not slow, an *allegretto,* and attains his necessary contrast by the low orchestral colouring—as opposed to the high colouring of the *vivace.* It is a marvellous movement, full of melancholy beauty.

The scherzo (*presto*) with its trio, said to be founded on an Austrian pilgrims' hymn, is warmer and brighter in colour, and has great rhythmic fascination. It is a midway stage of colour between the pensive *allegretto* and the astounding outburst of the finale, a movement which batters, hurtles, exults in a superhuman discharge of power. Beethoven is believed to have used a Cossack tune for it, but the tune is tame, compared to his treatment. There is one passage seething over a rising bass that always makes me wonder whether Beethoven really did know the sea. He might have seen it as a boy in Holland.

Throughout the whole Symphony Beethoven elevates colour almost to its modern position as a structural factor, while retaining his clear-cut intellectual lines.

The eighth Symphony is frankly a little darling—happiness incarnate and a masterpiece of character and conciseness. The four movements are extremely compact. Following the opening *allegro* there is again a quick 'slow' movement—this time an *allegretto scherzando* said to be designed as a skit on Mälzel's metronome. The *tempo di menuetto* is a delicious blend of beauty and humour, where the bassoon solo completes the enchantment, and the whole movement is very Viennese in the easy sway of the tunes. The opening of the finale is typical Beethoven, with immense vitality in the rhythms and violent dynamic contrasts. The second subject, however, is a piece of pure loveliness that rises suddenly into view by one of those step-of-one-degree harmonic transitions that Beethoven uses when he has something most special to say. This time it is the following melody:

Sir George Grove says it is one of those 'soft Lydian airs' which truly pierce 'the meeting soul'—and he directs attention to the fine example at bar 7 of what he calls the *appoggiatura* of passion. Beethoven usually reserved this melisma (denoted either by its sign, or, as here, written out in full) for moments of intense feeling—a practice in which Wagner followed him. I cannot get it out of my head that Beethoven had Amalie Sebald in his thoughts when he wrote this Symphony.

Over ten years passed before Beethoven completed the Symphony in D minor, his ninth and last, somewhere about the end of 1823 or early in 1824. It was one of his life-goals attained. Thirty years earlier Fischenich had written to Charlotte von Schiller: 'I am enclosing with this a setting of the *Feuerfarbe* on which I should like to have your opinion. It is by a young man of this place whose musical talents are universally praised and whom the elector has sent to Haydn in Vienna. He proposes also to compose Schiller's *Freude*, and indeed strophe by strophe.' The young man was Beethoven; the intention remained with him. It cropped out in the sketch-books of 1798, 1811 and 1822. It cried out from his second Symphony during the crisis of 1802. When the right time came he composed it, but not strophe by strophe.

Instead he made a selection from the verses, even re-arranged their order, and bound them into a compact text which could serve for the finale of a great symphony. The result was the stupendous ninth. In it three purely instrumental movements, an *allegro,* a scherzo, and an *adagio,* of a magnitude never before imagined, pass by a long bridge or transition into a choral finale where four solo singers and a full chorus are added to the score for the triumphant close.

The ninth Symphony, like the *Eroica,* is a composite work, but the synthesis is larger, the connecting thread wider and looser, for Beethoven apparently worked the two symphony schemes he noted in 1818 into this one.

Moreover the introduction of human voices was a disturbing element. Not that a choral finale was quite novel. Such minor composers as Winter and Maschek had already employed the idea; Beethoven himself had done so in the Fantasia for piano and orchestra in C, Op. 80, 1808. But for the ninth Symphony he enlarged his plan enormously to carry the great surcharge of feeling which the finale was to express. That he had a most definite poetic intention behind each movement of the work is certain, but it is easier to feel these meanings than to express them. The usual interpretation is that the first movement is Destiny and the inexorable order of the universe; the second (the scherzo) is physical exuberance and energy; the third is Love. With the finale there is no uncertainty—Joy is its dominant idea; and Joy was to Beethoven what Charity was to St. Paul, the one thing without which all else was incomplete. Milton perhaps dreamed of something of the same sort when he wrote: 'Joy shall overtake us as a flood.' Beethoven's initial inspiration came from Schiller. During the course of years his mind had voyaged out into a cosmic philosophy where, as he looked calmly at the great truths under the aspect of eternity, their different earthly manifestations were seen to be symbols mystically related. Thus he found nothing incongruous, when he wished to express Joy Divine, in combining Schiller with Bacchus in a finale, nor did he feel anything irreverent about it, since the symbolism of the True Vine runs all through the Christian religion. The utter simplicity and absence of sophistication in Beethoven are disconcerting, but they must be recognized. As W. J. Turner has well said:

> It is a peculiarity of Beethoven that he can use the words 'best' and 'noblest' without making an intelligent man laugh up his sleeve. . . . The very words 'good,' 'noble,' 'spiritual,' 'sublime,' have all become in our time synonymous with humbug. In Beethoven's music they take on a new and tremendous significance and not all the corrosive acid of the most powerful intellect and the profoundest scepticism can burn through them into any leaden substratum. They are gold throughout.

For the first movement of the ninth Symphony it is as if Beethoven took us out with him into the inter-stellar spaces. The loneliness is illimitable. Across the prelude-like bars of bare fifths and octaves shivering on the strings, there presently descends the famous first subject, the slow lightning stroke.

FIRST SUBJECT

Professor Tovey, in his magnificent analysis of the Symphony, says of the opening that it is a revelation of Beethoven's full power, and that of all single works of art it has had the deepest and widest influence on all later music. Professor Tovey's explanation of the means by which Beethoven attains his effect of gigantic size while keeping within the normal length for a first movement, and his wise words upon Beethoven's method of scoring (which is here practically all *tutti*), deserve close study. To describe the Symphony here is impossible; only the briefest pointers can be attempted.

The varied and lovely group of themes forming the 'second subject' must be noticed, and in the coda is a passage that is like a premonition of the Day of Judgment—'the famous dramatic muttering in semitones of the whole mass of strings beginning with the basses and rising until it is five octaves deep in the violins.'

The second movement is the 'greatest and loveliest of Beethoven's scherzos.' The idea for it is said to have flashed upon him as he stepped from darkness into light. In its way this movement too is almost terrifying, not from loveliness but from excess of vital power and rhythm. In the orchestration Beethoven is at his most explosive and the drum passages are amazing. Throughout his career it is characteristic of him that though he gives the drum a status approaching virtuosity he never allows it to unsettle the legitimate symphonic style.

In the trio appears that exquisitely happy passage which links it to the second Symphony in the past and with the coming finale.

'The supreme slow movement,' said Parry, 'is the finest orchestral example of that special type of slow movement,' viz., a theme and variations. It is a double set, with two themes. The first is beautiful:

But the second is even more beautiful. It is prefaced by a couple of chords in which the horns seem to arrest one's very heart to share in a melody which is the supreme utterance of love to the loved one.

Following three such magnificent instrumental movements, it was no light problem for Beethoven to pass logically to the choral finale. After long puzzling he devised the plan of a bridge, or introduction, from whence he could look backward and forward—as in little he had often done with his pivot modulations.

It is a passage of real drama. With fiercely clamouring cellos and basses Beethoven reviews and dismisses each move-ment in turn; then comes the earliest glimpse of the new order, a foreshadowing of the great tune which is to be the theme of the finale. This first reveals itself in the cellos and basses, then gradually shines out in full beauty in the orchestra; the realization, when it comes, is a moment to live for.

Beethoven's treatment of the accompanying string parts affords a wonderful example of his device for enhancing the beauty of his greatest melodies by placing living, pliable counter-melodies beneath the main themes. (See also the episode in the first movement of the *Eroica* and the *adagio* of the fourth Symphony.)

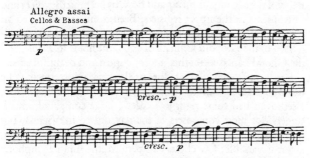

But even yet Beethoven is not satisfied. Again the clamour breaks out, to be calmed by the bass soloist with a recitative: 'O Freunde, nicht diese Töne; sondern lasst uns angenehmere anstimmen, und freudenvollere!' (O friends, not these sounds! But let us sing something more pleasant, and more full of gladness). Those words are Beethoven's own. He arrived at them, as at the bridge section, only after long thought.

Thence he 'swings himself up' into the choral finale, a

free set of variations. From now onwards the great movement sweeps forward on a tide of Joy whose waves sometimes
buffet, at other times lift one almost to the starry throne. In
the section marked *adagio ma non troppo, ma divoto,* Beethoven
reaches a height of spiritual devotion and ecstasy almost
unparalleled as he sets the verse:

> Ihr stürzt nieder, Millionen?
> > Ahnest du den Schöpfer, Welt?
> > Such' ihn überm Sternenzelt!
> Über Sternen muss er wohnen.

> (O ye millions, do ye abase yourselves?
> > Divinest thou thy Creator, World?
> > Seek Him beyond the canopy of heaven!
> He must dwell above the stars.)

Sir George Grove rightly points out here the beauty and originality of the accompaniments and how, by keeping the voices and
instruments in the upper registers, Beethoven has produced an
effect which is not easily forgotten. He notices, too, the premonitions—in the Leopold Cantata of 1790, the finale to *Fidelio,* and
the Choral Fantasia—of this 'most mystical and beautiful effect.'

Beethoven's scheme for the finale was transcendent. Its
triumph was hindered by the intractability of mankind.
Beethoven had some right to expect a large compass from his
singers, for most composers of the day did so in Vienna, but
his demands were wholly exceptional. Now the human
factor is variable; few choirs can perform the ninth Symphony
with the certainty he intended, and experts are still questioning
whether the choral finale is the crown or crime of the whole
Symphony. But Professor Tovey supplied what should be
the final answer when he wrote: 'There is no part of Beethoven's
Choral Symphony which does not become the clearer to us for
assuming that the choral finale is right; and there is hardly
a point that does not become difficult and obscure as soon as we
fall into the habit which assumes that the choral finale is wrong.'

The Choral Finale

Another assumption often made is that Beethoven did not orchestrate effectively. Judged by the virtuosity of a Berlioz, Tchaikovsky or Strauss, his scores may seem deficient in dexterity. Almost any conductor nowadays can point to passages where Beethoven might have taken a more directly effective course, especially with his brass instruments. But Berlioz began where Beethoven left off. Besides, the longest way round is often the shortest way home. Beethoven's scoring suits his music because it is an integral part of his thoughts. It belongs to the modern world — unlike that of Haydn which never quite outgrew the early *continuo* associations— and if less supple it is racier than that of Mozart. Beethoven's symphonies abound in scoring apt and eloquent for the most varied situations, and his concertos are if anything even finer in their imaginative solutions of the problems of orchestration.

The classical concerto, which received its final shaping and stabilization from Mozart, is a manifestation of sonata form closely allied to the symphony. But where a symphony is single-minded in its aim, a concerto exhibits the dual personality of soloist and orchestra. The virtuoso element must be combined with the symphonic structure. Roughly speaking one may say that in early times the orchestra and soloist were on equal terms; that in the mid-classical period the soloist gained predominance; and that the modern tendency is again to treat the soloist as one strand—important, but not all-important—in the *concertante* mass.

It is perhaps the difference between a master mind and the lesser man that one integrates, the other disintegrates, musical forms and materials. Beethoven, in the concertos belonging to his mature period, stands practically alone in his synthesis of all the factors, though for charm of solo idea Mozart and Schumann are his peers, and for symphonic structure Brahms and Elgar are his disciples.

Such equipoise was not reached immediately. Beethoven's

first attempts at concertos date from his Bonn days; namely, the youthful work in E flat major for piano and the fragment of a violin concerto in C major which was completed by Hellmesberger. Of the five concertos for piano composed in Vienna, that known as No. 2, in B flat major, Op. 19, is in reality the first, having been finished at latest by March 1795. Beethoven revised it for performance in Prague in 1798, but by 1801 he wrote very honestly to Hofmeister the publisher: 'I am valuing the concerto at only 10 ducats because, as I have already told you, I do not consider it to be one of my best concertos.' Beethoven was perfectly right. The Concerto, though elegant, is indeterminate. Its best touches are never made fully effective—as for example, the transition from C major *ff* to D flat *pp* at bars 39–43 in the first movement. The C major concerto, though called No. 1 and labelled Op. 15, is really a later work, composed in 1798. It marks some advance, even if the material of the first movement is in the manner of Mozart. The *largo* in A flat major is modelled on Italian cantilena, and the lively rondo is a good sample of a type then prevalent.

With the Concerto No. 3, in C minor, Op. 37 (composed in 1800) we reach Beethoven the tone-poet. Conventional elements are still retained in the disposition of the orchestral *tutti,* the cadenzas for the piano, etc., and even in the idiom of the subjects, but the imperious stride of the first subject, the impassioned quietude of the *largo,* the biting brilliance of the rondo and the subtle key scheme underlying the whole work are pure Beethoven. Indeed, I sometimes think this Concerto is as much a self-portrait of Beethoven at thirty as the *Eroica* is of Beethoven at thirty-three. Bekker remarks on the unusual key—E major—employed for the *largo.* 'Beethoven frequently set C major and E major side by side, but an E major piece between two C minor movements is quite extraordinary.' He surmises it had some special meaning.

It is remarkable, but I think one part of its meaning is that both Haydn and Beethoven had been experimenting with extensions of key relationship and that each stimulated the other to bolder innovations. Beethoven was quick to seize a good idea. In this instance he used his key of the mediant major against C minor with beautiful finesse. I have spoken before of his power of seeing things from two sides. Here is an example. In the C minor first movement the key of E flat plays a prominent part. Beethoven knows the note E flat will linger on vaguely in our ears. He changes it in his own thought to the enharmonic equivalent D sharp, which is the leading note of E major, and mentally steps up from it to the new key, which was intentionally remote from C minor. When he returns to C minor for the finale he confirms his E major *largo* by an enchanting passage well on in the rondo where he gets the orchestra on to the note G for two bars given in four octaves, then pushes it up to A flat for two bars; the piano enters, reiterating A flat for another four bars, next A flat in the bass floats up softly to E natural, A flat in the treble melts enharmonically to G sharp, the harmony hovers for four bars more and then the main subject is off into E major. The effect is magical.

Between five and six years elapsed before Beethoven produced his piano Concerto No. 4, in G major, Op. 58 (1805-6). Its beauty has an almost unearthly quality and its formal structure is so novel that only one concerto by Mozart affords a precedent for the manner in which Beethoven makes the piano speak first before the orchestra enters with its long *tutti*.

In the slow movement, *andante con moto,* Beethoven is said to have been inspired by the idea of Orpheus supplicating the powers of the underworld. The adamantine unison passages for the orchestra and the lovely hushed answers for the piano support the tradition. They are probably the most remarkable dialogue in instrumental music.

The rondo, though a little less distinguished, is still an exquisite finale to the Concerto. The pellucid nature of the themes and the limpid tone qualities Beethoven evokes from the piano are as lovely here as in the earlier movements.

The magnificent fifth Concerto, in E flat major, Op. 73, was completed in 1809. As in the fourth, Beethoven places the piano in the foreground from the outset, but here its imperial position is asserted by a couple of splendid preludings placed between ceremonial chords given out *fortissimo* by the orchestra before the real first *tutti* gets under way. The thematic material is so bold, ringing, triumphant, and its treatment so splendid that the origin of the nickname 'The Emperor' Concerto is easily understood. But Beethoven never gave it that title, nor by this time had he a spark of admiration left for Napoleon. A notable innovation in the first movement is the abolition (as Dr. Walker explains) of the customary interpolated cadenza in favour of something which is really nothing but a largely expanded coda, though it starts (as would a cadenza) with passages for the solo instrument after a pause on a six-four chord.

The *adagio un poco mosso* is mainly concerned with a melody of ineffable loveliness in the far-away key of B major. Beethoven sketched the theme in many forms before he reached the true one. Here are some of the first attempts. The final form is a melody which exercises a quite extraordinary spell of tranquillity and beauty, especially if played by the strings of the orchestra *very* softly with a pure solo quality of tone instead of the usually lifeless orchestral *pianissimo*.

SKETCHES

The choice of key is a perfect example of Beethoven's power of seeing a thing from two sides. B major may seem remote from E flat major, but he had subtly prepared for it in the first movement by making use of C flat major, a key quite easily within the sphere of E flat major, and which is the enharmonic equivalent of B major. Thus in the first movement he used the key in its *near* sense; in the *adagio* in its *far* sense. The transition back from B major to E flat major for the finale is achieved by one of his greatest strokes of genius—a step of one degree down from B natural to B flat. Though so direct and simple it never fails to bring a thrill, and the rondo following is splendidly exultant; a fitting finale for the right royal work.

This was Beethoven's last concerto for the piano. It had been preceded by his Fantasia in C, Op. 80, for piano, chorus and orchestra, an experimental composition in which he took his own early melody to Bürger's *Gegenliebe* and developed it as an imposing set of free variations for his strangely selected forces. It was followed after some years (1815) by the commencement of a piano concerto in D major, which he never finished, though as many as sixty pages were fully scored. They are said to be extremely fine.

Both Romances for violin and orchestra date probably from 1802, despite the fact that the G major one is labelled Op. 40 and that in F major Op. 50. They are beautiful in their way, not easy as to technique, very difficult to interpret satisfactorily, and not so effective for concert pieces as they should be. Their music leaves one where it found one. I suspect Beethoven had no strong poetic idea when he composed them.

The triple Concerto in C major, Op. 56, for piano, violin, violoncello and orchestra (1803–4) rouses expectations of great music it never fulfils, deals out platitudinous crafts-manship, and is, in fact, Beethoven animated by duty, not inspiration.

I have left the violin Concerto in D major, Op. 61 (1806) for the last because it is unique—the only one Beethoven gave to the violin, and still the finest in existence for that instrument. It was a 'Concerto per Clemenza pour Clement,' as Beethoven wrote in his punning way. This Clement, a Viennese, was among the best violinists of his day, and if the Concerto mirrors his playing, as seems likely (since Beethoven was very sensitive in these matters), then Clement must have been a singularly pure, strong, warm and lovable player. In spite of his abilities and the extreme beauty of the music, the Concerto made no permanent success on its first appearance in December 1806. How could it, when Beethoven only finished the work just in time for Clement to read it at sight at the concert? Under such conditions not even an angel violinist could have done justice to it, for the Concerto must be loved and lived with for years before the player really begins to understand it!

In form it follows the classical pattern, with a long orchestral *tutti* at the beginning and a place for a cadenza near the end of the first *allegro*; the slow movement is a *larghetto* which remains almost throughout serenely in the near key of G major; and the finale is a deliciously rhythmic rondo. That sounds simple enough, but actually the perfection comes near being miraculous. The scheme is exquisitely proportioned; the subject matter is of exalted beauty. A drum figure of four repeated notes that opens the first movement, and pervades it, is a marvellous foil to the melodic cantilena.

The episode in G minor which occurs just before the recapitulation is one of Beethoven's sacred moments—indescribable in its wistfulness and withdrawal from the world. Joachim used to play this so wonderfully that no one who heard him could forget that divine beauty.

Throughout the Concerto the scoring is extraordinarily fine; never more so than in the *larghetto*, where Beethoven places the solo part with consummate knowledge of the ethereal effects obtainable on the E string

and the strange lovelinesses of the D string (the heart of the violin), while he mutes the accompanying strings of the orchestra into a tender softness for the background, and uses the woodwind and horns with them lightly.

For perfection of string scoring the passage beginning at bar 46 should be specially noted, and towards the close of the movement Beethoven introduces the horns very softly with a call which has the effect of something from another world.

The rondo is made on a tune not far from a folk melody, and fairly dances with happiness. Constructively it ranks with the great rondos of the last piano concertos, but is quite different in type.

As in those concertos, so here, the key scheme for the entire work is extremely subtle. Most composers writing in D major would have veered naturally towards the dominant, A major. Beethoven avoided the harsh brilliance of too much A major by tending towards the sub-dominant G, which appears as G minor in the episodes of the first and last movements, and as G major in the *larghetto*. Altogether the Concerto is a noble work, and Beethoven thought so well of it that he made a version for piano—a curiosity now almost forgotten, though the cadenza with drum accompaniment is a notable feature. Such a transcription could not have the value of the original because the principal part in that is absolutely made out of violin texture. When Elgar composed his violin Concerto in 1910 he inscribed on the title page these words: 'Aquí está encerrada el alma de . . .' For Beethoven's violin Concerto I would paraphrase and complete the sentence thus: 'Here is enshrined the soul of the Stradivarius violin'—which is very much what Elgar's bio-grapher, Basil Maine, suggests as the inner meaning of the Elgar Concerto.

CHAPTER XII

DRAMATIC MUSIC

MUSIC for the stage, like the idea of marriage, attracted Beethoven throughout the major part of his career, and a survey of either produces a bewilderment akin to losing one's sense of the north. Where are the points of the compass by which to steer a right course? How shall one tell the dividing line between his music for the theatre and his music for the concert room?

With Mozart no such difficulty could occur because his thoughts and technique moved in separate ambits for the separate kinds of work. With Beethoven this was not so. Though he wrote one great opera, he was not a great operatic composer, and his genius turned on a symphonic axis, with sonata form and variation form as its magnetic poles. His symphonies are the most dramatic in existence; his stage works show a homing tendency towards the concert room. Indeed all his finest overtures, *Leonora* No. 2, *Leonora* No. 3, *Coriolan* and *Egmont,* have found their destiny in orchestral programmes.

Yet since Beethoven designed them for stage use, I propose to discuss them in this chapter coupled with his one opera. The *Ritterballet* and *Prometheus* ballet have been already considered in connection with his orchestral music. They led nowhere in his dramatic development, and served but as prologues to his great symphonic works. Let them rest at that.

If environment determined the cast of a man's genius, Beethoven might well have been a second and greater Gluck. During his prentice years in the opera orchestra at Bonn he had ample opportunity to absorb stage technique and sense of the theatre. But he absorbed little, and he learned nothing of the stage from Haydn in Vienna, for the excellent reason that Haydn understood it even less than Beethoven himself. Dear Haydn with an opera was almost as innocent as César Franck with Satan! Finally, Beethoven appears to have been somewhat indifferent to the stage during his first decade in Vienna. Beyond his studies with Salieri in Italian dramatic declamation, two bass arias, a prelude and a couple of songs written to be introduced into Umlauf's comic opera *Die schöne Schusterin,* there is next to nothing prior to *Prometheus* to show that he had any ambitions in that direction. It is said that Schikaneder engaged Beethoven in 1803 to compose an opera for the Theater an der Wien, on a subject said to have been that of Alexander. But Schikaneder passed out of power and the whole story is a tissue of 'ifs,' not worth pursuing here. Nor is it necessary to rake up the confused quarrels and changes at the Theater an der Wien, where Schikaneder was reinstated by the new owner, Baron Braun, and where in 1804 a novelty was badly needed. The astute Schikaneder, rather than Braun, was probably the instigator of the commission to Beethoven. If so, he deserves well of us, for to have evoked two such operas as Mozart's *Magic Flute* and Beethoven's *Fidelio* was a memorable deed.

The commission given, it remained to find a text. Joseph von Sonnleithner, a very cultivated man, secretary of the Court Theatre, offered to provide one. He suggested *Léonore ou l'amour conjugal.* The idea pleased Beethoven; it proved indeed to be the only opera subject that ever fully satisfied him throughout his career, except of course *The Water Carrier* and *The Vestal* which Cherubini and Spontini made their own.

Léonore was a 'pain and torment' story of a type very popular in a world which had witnessed the French Revolution. Its central incident had really happened within the jurisdiction of J. N. Bouilly, who administered a department near Tours during the Terror. When called upon to supply opera libretti (why are librettists nearly always amateurs?), Bouilly drew upon what he had seen, and produced the texts of Cherubini's *Water Carrier* and Pierre Gaveaux's *Léonore,* both performed in Paris with immense success. An Italian version of the latter, composed by Paer, was given at Dresden in 1804. Sonnleithner, third in the field, made a German version, but unwisely expanded the book to three acts. Thus Beethoven's text, like the framework of Shakespeare's plays, came to him from many sources, and the good points concealed the flaws from his inexperienced eyes. Treitschke, poet and stage manager of the German court opera, records that Beethoven had no fear of his predecessors and went to work with eager delight.

This first opera of Beethoven's was like a case of love at first sight. Sitting on the low-branching oak in the woodland at Schönbrunn, where he had once composed his oratorio of Christ as deliverer, he surrendered himself to this tremendous new experience. In his *Eroica* he had given to the world for all time his portrait of the ideal hero, the great man. In *Fidelio* he now enshrined the companion portrait of his ideal heroine, Leonora, the faithful wife, portraying in deathless music her undying love and devotion. She took possession of him; she took possession of the opera. No other character has any real existence except as it impinges on her, and the incidents, true to fact and necessary for the realistic presentation of the opera, are yet so infinitely more true as symbols of the inner life of the human heart that in a way the opera exists less as a stage construction than as a part of our own being.

The scene is laid in Spain. Florestan, for some political offence never disclosed, is being starved to death in one of the lowest dungeons of a fortress governed by his implacable enemy, Pizarro. News of Florestan's demise has already been circulated in the outer world. But Leonora—perhaps by the singular awareness of love to the loved one—believes he may still live, and resolves to rescue him. She disguises herself as a boy, takes the name Fidelio (so did Shakespeare's Imogen take the name Fidele!), and manages to enter the castle in the service of Rocco, the jailer. By another stroke of fortune Rocco's daughter, Marcellina, who is heartily sick of the suit of Jaquino, the porter, falls in love with the handsome Fidelio. Meanwhile Pizarro, seeing that starvation works too slowly, orders Rocco to kill Florestan before Fernando, the minister, can arrive to inspect the prison. Rocco, a kindly old thing, refuses, but consents to dig the grave if Pizarro will commit the murder. Leonora, overhearing these arrangements, per-suades Rocco to take her as his assistant. Meanwhile Rocco has permitted the other prisoners in the fortress to come into the courtyard for exercise. As they file out, haggard and weak, Leonora searches each face to see if her husband is among them. (Her intense gaze is a bit of 'business' that has come down probably from Beethoven's own time, and it is infinitely touching.) Pizarro is furious at finding the prisoners in the courtyard and rebukes Rocco. Meanwhile Florestan, lying in the last stages of exhaustion in his dungeon, dreams of Leonora. Presently Rocco enters with the 'boy' and orders her to help him dig a grave. In her anxiety to identify the prisoner, she nearly betrays herself, and can hardly suppress her emotion on recognizing her husband's voice. Pizarro arrives, tells Florestan he will kill him, attempts to stab him, and is stopped by Leonora, who flings herself as a shield in front of Florestan. Pizarro again tries to kill him; Leonora again defends him, crying out: 'First kill his wife!' Florestan's rapture and Pizarro's rage burst out uncontrolled; Pizarro exclaims: 'Shall I tremble before a woman?' and tries to murder both. Leonora, at bay, draws a pistol and retaliates: 'One word more and thou art dead'—when suddenly the sound of a distant trumpet strikes all else to silence. Don

Fernando has arrived; Florestan is saved. It is the great moment, the magnificent climax of the story. The last scene is simply the completion of justice and rejoicing.

This libretto appealed to the tremendous liberating passion in Beethoven which M. Closson believes was a mark of his Flemish ancestry. The very name Leonore too was dear to him for the sake of Eleonore von Breuning. Is it some unacknowledged link with her memory and the happy days at Bonn that, into the finale of the libretto—which M. Rolland says is a fairly close transcript of the French original—Beethoven introduced the lines:

> Wer ein holdes Weib errungen,
> Stimm' in unsern Jubel ein!

They are practically a quotation from that *Ode to Joy* by Schiller which Beethoven had resolved to set to music long ago at Bonn, and which he did compose at last in his ninth Symphony. For Beethoven the opera was always *Leonore*. It vexed him bitterly that the theatre authorities insisted it should be called *Fidelio*.

From the first performance in 1805 he became aware of the faults of Sonnleithner's libretto. I have already described in Chapter V the well-meaning council of friends who persuaded Beethoven to accept a revision by which Stephan von Breuning carried out such drastic cuts for the 1806 revival that the second state was almost worse than the first, except that the three acts were reduced to two and that Beethoven superseded the original overture by the astoundingly glorious overture known as *Leonora No. 3*. When *Fidelio* was revived in 1814, Beethoven secured G. F. Treitschke as his skilful collaborator, and he was himself in a better state than before to pass critical judgment upon the music. *Fidelio* in its present form is the result of their efforts.

Fidelio was designed along the lines of German *Singspiel*.

i.e. the musical numbers were interspersed with spoken dialogues. Admirable in comedy, the form is less suited to drama, where the alternations between song and speech play fast and loose with one's feelings. This is so in *Fidelio*, particularly in the first act, though there are places in the second act where the method seems a pure inspiration.

When beginning his opera it was natural Beethoven should examine the best models by other composers. Bekker says that *Fidelio* has some elements of style that look back to the lyrical opera, and others that belong to dramatic music. 'Mozart,' he adds, 'attempted to blend something of the German lyrical drama with the Italian form, and Beethoven carried the idea further with the help of French models, which were of a freer and more declamatory style than the Italian *cantabile* form.'

M. Rolland is very positive about Beethoven's French sources. After considering the French origin of the libretto, he continues:

This filiation between a robust junior and the elder members of a noble race . . . is not confined merely to vague moral resemblance. It is clearly marked in the music, with a precision that admits of no doubt. The symphonic style of *Leonore* derives in essentials from that of Méhul and Cherubini. We know that Beethoven, at the height of his genius (in 1823), wrote to Cherubini paying humble homage to this work (*Medea*). It is not surprising, then, that traces of this influence should be found in his own music.

Arnold Schmitz (1925) finds the resemblances particularly strong in the overtures. Rolland admits, however, that some of the analogues may be explained on the theory of a common source in Gluck; for example, the mighty unisons with which all Beethoven's tragic overtures open.

No doubt a close study of the scores of Gluck, Méhul, Cherubini and other composers of the period would throw interesting light on the studies which Beethoven quietly

conducted for himself, but the more one sees of his debt to
other men, the more entirely Beethoven he appears. His
great enveloping genius is the fact that dominates all else.

Of the four overtures to *Fidelio, Leonora* No. 1 has been shown
to have been the earliest, written before the first performance
and withdrawn by Beethoven as too insignificant. Some
affinities with his overture to *Prometheus* are relevant in this
connection. Thayer was mistaken in thinking that the evidence pointed to *Leonora* No. 1 having been composed for a
performance at Prague in 1807, which never took place.
Fanny Mendelssohn could not understand Beethoven's poor
opinion of it. 'Ah, Rebecca,' she wrote to her sister from
Düsseldorf in 1836, 'we have heard an overture to *Leonore,*
a new piece. It is notorious that it has never been played;
it did not please Beethoven and he put it aside. The man
had no taste! It is so refined, so interesting, so fascinating
that I know few things which can be compared with it.'

The overture *Leonora* No. 2, played at the actual first performance on 20th November 1805, is a far finer work, initiated
on a span of sonata form so great that even Beethoven himself
does not fulfil it. The slow introduction, the exposition and
development of the *allegro* are so large that there is no time for
a recapitulation and the coda is not big enough to compensate
its absence. To-day such a scheme would be accepted as
satisfactory, but it did not content Beethoven. Before the
revival of his opera in 1806 he rewrote the overture. The
result was the incomparable *Leonora* No. 3. Into it Beethoven
put everything that was vital in his conception of the opera.
He succeeded only too well. No. 3 is not the overture to
Leonora—it is *Leonora*. It does not arouse anticipation; it
fulfils everything.

By a close comparison between *Leonora* No. 2 and No. 3
one gains an absorbing lesson in Beethoven's mental processes,
and also a wonderful lesson in musical construction. To all

intents and purposes his material is the same in both overtures, but the structural use is different. Where in No. 2 the abstract scheme is grand but unbalanced, in No. 3 it is tense, superb, magnificently proportioned, underlying the music as bones underlie muscles. Moreover, the emotional details are better picked and placed. Compare the immensely more noble effect in *Leonora* No. 3 of the passage between the two trumpet calls played 'off stage' with the corresponding passage in *Leonora* No. 2.

Those trumpet calls are among the most famous things in music. Rolland, following Schmitz, declares they derive from Méhul's overture to *Hélène*, but why Beethoven could not have got the suggestion nearer home from the trumpet call in Haydn's Military Symphony, is a nice point for the French! Rolland and Schmitz also attribute the 'boil and swirl of the unison strings in the coda of *Leonora* No. 3' to Cherubini's *Elisa* overture, besides finding other analogies of rhythm, syncopated chords, etc., with Cherubini and Méhul. These things show how Beethoven, by the alchemy of his genius, made everything into his own gold.

Here is the great unison beginning of *Leonora* No. 3; pure Beethoven, whatever its origin in Gluck or Cherubini:

Even yet Beethoven was not satisfied. When he revised *Fidelio* in 1814, he realized that a great dramatic overture was an unsettling preface for a lyrical drama. He therefore replaced *Leonora* No. 3 by a new work called the overture to *Fidelio*. The change of name coincided with a change in character. E major, not C, was now the chosen key, fresh themes were employed, and the bright texture of the music was evidently intended to provide a light curtain-raiser that could pass smoothly into the opening scene where the small fry of the cast, Jaquino and Marcellina, 'sing in' the opera quite conventionally with a duet about their small love affairs. What an example of Beethoven's acute dramatic sense, one exclaims! Well, yes, but also of his vacillation, for in that same year he certainly acquiesced in the substitution of his overture to *Prometheus* for one performance of the opera, and (possibly) of his overture to *The Ruins of Athens* for another.

Of the two acts now constituting *Fidelio*, the first contains ten numbers (exclusive of overture) and the second six, several of which are so wide in scope that the opera has often been called symphonic. Beethoven, by his nature, could seldom help bringing symphonic traits of melody, harmony, instrumentation, even symphonic texture itself into music written in the grand manner. But it is totally untrue to suppose that because his opera is symphonic, it is therefore not of the stage. In some extraordinary way the spiritual reality of his drama gets right through the formal operatic mould stiffened with symphonic technique, and the music makes its compelling effect sometimes by direct truth of expression (as in the dungeon scene) and sometimes by a general symbolic artistic evocation, which, by carrying forward the listeners on a broad stream of music conveys their thoughts in the intended direction, even when there is no particular attempt at expression and characterization.

Moreover, behind the musical plan there is a sort of metaphysical design. Each act opens simply, with few characters, then gradually gathers its forces until it expands into a broad concerted finale. But while Act I begins in bright daylight and banter with the simplicity of little everyday affairs and moves from them steadily downward into the shadows of tragedy and the sighing of all that are desolate and oppressed in the prisoners' choruses, Act II begins below the threshold of hope, and from that lowest prison of the human soul in loneliness, as typified in Florestan, passes gradually upward to faith fulfilled in a burst of light more glorious than any sunrise.

Of the separate pieces in Act I those allotted to Jaquino and Marcellina are of secondary interest. On Leonora's entrance the music moves to a higher plane, though the quartet between Marcellina, Leonora, Jaquino and Rocco, (a delightful and admired example of effective canon), fails to give any expression to the extremely varied emotions of the characters taking part. For Rocco's song I suspect Beethoven cast back to Bonn associations—anyhow there seems a good Rhineland ring in the tune about gold. In the trio that follows Beethoven begins to get to grips with the true meaning of things. If he had never done anything else, one would love him for his wonderful understanding of the difference between Leonora's and Marcellina's ways of loving. Each in turn is given a musical phrase that opens similarly and ends with a melismatic passage. But where Leonora, thinking of Florestan, intensifies her phrase by a change to minor harmony and then clinches it by that 'appoggiatura of passion' which Beethoven reserved for feeling at its strongest, Marcellina's melody remains undisturbedly in the major and dissipates its sentiment in a superficial florid cadence.

LEONORA

199

MARCELLINA

der Lie - be Glück, der Lie - be Glück und un - nenn - ba - - - - - - - - - re Freu - den.

After a march, Pizarro's aria with chorus enters in the approved way, the villain uttering 'Ha! ha! ha!' the third time on a resonant high D. Beethoven here adopted the operatic conventions for villainy with force and success—his dark mood of D minor a little stimulated, I sometimes think, by the so-called motet from Haydn's *Ritorno di Tobia,* which we know in England as the anthem *Insanae et vanae curae.* Beethoven's chords of the diminished seventh in connection with Pizarro should be noted; also the letting loose of the orchestra at this point for the first time—an application of Gluck's theory that the instruments should be employed according to the degree of interest and passion. In the duet following with Rocco, Bekker considers that Beethoven brings out the 'beast of prey instincts' in Pizarro with great vividness, especially in the 'furtive unison passages.'

But all such matters go by the board when Leonora begins her recitative and aria, 'Abscheulicher! wo eilst du hin!'— the grandest thing in the first act.

Between the original version of 1805 and the final one of 1814, Beethoven made changes which do not meet with the approval of all critics, on the ground that he sacrificed the womanly elements of her character to the heroic. Yet the mere placing of the floriated passages is enough to show how Leonora's heart expands at the thought of hope fulfilled and how she gathers strength from the consciousness of her noble duty as a loving wife. Besides, this was the moment for heroic resolve. Beethoven met it with this magnificent aria, where every bar is packed with meaning, even to the orchestration of the accompaniment, in which we get privileged glimpses into Beethoven's own associations between certain ideas and special orchestral colours—for example, in his use of the horns. The great finale that follows is buttressed at the beginning and end by two choruses for the prisoners, one as they steal into the light, the other as they descend again into darkness. The second chorus is enriched by the solo characters, who in the intervening section have passed through a crisis, vividly portrayed in the music, where Leonora's hope of reaching Florestan is nearly frustrated by Rocco's misplaced consideration, and have endured the eruption of Pizarro's rage at Rocco's kindness (not misplaced!) to the prisoners.

This great finale, with its shadowy progressions, and heart-rending use of *piano* and *pianissimo,* is a piece of pure genius only less magnificent than the beginning of Act II, where, in the dungeon scene, Beethoven's incomparable music rises from inspiration to inspiration. First there is Florestan's air, 'In des Lebens Frühlingstagen ist das Glück von mir geflohn' (In the springtime of life, happiness has fled from me), so poignantly beautiful and (like Leonora's great aria) giving one an extraordinary glimpse into Beethoven's own mind and heart as man and musician. Berlioz, not usually afflicted with dumbness, found himself unable from sheer emotion to complete his description of this aria. He does mention, however, specially 'the continued song of the oboe that follows the song of Florestan like the voice of the adored wife which he imagines he hears.' And what a wonderful touch that is in the introductory recitative where, as the thought of God first comes to Florestan out of the darkness, Beethoven reflects it by an enharmonic modulation out of the muffled harmony of G flat into the pure brightness of F sharp and B major!

In the melodrame and grave-digging duet between Leonora and Rocco the terrifying quiet in which most of the music passes, the tense, short sentences of the diggers, the strange touches of realism in the orchestra when the stone moves, and the suppressed emotion in Leonora's music are as indescribable as unforgettable. The orchestral parts are minatory with meaning. Beethoven's use of the exceptional colours of double bassoon and trombone, the muted triplets in the violins, the eerie figure in the basses—what a marvellous score! Surely this scene formed the starting-point from which Schubert's genius leaped forth in 1815 to set Goethe's *Erl King*—as Richard Capell noted in his authoritative book on 'Schubert's Songs.'

As the action intensifies, Beethoven expands his treatment, though the melodious trio between Florestan, Leonora and Rocco is rather a widening of means than of music. The quartet which follows Pizarro's entrance is the superb culmination for which all the rest of the opera exists. The music sweeps the main action forward on a great wave, within which Beethoven develops the interplay of characters and motives with extreme truth and insight. The first transcendent moment is reached at Leonora's cry: 'First kill his wife!'

Beethoven altered the notes several times before he achieved what he considered sufficient intensity for the phrase. It is a striking example of the consistency of his imagination that he should have set this greatest act of heroism to a chord of E flat major, the key of his *Eroica*. The second and supreme climax of the scene comes with the trumpet calls which announce the arrival of the governor; in Beethoven's music the shadow of death rolls back like the passing of a solar eclipse.

The beautiful duet of joy between the reunited Leonora and Florestan that ensues fits well, despite its having been taken over by Beethoven from an earlier sketch which Bekker believes to have belonged to the projected opera of 1803.

In the second part of the act, with its broad ceremonial consummation of rejoicing, Beethoven also employs music from an earlier work to express the divine happiness when Leonora frees Florestan from his chains. The movement comes from the Cantata on the Death of Joseph the Second, and I cannot help feeling that Beethoven had been strongly influenced for both by Eurydice's air, in Gluck's *Orpheus*, describing the tranquil loveliness of the Elysian fields. All three arias are in the same key, F major; they have a wonderful musical affinity and are used to express the same sense of emancipation into heavenly calm and blessedness. In *Fidelio* this is immediately followed by the chorus on those lines from Schiller, 'Wer ein holdes Weib errungen,' which Beethoven interpolated into the work of his librettists. The sequence of his Bonn associations sets one thinking very hard. Leonora? Eleonore von Breuning? Beethoven's ensembles and choruses for the end of *Fidelio* more than fulfil the require-ments of operatic convention in the early nineteenth century, and are a sort of foretaste of his ninth Symphony, but never-theless they leave one with a little of the same disquiet. Is the big choral finale right or wrong? Treitschke thought the opera should end with the dungeon scene.

But here Beethoven was even more sure of himself than in the ninth Symphony. Whatever the world thought, or still thinks, of *Fidelio* as an opera, Beethoven believed in it passionately, not only for itself, but for the future of music. When dying he told Schindler that of all his 'children' it was the one most dear to him, and: 'Before all others I hold it worthy of being possessed and used for the science of art.'

Beethoven's words should be very carefully pondered. Though the world has passed a different verdict, it is quite possible *Fidelio* may yet show that he knew more than we do. And one thing is sure: the opera goes straight to the heart of humanity. A doctor from the Dominions who saw for his first opera a performance of Beethoven's *Fidelio*, and exclaimed enthusiastically: 'I shall go to every opera he wrote!' found the right verdict.

Ah! if only Beethoven had written those other operas! Libretto after libretto was sought or sent, considered and rejected. 'And now there must at all costs be *magic*—I cannot deny that on the whole I am prejudiced against this sort of thing, because it has a soporific effect on feeling and reason,' he wrote when offered a fairy opera, *Bradamante*. He rather thought he would like 'some grand subject taken from history and especially from the dark ages, for instance, from the time of Attila or the like!'[1] He revolved the idea of *Macbeth* with almost demonic excitement; *Faust* stirred his imagination; an Indian opera left him frigid. *Melusine, The Return of Ulysses, Bacchus, Romulus and Remus, Alfred the Great, Romeo and Juliet,* Schiller's *Fiesco* and Voltaire's tragedies were among the subjects considered and declined. The overpowering solemnity of the list bears out what Beethoven said to Rellstab when the latter offered him a libretto. 'I care little what genre the works belong to, so the material be attractive to me. But it

[1] Did this hint direct Wagner to the *Nibelungenlied*?

must be something which I can take up with sincerity and love. I could not compose operas like *Don Juan* and *Figaro*! They are repugnant to me. I could not have chosen such subjects; they are too frivolous for me!'

But though Beethoven never composed another opera, his connection with the stage remained fairly steady through the incidental music he supplied for various dramas. *Egmont,* the most extended and also the greatest of these sets of pieces, was written, he said, for pure love of Goethe's poem in 1810. The subject set ablaze the Flemish elements in Beethoven's character: the 'liberating passion' was at work again; he poured out music alight with genius. The overture is a superb example of a type which Beethoven made especially his own—the dramatic overture. He had arrived at it during the course of his *Leonora* experiments. As Bekker well says, it was Beethoven's own form of music-drama; he projected the whole spiritual content of the drama into the overture.' A tremendous compression—comparable to the locked power of atomic force. Into the *Egmont* overture Beethoven packed the whole scene and course of the heroic story. Perhaps the most astounding example of his compression is the passage immediately following the very softly held chords that denote the patriot Egmont's death, when Beethoven conveys in *eight* bars the gathering together and uprising of a nation in revolution.

The four orchestral entr'actes, the music depicting Clärchen's death, the melodrame for Egmont's dream, and the victory symphony are all worthy of the overture. Clärchen's two songs, though not equal to Leonora's music in *Fidelio,* are nevertheless among the best lyric songs Beethoven ever wrote, and are beautifully characteristic. Everywhere, too, in *Egmont* Beethoven profoundly enhances his meanings by his orchestration, a fact that can be proved by comparing the *Egmont* score with his procedure in the *Eroica* and *Fidelio.*

The overture to *Coriolan,* written in 1807 as preface to

Collin's (not Shakespeare's) play on that subject, is another of those tremendous overtures which contain the whole drama. Its delineation of catastrophic pride and power is too well known to need description, yet I cannot resist one word about the way in which Beethoven, after launching his tender second subject in the major key, diverts it into the minor before the end—as if he realized that had the full loveliness continued, it would have been almost more than heart could bear.

The overtures and incidental music for Kotzebue's *Ruins of Athens* and the same poet's *King Stephan, Hungary's First Benefactor,* date from 1811. Beethoven is said to have composed the lot in a month. He possibly repented at leisure, for though the works were received at Pesth with clamorous applause on their first performance, and though he once called them his little operas, their overtures (when he sold them to the Philharmonic Society of London in 1816 as new) so disappointed his English admirers that they wrote to Charles Neate who had been one of the go-betweens: 'For God's sake, don't buy anything of Beethoven!'

Both *The Ruins* and *King Stephan* have fallen into a desuetude that is the complete comment on their place among Beethoven's works. Perhaps, however, one ought to mention the Turkish March in the former because the theme had already been used by Beethoven in the Variations in D he dedicated to Oliva. The tradition runs that it was Russian. What a glorious medley!

Among Beethoven's other 'occasional' pieces of dramatic music were the Triumphal March for *Tarpeja* (1813), which is effective in the conventional way of such things; also in 1815 a Soldier's Chorus for male voices unaccompanied, a romance with harp, *Es blüht eine Blume*, a melodrama with glass harmonica, and an orchestrated version of the Funeral March from his piano Sonata, Op. 26, all for a drama called *Leonora Prohaska* that was never performed, because, it is said, the censor vetoed it. As the Soldiers' Chorus was a glorification of 'die Freiheit' (freedom), and as the story was concerned with a heroine who fought through the war of liberation, one sees at once why the play attracted Beethoven and displeased the censor. A chorus, *Germania, wie stehst du*, was supplied by Beethoven for a *Singspiel*, called *Gute Nachricht* (*Good News*), which Treitschke put together to celebrate the occupation of Paris in 1814.

Next year history repeated itself. Paris again capitulated; Treitschke prepared another jubilant piece, *Die Ehrenpforten*, and Beethoven composed for it the chorus *Es ist vollbracht*.

These compositions served their topical purpose, but Beethoven's last work for the stage stands in a wholly different category. The Josephstadt Theatre was to be opened on the emperor's nameday, 3rd October 1822, and the first piece down for performance was a paraphrase of *The Ruins of Athens*, now changed and adapted by Carl Meisl into *The Consecration of the House*. New words, with misfits that worried Beethoven, were for the most part set by Meisl to the old music. However, at one point Beethoven supplied a fresh and stately chorus leading to a tableau and—far more important—discarded the old overture to *The Ruins of Athens*, composing in its place the one we now know as *Die Weihe des Hauses* (*The Consecration of the House*), Op. 124. If ever music was rich with mellow wisdom it is this noble and strangely neglected work, whose significance in the sequence of Beethoven's thoughts is not sufficiently recognized. It stands in the same relation to his latest period as does the *Prometheus* overture to his middle period, and, by a beautiful inevitability like a natural law, Beethoven returned here to the reflective, non-dramatic type which had served him for *Prometheus*, but which he now employed with infinitely greater mastery. Schindler tells a valuable anecdote of its composition. Beethoven, already at work on the *Consecration*, was walking one day with his nephew Karl and Schindler in the Helenenthal, when two motives suddenly came to him, one in the free style, the other in the strict. He sang them to his companions and asked which they liked better. Karl voted for both, but Schindler expressed 'a desire to see the fugal theme worked out for the purpose mentioned. It is not to be understood,' continues Schindler, 'that Beethoven wrote the overture *The Consecration of the House* as he did because I wanted it so, but because he had long cherished the plan to write an overture in the strict, expressly in the Handelian, style.'

This story tallies with the overture itself, which may be described in a rough and ready way as consisting of blocks of *tutti* in free harmonic style, and blocks of close-reasoned fuguing. Better still, it illustrates the principle of duality which had shown itself in Beethoven's mind from early times, and which became a governing force in his latest compositions. I feel sure that this overture, intended by Beethoven as homage to Handel, must have been planned by him as a companion piece to the overture on the name of Bach, which he sketched about this time, but never completed. With beautiful perception the overture for Handel was written for the theatre, the one for Bach designed for the concert room. The fact that the overture to *The Consecration of the House* also owes something to Mozart's overture to *The Magic Flute* is perhaps only a further acknowledgment of Handel as a common source.

Bekker says of this great piece of ceremonial music that it is 'a perfect expression of the joy of a creator in his creation . . . an apotheosis at once secular and religious, of the priestly quality of the artist.'

Thus out of the *Ruins of Athens* was built a new and glorious temple—one which, 'never built at all,' was therefore 'built forever.' Beethoven's last work for the stage was not an end, but a beginning.

CHAPTER XIII

VOCAL MUSIC

On a rough computation Beethoven's vocal works amount to close on one hundred songs, one hundred and sixty-four settings of folksongs, forty canons, five cantatas, one oratorio, two masses, and some miscellaneous pieces for chorus or smaller vocal ensemble. Of all these only a few songs and the great *Missa Solennis* remain in use. To confine this chapter to the survivals, displaying them under the spectacular aspect of the scrap of paper, the billiard ball and the cannon ball which a famous variety artist used to juggle in the air simultaneously, would be to present Beethoven's vocal works in a misleading way. For though Beethoven was no virtuoso with vocal music, his works in that medium possessed a precious quality that made them vital even while it rendered them vulnerable. Wagner seized on it when he said that, apart from sonata form, 'the other forms, particularly the mixed ones of vocal music, he only touched upon in passing, *as if by way of experiment,* despite the most extraordinary achievements in them.' (My italics—not Wagner's.)

Experiment. In that word is a key to the songs, the cantatas, the oratorio, the masses, and a clue to the subconscious discontent which I think Beethoven experienced when dealing with voices; discontent with the limitations of the human voice; discontent with existing conventions of word setting, vocal formulae, singers' demands; discontent with himself for the intractability of his choral writing. To match his work against Handel's sweeping power and infallible directness made him very humble. Schulz, who visited Beethoven in 1823, records:

I cannot describe to you with what pathos and, I am inclined to say, with what sublimity of language he spoke of *The Messiah.*

. . . Every one of us was moved when he said: 'I would uncover my head and kneel down at his (Handel's) tomb.'

At that time Beethoven had but just emerged from his four years' life and death struggle in writing the *Missa Solennis*. Handel, his model, had composed *The Messiah* in less than a month.

In song writing Beethoven had no great models. His own works are the bridge between the ingenuous songlets of the eighteenth century, written for domestic performance, and the exquisite *Lieder* of Franz Schubert. At the outset Beethoven relied largely on instinct. Indeed, looking at his songs com-posed during the Bonn period, there are moments when I wish he had never studied under Salieri. The jolly bass arias with orchestra (*c.* 1790), *Prüfung des Küssens* and *Mit Madeln sich vertragen,* have a youthful sing-yourself zest that is most attrac-tive, and the simplicity and pathos of *Elegie auf den Tod eines Pudels* (*c.* 1787) still go straight to the heart. It is true many of the early songs show weak spots in the workmanship and even a vein of sentimentality, but they have lyric impulse and that young man's freshness which can never be recaptured in mature composition. With Beethoven it vanished—so far as his songs were concerned—under the ministrations of Haydn and Salieri in Vienna. Haydn simply confirmed Beethoven in the convention of doubling the vocal line with the top part in the accompaniment, a bad habit that, under guise of supporting the voice, trammelled it, and Salieri led him back to Italian models which, excellent in themselves, were alien to Beethoven's genius. I must honestly admit, however, that *Adelaide* (1795–6), the most famous of these Italianate songs, is really most beautiful and has the genuine Beethoven passion breaking through its formal mould in the lovely and ever-new phrases to which the lover reiterates the name of Adelaide. The style is pure *bel canto*. Few singers now possess the method, and the song is seldom sung.

Early Songs

The great dramatic scena for soprano and orchestra, *Ah, perfido! spergiuro* (1796), the arietta, *In questa tomba* (1807) and the six sacred songs to poems by Gellert (1803), which include the impressive *Vom Tode* and *Die Ehre Gottes aus der Natur* (foreshadowing Schubert), are all remarkable, but nowadays they are rather avoided in England, because they demand the reserves of physical power associated with the Central European types of voice.

To examine Beethoven's songs of his middle period is to see how he wavered between the past and that magic new world of the German *Lied* whose coming he sensed, but which he never saw clearly till some of Schubert's songs were put into his hands on his death-bed. So, at times turning towards the past, Beethoven over-rode the verbal quantities in his songs as ruthlessly as any opera composer of the mid-eighteenth century. At others, gazing into the future, he showed himself exquisitely sensitive to the inflexions of the poems set. So too with his accompaniments. Some are non-contributive, and express only the harmonies implied in the melody; others stand in a living partnership with the voice; others are hybrids. Nearly all the songs bear the marks of a transition period. With one notable exception Schubert learnt far less from Beethoven the song-writer than from Beethoven the symphonist.

That exception was the song cycle *An die ferne Geliebte* (*To the Distant Beloved*), Op. 98, which Beethoven composed in 1816 to six poems by Jeitteles. So far as is known Beethoven originated the form—*Liederkreis,* as he called it—and his solitary example is still considered the most perfect, though Schubert's *Schöne Müllerin* and *Winterreise* and Schumann's *Dichterliebe* contain songs which are individually greater. The poems of the *Ferne Geliebte* express the wistful longing and loneliness of the lover as he sits upon a little hill, feeling his heart drawn into the distance towards the loved one.

Beethoven has set the poignant little poems to music of a tenderness and simplicity that conceal the consummate art with which he links song to song, and finally completes his circle by a long coda made from the material of the first song, now greatly intensified in emotion. The changes of key, tempo and rhythm are so subtle, and the touches of expression and word painting in the accompaniment give such an intimate sight of Beethoven's heart, that I doubt whether any performance, however good, could produce quite the same exquisite impression as a perusal of the score. Take such a song as No. 2, which enters poised on the least defined position of the common chord (technically known as the $\frac{6}{4}$), and hangs there more or less for bars on a dominant pedal note as the lover looks at the distant blue mountains. Then when his thoughts pass to the deep peace of the valley enfolding the loved one with whom he longs to be, the music modulates to C major and floats in an almost clairvoyant quiet upon the pedal note G, on which the voice monotones the words very softly. Or take Beethoven's tiny picture in the accompaniment of No. 3 at the words 'Und du, Bächlein, klein und schmal' (And thou, brooklet, narrow and small), where one sees his wealth of affection for the little stream he had already painted in the Pastoral Symphony. Or look at such a passage as the opening of No. 4, where by the simplest means Beethoven gives the very feeling of clouds sailing high in the blue. Could any singer or pianist convey these impressions with Beethoven's reticence and clarity? Some sonnets, we are told, are so beautiful that they should be heard by the inner ear only as the eye reads them silently. Beethoven's *Ferne Geliebte* has that inexplicable loveliness. It has, too, Beethoven's strange secrecy. Though, like the lover in Robert Bridges's poem of praise to the gentle maid and tender flower, Beethoven seems to say:

> So in my song I bind them
> For all to find them,

212

yet in reality he never lets us know the woman who inspired his greatest songs. He dedicated his *Liederkreis* to Prince Joseph von Lobkowitz!

Beethoven's folksong settings were begun at the request of the Scotch publisher Thomson, who had already enlisted Pleyel, Koželuh and Haydn in the enterprise. Since it was profitable for all concerned, the number of Scotch, Welsh and Irish tunes thus provided with piano accompaniment and violin and cello parts *ad libitum* rose to a high total. Beethoven got so bitten with the work that he extended his attentions to Portuguese, Spanish, Italian and Russian folk-songs, these exotics being published by Schlesinger, the cautious Thomson refusing to have anything to do with them. Apart from the fundamental error of forcing modal tunes into diatonic harmonies—a crime which nowadays makes the fur of folksong experts rise fiercely—many of Beethoven's arrange-ments are not unattractive, while some contain really fine work.

Haydn had been a great hand at canonic writing, so it is possible Beethoven adopted from him the habit of throwing off short canons on special occasions. Some were for cere-monial and academic purposes; others were of social or convivial kind. Once he obviously had doubts next day whether he had written sense overnight. The words of the canons are an index of what thoughts happened to be upper-most in his mind. Here are some samples: *Das Schöne zu dem Guten* (1823 and 1825); *Ars longa, vita brevis* (1816 and 1825); *Gedenkt heute an Baden* (1823); *Hol Euch der Teufel! B'hüt Euch Gott!* (1819). The workmanship is always firm, betraying the Beethoven touch, and though I do not think his canons equal Haydn's in distinction, they served excellent purposes, one of which was to keep his counterpoint well oiled. The punning example on the next page belongs to the sombre year 1825. Beethoven wrote it for Dr. Braunhofer, who had attended him through a serious illness.

Doctor, close the door 'gainst death,
Notes will also help in need.

Beethoven's cantatas began on a grandiose scale: they ended by being little more than choral songs. The Cantata on the Death of Joseph II and its companion piece on the accession of Leopold II to the imperial throne, both composed in 1790, were designed for special occasions which fortunately fired the young man's imagination. Brahms declared the Joseph Cantata to be 'Beethoven through and through,' and Beethoven thought well enough of it to adopt a movement for *Fidelio*, as described in my previous chapter. The perception of choral and orchestral possibilities shown by Beethoven at twenty was remarkable. The opening chorus of the Joseph Cantata, with its weeping phrases in the woodwind of the orchestra, the antiphonal effects between chorus and orchestra where the voices enter ejaculating the word 'Tod,' the sudden rise to a *fortissimo* outburst, are wonderful instances of Beethoven's emotional power even when very young. The massive final chorus of the Leopold Cantata deserves consideration for the bearing it has on the finale of Beethoven's ninth Symphony.

Whether the Joseph and Leopold Cantatas were ever performed is an open question, with a trend towards a negative answer. Years later, in 1814, Beethoven's occasional cantata *Der glorreiche Augenblick* was performed in Vienna before an audience of sovereigns and princes assembled to celebrate Napoleon's defeat—an audience almost unparalleled in social brilliance. It is symbolic that the music should have had no lasting value. Bekker cautiously says that without being actually inferior the cantata offers no new material to the critic. The Lobkowitz Cantata (1823) is one only in name. Actually it is a short greeting piece for the sixteenth birthday of Prince Ferdinand. A soprano solo is punctuated by outbursts of harmonic support from a second soprano and two basses, above an accompaniment written for piano. Drawing-room music.

The cantata *Meeresstille und glückliche Fahrt* is quite another affair. Composed in 1815 for four-part chorus and orchestra, Beethoven linked together in it a couple of poems by Goethe, because, as he told the poet when sending him the dedication: 'Both, on account of the contrast which they offer, seem to me most fitting to be expressed musically. And how thankful I should be to know whether my harmonies are in unison with yours.' Goethe, presumably 'puffed up with majestick pride,' never replied. Beethoven's *Meeresstille* is a lovely little thing, almost a first-class work. If its 'cadences' have dated somewhat, their dominant-tonic familiarity is compensated by the imaginative treatment of the voices and the hypnotic long *pianissimo* of the opening where Beethoven literally makes us see the glassy ocean and then feel its becalmed horror by unleashing the four voices into a wide *fortissimo* chord that spreads to the immensity of circling horizon at the words 'In der ungeheuern Weite.'

Beethoven's word-painting should be noted all through the cantata.

Among Beethoven's other short vocal works the *Elegischer Gesang* ('Sanft wie du lebtest') written in memory of Baroness Pasqualati is simple and touching. Bekker points out its kinship with the slow movement of the great B flat major Trio, Op. 97. The four settings of Matthisson's *Opferlied*, done at various times, prove, as do some other poems which Beethoven set and reset, that in vocal music his instinct was often dissatisfied with what his intellect accomplished. The Monk's Song from Schiller's *Wilhelm Tell* (1817), the *Bundeslied* and other small things are unimportant.

The oratorio and two masses, on the contrary, are precious records wherein may be read not only the changes of Beethoven's technique but the growth of his religious thought.

Christus am Ölberge, the oratorio, was composed in 1803. When Beethoven revised it in 1804 he said it was written in a few weeks. By 1811, when it was published, 'a few weeks' had become 'a fortnight'; many years later, in 1824, he went further and said that this included the writing of the text. The text was nominally founded on the New Testament narrative of Christ in the Garden of Gethsemane and partly invented by the poet Franz Xaver Huber, with whom Beethoven constantly talked it over. The two evolved a work which in its illusionless secularism was a reflection of the French Revolutionary attitude towards religion. Beethoven always approached a hero with readiness and admiration. But here, one cannot help feeling, Christ was less real to him than, say, Prometheus, and that the Christ spirit was hidden from him by the material images and gorgeous ceremonial which had prevailed in Bonn and old Vienna. A good deal of baroque and rococo certainly got into the music. There was also a good deal of the theatre. Beethoven intended to be 'modern.' As often happens where modernism is deliberately adopted, the work had a striking success at the time, but is now *démodé* and too comic to perform. Yet portions have some nobility.

The orchestral introduction in E flat minor is the finest thing in the whole. Beethoven used it to create a clairvoyant vision of the dark garden of Gethsemane and Christ praying in agony. Apart from the intrinsic beauty of the music, it is valuable as an early indication of Beethoven's feelings about certain keys, for he employed the muffled darkness of E flat minor, a key he seldom used, and modulated to B major—

a transition he repeated long after with almost supernatural effect in the C sharp minor string Quartet. The introduction leads to a striking recitative for Christ, followed by an aria in C minor (for Beethoven the key of Fate) in which Christ prays that the cup may be taken away from Him. The treatment is tolerable, though operatic, but from the moment the Seraph, very baroque, caracoles on to the scene (with a recitative and aria written for a voice I have heard called 'a high caricatura soprano'), it is no longer possible to retain reverent sympathy for the oratorio. For one thing Beethoven employs the chord of the diminished seventh with melodramatic, almost sentimental frequency and the bits of word-painting are naïve—as for example the quivering demisemiquaver figure where the Seraph palpitates with fear in No. 8. In the trio between the Seraph, Christ and Peter there is a forecast of *Fidelio*. The fugal entries of the chorus where the soldiers seize Christ sound as if Beethoven, before he wrote it, had studied Handel's fugue in *The Messiah*, 'He trusted in God that He would deliver Him.' The final chorus is undeniably rather imposing. Beethoven is said to have thought of composing a companion oratorio, *The Redeemer's Journey into Hell*. It was like him to wish to follow into the unseen, but he was not yet ready for such a tremendous metaphysical experience and he wisely left the oratorio unwritten.

The Mass in C major, composed in 1807 at the request of Prince Esterházy and designed for normal liturgical use, bears the imprint of Catholic custom, but is nevertheless a direct approach by Beethoven to the words set.

It shows how far he had travelled as man and musician since 1800. His creative powers had matured—he was at work on the C minor Symphony—and his spiritual understanding had quickened. Where his honesty had once betrayed him into the religious crudities of the *Mount of Olives*, that same honesty now led him to study the text of the Mass free from any dogmatic or ecclesiastical intermediation between himself and his Maker. Given such a mind as Beethoven's, the results were bound to be remarkable. 'I am reluctant to say anything about my Mass, and indeed about myself,' he wrote to Breitkopf. 'But I think that I have treated the text in a manner in which it has rarely been treated.' He was perfectly right. Looking at his Mass to-day, we can see that the familiar words had become translucent for him to the truths behind. His setting followed the words and painted their ideas with extraordinary fidelity. At the same time he strove for a musical design that should evolve logically, without depending on the verbal clauses to make it intelligible. The Mass, in fact, was to be as self-sufficing as a symphony or sonata. It was planned on a noble scale for a quartet of solo singers, chorus and full orchestra—a decision justified by the ample resources of the Esterházy musical establishment. Unfortunately there is reason to believe the rehearsals were grossly inadequate, so when the Mass was performed on 13th September 1807 it was a fiasco. 'But my dear Beethoven, what is this you have done now?' quizzed Prince Esterházy. Hummel, standing by, smiled. The Esterházy family taste in masses was distinctly 'tuney.' But Beethoven believed the smile had been directed at himself. It hurt atrociously.

The cold-shouldering of the Mass continued. When Beethoven tried to make terms for publication, Breitkopf assured him there was no demand for church music. At one time Beethoven would even have given Breitkopf the Mass to ensure its future. 'The reasons why I particularly wanted to bind you and no one else to publish this Mass are (1) because notwithstanding the utterly frigid attitude of our age to works of this kind, the Mass is especially close to my heart . . .' he wrote. Ultimately it was published, and received chastened approbation, which in Victorian days swelled to adulation mixed with revolting patronage. Latterly it has returned to the list of works more honoured in name than in deed.

The Esterházy entourage were not altogether wrong in detecting the experimental element in the Mass in C. The Victorians can be excused for surprise at what they called Beethoven's 'singular ideas.' But our business now is to revalue the Mass both for its own sake and for the light it brings to Beethoven's *Missa Solennis* and his still later works.

On the constructional side the Mass in C is divided into the customary movements, the Osanna being repeated after the Benedictus. During the first three numbers, the Kyrie, Gloria and Credo, Beethoven employs the key of C major, as the point of departure and arrival, but the modulations within those movements follow a different circle in each case. Then, as if to show the change to some condition above the earth, he sets the Sanctus and Osanna in A major, while between them comes the Benedictus in F major—a favourite key with him to express tranquillity and blessedness. For the Agnus Dei he uses C minor, and comes back to C major for the 'Dona nobis.' But to confirm the scheme he does a thing which is an æsthetic and psychological master-stroke: he repeats the pleading music with which the mass had opened on the words 'Kyrie eleison' as a coda to the whole work on the supplication 'Dona nobis pacem.' Thus he unified the work and linked its emotional sequence into a perfect circle. Here was the principle of his *Liederkreis,* applied nine years ahead of the time when he is said to have invented it.

This rounding of the work was all the more valuable that the relative proportions of the movements were not quite perfect. But the choral writing in the Mass in C is more feasible for singers than that of the *Missa Solennis,* and the orchestration is beautiful. The instruments take their part beside the chorus almost like living creatures. It is possible that the loveliness and depth of Beethoven's intentions were a little greater than the thematic material in which he expressed them, but every movement of the mass has wonderful beauties. Note the Kyrie, in which the first long-phrased melodies are followed by short points of imitation and brief ever-shifting modulations, as if Beethoven looked out and saw imploring hands lifted everywhere over the world beseeching help. The broad diatonic harmonies and the stability of the choral writing in the following Gloria give a wonderful impression of the unchanging eternal strength of God. Beethoven's close illustration of the text is seen at his setting of the words 'Laudamaus te, benedicimus te, adoramus te, glori-ficamus te,' where at 'adoramus' he bows himself down clean out of C major into the chord of B flat major. (The Victorians called it a Gothic progression!):

For the 'Qui tollis' Beethoven goes into F minor—a key which he seemed to associate with suffering and punishment borne by the innocent, since he used it in *Fidelio* for Florestan and in the overture to *Egmont*. At the words 'Qui sedes ad dexteram Patris' he reduces the voices from four-part harmony to octaves for the first time, as if to show the oneness of Christ with God, and thereafter throughout the work, octaves or nnison are often employed in connection with the idea of God as the One, for example, at the words 'Quoniam tu solus sanctus' and later in the Credo at 'Deum verum de Deo vero.'

Up to the 'Quoniam' the style has been mainly melodic and harmonic, with some canonic imitation, but at the words 'Cum Sancto Spiritu,' Beethoven introduces a movement in fugal style which is developed with brilliant effect. The Credo, musically very fine, is psychologically profoundly interesting. If the descending phrases at 'descendit' might have been done by any composer, no one except Beethoven would have set the 'Et incarnatus' thus, with so much meaning in such subtle simplicity. As if to make his progressions clearer, he allots this section to solo voices. The poignancy of the harmony in the orchestra at the words 'et homo factus est' gives an indescribable impression of Beethoven's view of manhood—just as if he said: ''Tis glorious misery to be born a man'—and the extraordinary slither of semitones at 'sub Pontio Pilato' (like water falling away) expresses Beethoven's contempt for Pilate's despicable weakness:

The fugal element reappears briefly at 'Et resurrexit' and at the 'Et vitam venturi saeculi, Amen,' a great choral fugue rolls forward on glorious waves of melody.

This association in Beethoven's mind between the idea of Life Everlasting and fugue as its musical symbol is not a mere chance, nor even a second-hand acceptance of the practice of other composers who had introduced fugal writing at this point. I am convinced he adopted it deliberately.

Beethoven never accepted anything for his great works to which he could not subscribe with his whole being. Fugue and invertible counterpoint offered him material almost as sure as the progressions of pure mathematics. For example, the interval of the perfect fifth when inverted can only produce the perfect fourth and vice versa; the major third can only become a minor sixth, and so on. Musically, therefore, fugue would be right as the symbol for Beethoven's conception of the life of the world to come, and metaphysically he was right in identifying that life with God 'in knowledge of whom standeth our eternal life,' as the collect says.

The Sanctus is a short movement like a sojourn in heavenly peace. It contains beautiful harmonic textures, and an enharmonic modulation so characteristic of Beethoven that I quote it:

The Benedictus is a long flowing movement, beautifully orchestrated; the Agnus Dei is heartfelt; the 'Dona nobis' contains an almost too graphic passage in which the voices mutter antiphonally 'miserere, miserere,' and the mass ends—as I have already said—with a return of the lovely melody with which it had opened.

It has been hard to give even a bare outline of the C major Mass in the space available, but the difficulty dwindles to nothing when compared with that of describing and assessing the Mass in D major—the *Missa Solennis*—one of the masterpieces of the world, which occupied Beethoven from 1819 to 1822. As well try to fix Mount Everest on the point of a pen!

'Missa Solennis'

Historically the Mass in D arose from Beethoven's wish to compose something for the enthronement of his pupil, the Archduke Rudolph, as Archbishop of Olmütz. He produced a work so stupendous and so exacting that for over a century the world has relegated it to the concert room. Beethoven himself never heard a complete performance. Nevertheless it was designed for a religious purpose, and Bekker goes rather beyond the mark when he asserts that it took no account of liturgical customs, that it was a logical pursuance of the path struck out in the symphonies and that 'only the outward form, words, plan and structure were borrowed from the ecclesiastical Mass; inwardly the work is the appropriate link between the eighth and ninth Symphonies —a sacred symphony with solo and chorus.'

Certainly the *Missa Solennis* is laid out for four soloists, a large chorus and full orchestra, such as no ordinary church could produce. Also it is far too long for liturgical use, and the treatment of the words sometimes departs from Catholic dogma and the rubric. But Beethoven had in view a ceremony of exceptional grandeur, in which a prince of the imperial house was to be enthroned as a prince of the Church, while above all was the thought of God the King and Father, before whose Throne these earthly and spiritual splendours were no more than the drift of star-dust. For such purposes the Mass in D was not unsuitable—it was only too great for average human beings, a fault of which few composers are guilty.

Perhaps recollections of the installation of Maximilian Franz long ago as Elector of Cologne had lingered in Beethoven's memory. Or he may have witnessed when a boy some such tremendous festival in Cologne Cathedral as that which inspired Schumann to his Rhenish Symphony. Old Memories united with the present; the Mass would indeed be for Cologne Cathedral since the Archduke Rudolph's enthronement was to take place there. The proof that Beethoven intended the *Missa Solennis* for a liturgical purpose can be found in his division of the text according to the Catholic use (quite unlike Bach's B minor Mass), in the introduction of a solemn *Präludium* for orchestra alone at the place where the elevation of the Host should take place, and in his intention of adding to the finished work a Gradual, an Offertory, and a setting of the hymn *Tantum ergo,* movements which apparently were never written out though they existed in Beethoven's mind.

To compose the *Missa Solennis* Beethoven restudied the text of the Mass. The results were yet more amazing than before. Where he had approached the words as a musician, he now administered their meaning with the authority of a priest. A comparison between his two settings, noting those views which he retained and those which he altered, is an experience enriching to one's own life. The great fugue in the *Missa Solennis* on the words 'et vitam venturi saeculi' lifts one to such an exultation as cannot be described when its meaning is confirmed by the recollection of Beethoven's earlier fugue on these words, and I know no pages in music whose mere look conveys such a sense of the teeming millions of eternity as the pages of the full score at this point. Little wonder Beethoven forgot time when wrestling with Eternity. (Poor Schindler, surprising Beethoven in the act of composition, ascribed his fearful look to his hatred of contrapuntists!) On the other hand Beethoven's feeling about the Incarnation had changed. Formerly at the words 'homo factus est' Beethoven had been penetrated by the misery of manhood. Now he had suffered still more deeply and had won to an inner, transcendent serenity in which his whole heart flowed out with thankfulness to God become man; the mystical joy and beauty of Beethoven's music for the Incarnatus are not expressible save in terms of music.

But though he came to the *Missa Solennis* as a man far in

advance of the Beethoven of 1807, the years of concentration on the Mass affected him profoundly. The work carried him into spiritual regions beyond common experience. Musically it drew him into the new developments which mark his third period.

In form the mass is as perfectly organized as any of Beethoven's symphonies—its peculiar glory being that while every detail is suggested by the text, 'the multiplicity of words gives Beethoven occasion to produce some of his most gigantic symphonic designs,' as Professor Tovey comprehensively says, adding: 'I say "symphonic" in full view of the fact that the forms that Beethoven has thus produced are in no way *a priori,* but are dictated at every point by the course of the words.'

The texture is infinitely richer than that of the Mass in C. The distinction between themes and *tutti* often observable in the earlier work has now merged into that later style where the melodic on-flow is inexhaustible as the waves of the sea, and (like waves to the wind) as endlessly mutable to the Spirit that bloweth where it listeth. In this sea of music Beethoven holds his harmonic and contrapuntal elements in solution with astounding success.

The choral writing shows a similar synthesis. Beethoven's perception of choral style and his evocation of the effects possible only to voices is far greater here than in other work of his, yet one is conscious also that he is imagining and employing the two bodies of voices and instruments as a kind of double orchestra. In most instances this is deeply impressive; but voices cannot bear such long strains of effort as instruments, nor will they produce such rhythmic accentuation as Beethoven often required, so moments occur when the means attract attention rather than the end.

The Kyrie follows the same ternary form as that of the Mass in C, and again for the middle section (the 'Christe eleison') the modulation is to a key a third away from the tonic. But whereas the C major movement modulated to E major, the third above, this one goes to B minor, the third below. Whether this insistence on the number *three* was suggested by the idea of the Trinity, or sprang from a purely æsthetic impulse, we shall never know. The two following quotations taken almost at random from the Kyries of the two masses, show the differences in their texture and style better than any words:

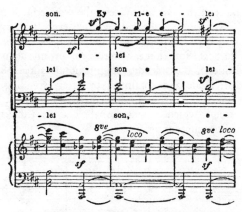

The Gloria of the *Missa Solennis* is an enormous conception in which the contrasting sections (moulded by the successive meanings of the text) are united with consummate power to lead forward to a final fugue on the words 'Cum Sancto Spiritu in gloria Dei Patris. Amen.' This starts on such a gigantic scale that had 'a more guileless composer worked it out normally he would not have got through it in twenty minutes'—as Professor Tovey points out—but 'what happens with Beethoven is that within the compass of six bars he contrives to give a sense that this passage (bars 435—40) has gone round the universe.' The effect is obtained by rapid and remote modulations which obliterate the hearer's sense of key.

The Credo (B flat major) is yet more gigantic than the Gloria—a magnificent movement unfolding a chain of movements bound together by the use throughout of the same phrase for the word 'Credo'—as if here Beethoven touched the points in it which are like the nodes in a vibrating string. The grandeur of the opening 'Credo,' the mystical beauty of the 'Et incarnatus' (in which Beethoven goes back to the sixteenth century and forward one hundred years to use the

227

'pure strains of the Dorian mode'), the wonderful setting of
the Crucifixus where at the end he brings everything down to
a low open octave on D flat at the words 'et sepultus' (a
piece of musical expression easy to read for any one acquainted
with his ideas), the splendid Resurrexit announced in the
Mixolydian mode and continued by great ascending lines,
all these unforgettable things lead to the final fugue, 'Et vitam
venturi saeculi' which crowns the whole as with life eternal.
Here is the opening for the voices:

At the beginning of the Sanctus (D major) Beethoven had
written the same direction as for the first Kyrie—*Mit Andacht*
(with devotion). This mystical, intimate movement kindles
into an Osanna that is like sacred fire, and it is followed by

the exquisite orchestral *Präludium* at the elevation of the Host. Then, from the high quiet B natural on which it has floated into our consciousness, there descends a violin solo that streams on in endlessly blessed, beautiful melody through the G major Benedictus. This loveliness must be heard to be believed—and only after it has gone do we realize the genius of Beethoven's melodic, harmonic and canonic devices, or the perfect tone-values of his choral and orchestral texture.

The Agnus Dei (B minor) is rightly dark and agonized. It leads direct into the 'Dona nobis pacem,' where Beethoven has taken the course of explaining his intentions by the inscription *Bitte um innern und äussern Frieden* (Prayer for inner and outward peace). The earliest movements in the Mass are the most liturgical. At its ending Beethoven makes his own comments on the horror and terror of war. He had lived through the Napoleonic invasions. The symbolism of his military sounding passages goes straight now to the heart of people who lived through the Great War, as it could not to comfortable Victorians who saw in the music (an irony worthy of Hardy's Intelligences) Beethoven's compliance with the convention of a cheerful ending! Beethoven never shirks a responsibility, and never leaves problems unsolved. He knew that prayers are answered, deliverance sure. With peace that descends like the Holy Dove, the mass ends.

While writing the Mass in D Beethoven planned two other masses as companion works. A few sketches exist for one in C sharp minor, but though this was designed for the emperor, Beethoven ultimately abandoned the idea, and the other mass remained only a project.

What would have happened had they been written? On the evidence of the Mass in D and the ninth Symphony Professor Tovey suggests that Beethoven might have become as great in choral music as in symphonic composition. That precious, young man's quality of experiment remained with him to the last.

CHAPTER XIV

CHAMBER MUSIC

A COSMOS, not a chapter, would be the comfortable place in which to review Beethoven's chamber music, for he began composing in this medium when still a boy; he continued to do so all through his career, and his last completed works were for string quartet.

That being so, only two courses seem possible here. Either each work must be described in the manner of a museum catalogue, or the great works must be concentrated upon and the rest merely indicated. I have chosen the latter course, helped thereto by Bekker's three-group scheme of classification: (1) chamber music for wind instruments (occasionally supported by piano or strings); (2) chamber music for piano and strings; (3) chamber music for strings alone. It is significant that the first group coincides with Beethoven's early period, the second covers his early and middle periods, the third extends over all three. To this several causes are contributory, but I believe myself that one of the most important and least recognized is to be found in the nature of his hearing. In youth Beethoven could tolerate, from everyday association, the discrepancies of intonation and the compromises of the tempered scale; later, when deafness shut him into the ideal world of imagination, his ideas came to him in the pure scale, unsullied by equal temperament. Thus he employed increasingly the media capable of pure intonation—a habit of thought that in turn reacted on the character of his ideas.

Apart from this, there are plenty of historical reasons to explain Beethoven's youthful preoccupation with chamber music for wind instruments. Eighteenth-century folk, like

those of the seventeenth, had a strong taste for 'wind musique.'
Out of doors it sounded better than strings; indoors it could
hold its own against the clatter of dishes. The Elector Max
Franz at Bonn was daily 'entertained by a small orchestra
consisting of two oboes, two clarinets, two horns and two
bassoons.' The players were good artists and their library
cannot have been large. Beethoven was probably invoked.
Young as he was, he gave them some additions which have
outlived the elector, his court and his century. The Octet in
E flat major (*Parthia in Es,* as Beethoven named it), for two
oboes, two clarinets, two horns and two bassoons (known as
Op. 103), and the Rondino in E flat major for the same
combination of instruments, are both supposed to date from
1792. Thematically they are elegant, and the art with which
the instruments are combined is remarkable—well in advance
of Haydn and quite as good as, if not better than, anything
Mozart had done in that direction. For purposes of convenience the Octet and Rondino were subsequently made
available in other forms—a fashion characteristic of the late
eighteenth and the nineteenth century, when even orchestral
works were reduced to chamber dimensions. It was not a
bad idea, since it enabled music lovers, in the absence of
regular concerts, to become acquainted with works they would
otherwise hardly have known. That it can be pushed to
absurdity is true—as in the case of Wagner's overture to
Tannhäuser arranged for mandoline and piano—but Beethoven
tried to ensure that his arrangements should be well done, and
sometimes they were better than the original. The arrangement of the Octet as a string quintet was so radical that when
it appeared in 1796 it was advertised as 'wholly new,' and
some people consider the arrangement superior to the original.
The quintet arrangement was reduced, by another hand, to
a Trio for piano, violin and violoncello. The Rondino also
emerged in the guise of a string Quintet with two violas.

Other 'wind' works of the Bonn period were an early Trio for piano, flute and bassoon (1787), possibly composed for Count Westerhold; a Duo in G major for two flutes written 'For Friend Degenharth by L. van Beethoven, 23rd August 1792, midnight' (what a queer feeling of sharing the warm August darkness that word 'midnight' gives one); and three Duos for clarinet and bassoon. A piece for a musical box (?) may belong to this period; it might as well be mentioned now to get it out of the way.

On settling in Vienna Beethoven found almost as wide a field for wind music as in Bonn. Not in vain had the Elector Max Franz been a Viennese. Moreover, the best of the world's wind instrument players visited Vienna at one time or another. The Trio in C major for two oboes and cor anglais which Beethoven composed in 1794 was probably inspired by the three brothers Teimer. The work is very artistic and provides an early proof of Beethoven's affectionate understanding of the oboe. The same Trio appeared in a version for two violins and viola, and (final metamorphosis) as a Sonata for piano and violin. A set of variations for two oboes and cor anglais on Mozart's *Là ci darem* dates from 1796-7. A year or two earlier, in 1794-5, came the Sextet in E flat major for string quartet and two horns (not one of Beethoven's best successes), and in 1796 another Sextet in E flat major for two clarinets, two bassoons and two horns, which also appeared as a wind quintet. Yet another Quintet in E flat, now for piano, oboe, clarinet, horn and bassoon (1796-7), went through two incarnations, first as a piano quartet and then, according to Ries, as a string quartet.

Beethoven fairly wallowed in E flat major at that time. But there was method in his monotony. E flat was by far the best key in which to draw together his disparate teams of wind instruments. He emerged from it to compose the delicious Serenade in D major, Op. 25, for flute, violin and viola in 1795–6—a work fit for a fairy. Yet its fairylikeness in no way interfered with its practicability. It could be played in the streets by players as mobile as any for whom Haydn had written *Gassadenmusik* forty years before, and it followed the old plan of grouping together a number of short movements, such as had served Haydn in his *notturni* and cassations. Beethoven wrote here for the flute with real understanding of its nature and an enchanting humour. Just think of the *entrata*, where the tiny flute prances on first all alone with a fanfare that might come from a fairy turned gamin; or look at that lovely variation iii in the *andante* where the viola sings a solo to an accompaniment that uses with consummate skill the violin's capacity for flowing sostenuto and the flute's dexterity in skipping. To arrange such a work for piano and flute (or violin) was almost a vandalism, but Beethoven had to allow it.

The Trio in B flat major, Op. 11, for piano, clarinet and violoncello is dull compared to the Serenade. It is said to have been written at the request of a clarinet player—possibly Beer—but whether Beethoven was bored by the instrument or merely disliked the man, the Trio comes near being a dud. Nothing in its suggests that Beethoven had grasped the nature of the clarinet as he divined the souls of the flute and oboe; the subject-matter is formal, and the instruments are often treated in that old-fashioned way where the piano is master, and the clarinet and cello are two good dogs on a string. Haydn's influence is apparent (not always as an enlightened guide), and a theme by Weigl is used for the variations. Perhaps the most interesting point in the Trio is the *adagio*. It is supposed to show a version of the theme Beethoven employed in the Septet (1800) and in the *menuetto* of the piano Sonata in G major, Op. 49, No. 2 (1796). The Trio is now usually included in the series for piano, violin and violoncello, with a violin as substitute for the clarinet.

The year 1800 brought the Sonata for horn and piano which Beethoven composed specially for Punto, a great virtuoso even in an age of brilliant horn players. Considering the Sonata was written on the last day before Punto's concert, the workmanship does the composer credit. Punto's feelings are unrecorded.

The famous Septet (1800) forms the apex of Beethoven's wind ensembles. Here at last, by binding together the wind instruments (clarinet, bassoon and horn) with the ever adapt-able strings (violin, viola, violoncello and double bass) in the score, Beethoven secured a blend that softened the asperities of wind intonation and charmed the ear under all conditions. The elimination of a second violin in favour of a double bass was strategic, for it gave the woodwind and brass a foundation tone that set everything they did on the right basis. Moreover, lest the team of instruments should still seem a little undisci-plined, Beethoven adopted suite form instead of the more closely reasoned order of movements in the sonata group, which would have exposed their shortcomings. As might have been expected the Septet was in E flat major, and Beethoven's subject-matter was always melodious. The theme of the variations is said to be a Rhenish folksong; it may very well have been so despite the failure of investigators to establish the claim. The Septet is beautifully scored, and altogether it is an example of a work arriving at the exact moment when its arrival would be welcome. It had a *succès fou*. Every one lauded its 'taste and feeling,' and praised it as a model till Beethoven could scarcely bear it mentioned.

Possibly it gave him a distaste for further wind music, except in the orchestra. Apart from some odds and ends in the way of variations on national themes for piano and flute (or violin), there is nothing else demanding attention except the magnificent three *Equali* for four trombones which Beethoven composed for All Souls' Day at Linz in 1812.

Each one is quite short, depending for its nobly pathetic effect upon the nature and placing of solemn chords rather than upon melody. The first is in D minor, the second in D major and the third in B flat major. Brief as it is, this last carries within its sixteen bars a transition to the chord of D flat major, which for Beethoven was like the cartouche of Death. Arranged for voices the *Equali* were sung at his own funeral.

In surveying Beethoven's works for piano and strings the first thing to be noticed is that after the early quartets of 1785 for piano, violin, viola and violoncello, he never again wrote for a combination where the strings were sufficiently numerous to form a full harmonic group of their own against the piano: in other words, he avoided pitting blocks of pure intona-tion against blocks of tempered intonation. Schumann and Brahms, brought up on the piano, could amalgamate the two without scruple and with splendid results. But Beethoven would not force the issue. His one so-called piano Quartet (other than the Bonn works) was really the arrangement he made of the Quintet, Op. 16.

Thus his compositions for piano and strings follow three clear lines, namely, works for piano and violin, works for piano and cello, works for piano with violin and cello. In each he initiated a new era. He enlarged the scope of his piano and violin sonatas far beyond the pattern set by Mozart; he did for the cello what neither Mozart nor Haydn had accomplished, and gave it sonatas with piano for its very own; in his trios he was quick to realize the ideals of eman-cipation for violin and cello which had dawned in Mozart's and Haydn's latest works.

Some of the smaller things for piano and violin, such as the Variations on Mozart's *Se vuol ballare* (1792-3), the six German Dances (1795-6), the Rondo in G major (1793-4) and the varied themes already mentioned for piano with flute or violin *ad libitum* (1818), have fallen into desuetude.

But the ten sonatas for piano and violin are a heritage no violinist could surrender. They are true duos, where the instruments are equal partners, and under the conditions for which they were written (with the early, less resonant type of piano, instead of the modern mammoth) the distribution of material and tone balance is wonderfully adjusted. This is as noteworthy in the three early Sonatas, Op. 12 (1797-8), which Beethoven dedicated to Salieri, as in the comparatively late (and last) Sonata, Op. 96 (1812-13), composed for and dedicated to Rode. Players who do not reproduce this original balance inflict on Beethoven a grave injustice. Admittedly the old type of piano has gone for ever, but it is perfectly feasible to restrain the enveloping tactics of the modern piano. Failure to do so simply means an imperfect equipment on the part of the pianist. And both pianists and violinists should combine in thinking out Beethoven's real intentions in the matters of phrasing and tone-matching. The take-it-for-granted tone conventions are not good enough for his music, nor the easy-going thought-habits which do not discriminate between the styles of one composer and another, one age and the next. These early Sonatas of Op. 12, though they abound in freshness and vitality, have also a good deal of the eighteenth century in their make-up. They follow the three-movement type found in the bigger sonatas by Haydn and Mozart. The first, in D major, starts with a first subject that is a typical eighteenth-century statement of the tonic chord, though the opening of the development, with its swift step into F major and *sotto voce* allusion to the cadence subject, is pure Beethoven. The second movement, a theme and variations, and the final rondo are charming in a simple way, and effective even to-day on a concert platform. Sonata No. 2, in A major, offers so good an example of Beethoven's part-placing that it will serve as well as any later work to show his master craftsman's cunning. The first subject opens thus, with the theme in the piano, the accompaniment in the violin part:

When this is repeated the parts are reversed, yet not exactly, because Beethoven's perception told him that while it was quite satisfactory for the piano to carry the melody notes across the low, jog-trotting accompaniment of the violin, it would not sound well if the violin, when charged with the melody, got mixed up with the middle of the piano chords. Beethoven not only solved the problem but strengthened the musical interest by his solution. Here it is:

The second and third movements, an *andante* and an *allegro piacevole,* are conceived in an idyllic vein—one pathetic, the other graceful.

In the Sonata No. 3, in E flat major, which is more largely planned, the piano plays a brilliant role in the first movement and the violin sometimes endures a slight eclipse from being forced to play passages that properly belong to piano technique.

The fiddle, however, gets its turn in the second subject and in the lovely C flat major episode just before the recapitulation, where Beethoven gives an early instance of that interrelation between E flat and C flat, which he used later in his 'Emperor' Concerto with such glorious effect. The *adagio con molt' espressione* is among the finest of Beethoven's first-period slow movements. It is a true song, grand, slow, sustained. In the middle episode the violin sings a melody that seems to pierce beyond the veil of earthly things, while the piano has an accompaniment which I think is one of the first places where Beethoven caught the sound of 'that murmur of the outer Infinite.' The last movement is a Mozart-like rondo.

For the Sonata in A minor, No. 4, Op. 23, composed in 1801, Beethoven still adhered to the three-movement plan, but for the Sonata in F major, No. 5, Op. 24, he enlarged the scope to four movements, the addition being a short, witty scherzo and trio. This F major Sonata has great felicity of matter and manner, and its 'safety margin' in scoring is so wide that it never fails to sound well in any performance approaching adequacy. Beethoven was not responsible for its nickname of the 'Spring' Sonata, but if one thinks of Orpheus who made 'a lasting spring,' then the sobriquet is not far wrong.

The A minor Sonata, Op. 23, has never enjoyed such popularity as the F major, Op. 24, nor is it so good a work, in spite of the deliciously playful *andante scherzoso,* which combines the functions of a slow movement and scherzo in one. The A minor finale, *allegro molto,* develops some of that dark energy which was later to drive through the Kreutzer Sonata with such terrific effect.

Sonatas Nos. 6, 7 and 8, Op. 30, form an arresting group dedicated to the Emperor Alexander I. Dating from 1802, the year of the second Symphony and the piano Sonatas, Op. 31, they show less markedly than these the signs of change between Beethoven's early and middle periods, but one, at least, the Sonata in C minor, offers an astounding contrast to anything that had been composed before in this genre. The Sonata in A major, first of the group, is a gracious work that fulfils the most elegant ideals of Haydn's three-movement type of sonata. The 'little G major,' last in the set, also depends to some extent on stylistic elements for its themes and texture; yes, even in spite of the pastoral freshness of its first movement, the easy-swaying rhythms—real Viennese—of the *tempo di menuetto,* and the sparkling finale with its fascinating pivot modulations. But the middle Sonata, the C minor, strides forward like Beethoven himself, dark-browed, tempestuous. The four movements follow an almost symphonic plan. Beethoven's abolition of the customary repeat mark in the first movement was a bold course dictated by the urgent nature of the music. The impression of a 'poetic idea' behind the work is insistent. Five or six years later he would have made his meaning so clear that no one could miss it—as in the *Sonata Appassionata*—but there is no gainsaying that the C minor Sonata has a Protean quality that provokes opposite views. Dr. Walker calls it one of the great masterpieces and says of the first and last movements that 'their wonderfully strong, sombre energy and passion strike a note hitherto unheard in Beethoven's music.' Bekker describes the Sonata as pathetic in character, with 'no logical development of the subject . . . but rather a stringing together of ideas in different shades of tone-colour, the unity of the whole being temperamental rather than logical.' Beethoven experienced no vacillation over the first and last movements, but was less certain about the *adagio cantabile* and the scherzo. As originally planned, the *adagio* stood in G major. Its opening theme would have sounded heavenly on the violin in that key. But Beethoven transposed it into A flat major, perhaps thinking that key better for the piano, or that the *barbaresco* (his own word) nature of A flat was more suitable in this stormy sonata. One cannot feel convinced by Beethoven's after-thought. The key finally chosen did not afford enough change from the note C which persists throughout the Sonata with almost Russian monotony. Moreover, A flat, a closed key on the violin, muffles its capacity for *cantabile*. The scherzo is a most piquant movement. Later on Beethoven talked of it as out of keeping with the rest and wanted to remove it; he even wanted to reduce all his four-movement sonatas for piano and violin to three. Fortunately he was dissuaded.

Sonata No. 9 in A major, Op. 47 (1803), the famous 'Kreutzer,' formerly enjoyed such a reputation that Tolstoy (who felt, feared and hated music) named one of his stories from it. The Sonata is certainly very remarkable, but some-what overrated, since a masterpiece should begin, continue and end on the same plane of inspiration. The 'Kreutzer' opens with an introduction and first movement on a scale of emotional and executive magnificence unmatched in any other violin sonata. The second movement, a set of varia-tions on a theme that is grace personified, maintains the same executive beauties, though the emotional temperature has cooled. The finale (*presto*) is practically a long tarantelle in sonata form, where the leaping rhythm runs through with hardly a break from beginning to end. It was just such a rhythmic *tour de force* as Beethoven had set himself in the finale of the D minor piano Sonata, Op. 31, and would have been equally successful in its own place, that is to say, as the finale of the violin Sonata in A, Op. 30, for which it was written. There it would have energized a work which seems over sedate, though Ries notes that Beethoven thought the first finale too brilliant. Transplanted into the 'Kreutzer' it is neither sufficiently strong nor conclusive enough for such a situation. It is as if after having begun as Othello and Desde-mona, the characters suddenly turned into Figaro and Susanna.

The Kreutzer Sonata

Beethoven had promised to compose the Sonata for the violinist Bridgetower, a British subject who was then on a visit to Vienna, and it was to be ready in time for the latter's concert. As usual Beethoven was late. Czerny says the first movement was written in four days. Ah! if only the concert had been a week later, we might then have had the whole sonata white-hot with genius, but as with Coleridge's *Kubla Khan*) the inspiration once cut short did not return. It must have taxed Bridgetower's courage to play the tremendous first and second movements almost at sight. Beethoven expressly described the work as 'Sonata scritta in uno stilo molto concertante, quasi come d'un conzerto.' Bridgetower, however, had plenty of assurance. When Beethoven played the cadenza-like 'flight'—bar 18 of the first *presto*—Bridgetower promptly imitated him on the violin. According to Bridgetower Beethoven was enchanted. Nevertheless the addition was not adopted, and in the long run the Sonata was dedicated to Kreutzer.

Beethoven had clear views of the function of ornament in music. While retaining the eighteenth-century skill and elegance in this art, he absolutely excluded ornaments save where they ministered to the meaning and emotion of his music, or genuinely adorned it. This cannot be too carefully considered, and it shows how completely Beethoven, following Haydn, refused to allow his works to be mauled about by executants who 'graced' by habit; it also shows how greatly modern performers wrong him if they play his ornaments coarsely and carelessly.

This question of ornament is intimately bound up with his Sonata No. 10 for piano and violin, in G major, Op. 96, last and loveliest of his works in that form, composed for Rode, the violinist, in 1812–13. Something of its calm, ethereal beauty is due to Rode's style of playing. Beethoven wrote to the Archduke Rudolph in December 1812: 'I have not hurried unduly to compose the last movement merely for the sake of being punctual, the more so as in view of Rode's playing I have had to give more thought to the composition of this movement. In our Finales we like to have fairly noisy passages, but R[ode] does not care for them—and so I have been rather hampered.'

In suiting Rode, Beethoven produced a perfectly homo-geneous sonata, where each of the four movements is the natural complement of the other three. In the first and last the ideas are irradiated with a light that is like the clear-shining after rain. The slow movement has greater depth of feeling, but no unrest; its beautiful theme is like the granting of a heart's desire. The scherzo, with its back-and-forth sforzandos, and the trio, gliding into a long dance rhythm, disturb this tran-quillity no more than the blessed spirits at play disturb the Elysian Fields in Gluck's *Orfeo*. This Sonata is a searching test for the players. Everything must be right, from the very first trill. How easy that opening looks on paper; in reality how hard it is; as difficult as the great passage in double-stopping which opens the Kreutzer Sonata—perhaps even harder, for the G major opening must sound as if the music had been flowing from eternity and had just emerged into hearing:

The trill on the first note is an integral part of the subject. Whether it should be executed with or without a turn at the end is one of the unsettled questions of interpretation. According to the tradition handed down from Joachim and Clara Schumann, the trill should always have the turn at the end.

Beethoven's five Sonatas for piano and cello, and three sets of variations on themes by Handel and Mozart, are still among the best things in the cello repertory. Not that the variations are important, for all are practically first-period work; but they do meet a real need.

The cello sonatas cover a longer stretch of Beethoven's career than the violin sonatas, and what has already been said of tone balance between the instruments applies here even more strongly than to the violin sonatas. The modern piano has enormously increased its power since Beethoven's day; the cello remains the same. Result, the cello is swallowed up unless the pianist adapts to the cellist and avoids too much use of the pedal, though of course where the piano has a solo it can do what it likes. If the balance goes wrong, the fault is with the players; Beethoven's cello parts 'lie' perfectly for the instrument. He was at pains also to leave a 'breathing space' for the cello in the piano part—a notable change from the old idea of the cello as a reinforcement of the *continuo*. This 'breathing space' is particularly noticeable in Beethoven's earliest cello Sonatas, No. 1 in F major and No. 2 in G minor, Op. 5, composed during his visit to Berlin in 1796 for Duport, first violoncellist to King Frederick William II of Prussia. The king was a good cellist himself, so it seems probable that Beethoven (like Mozart before him in his Prussian quartets) made special efforts to ensure the dignity and independence of the cello part. At the same time Beethoven evidently felt the *sostenuto* and *cantabile* powers of the cello were so much greater than those of the piano that to unite the instruments successfully in a true duo sonata it would be wise to keep them as far as possible to quick or moderate paced movements, thus avoiding an exposure of the piano's short-lived notes.

The F major sonata opens with a brief *adagio*, acting as introduction to a very long *allegro* in sonata form, which is followed by a rondo with a first subject flavoured by the old 6/8 *gigue* rhythm. The G minor sonata is on much the same pattern, save that the slow introduction is more important, the *allegro* has cleaner-cut workmanship and the rondo disports itself with a tune that might have come from Haydn.

While the G minor Sonata is better than the F major, one feels in both that Beethoven had not yet found his direction as a composer. Later in his career he would have avoided such mannered chromaticisms and melodramatic chords of the diminished seventh.

Sonata No. 3, in A major, Op. 69, sketched in 1807 and completed in 1808, is music as perfectly imagined and constructed as the 'great' G major violin Sonata, though Beethoven still avoided the issue of a real slow movement. The opening *allegro* in sonata form, and the scherzo (*allegro molto,* a most tricky movement on account of the rhythm and *acciaccatura* in its principal subject), are followed by a very short *adagio* in the dominant where 'the gradual harmonic over-balancing' (to use Dr. Walker's happy phrase) 'in the direction of the finale is so perfectly managed that the whole sounds quite natural and inevitable.' The finale is an exceptionally lovely movement on an exceptionally beautiful theme:

The Cello Sonatas

The **A** major Sonata, deservedly a favourite with cellists and the public, is yet least feasible of the five for less competent players because it covers the greatest compass for cello.

Sonatas Nos. 4 and 5, forming Op. 102, were composed in the July and August of 1815 for Linke, cellist of the Schuppanzigh Quartet. Outwardly they are somewhat dry; inwardly they are precious records of the changes going forward in Beethoven's mind. The Sonata No. 4, in C major, still shows his old unwillingness to face out a real slow movement for the cello. An *andante* prefaces the main *allegro*; then follows a short *adagio* like an extemporization, which leads into an even shorter allusion to the *andante,* this in turn passing into an extended final *allegro.* Beethoven intended it as a 'free sonata,' but its freedom is somewhat negatived by the nature of the material.

In the D major Sonata Beethoven at length grappled with the cello slow movement problem and adopted the order of movements normal for classical sonata form. A bold first *allegro,* and an *adagio con molto sentimento d'affetto,* lead to a vigorous finale, which is really a fugue. In that stands the innovation, and one of the earliest signs of Beethoven's new orientation towards counterpoint. Hitherto in instrumental music he had treated fugue as ancillary to variation form or sonata form; now he employed it in its own right. He told Holz later: 'To make a fugue requires no particular skill. In my student days I made dozens of them. But the fancy wishes also to assert its privileges, and to-day a new and really poetical element must be introduced into the traditional form.'

The list of Beethoven's duo sonatas would be incomplete without the little Sonatina for mandolin and piano (cembalo) and another slight piece for the same odd pair of instruments. They were first-period works, probably written for his friend Krumpholz.

Beethoven's Trios for piano, violin and violoncello are of

extreme interest and beauty, but (like sheep) a shifting flock to number on account of the arrangements. The Trio in C minor, Op. 1, No. 3, originally for piano, violin and cello, appeared as a string quintet for two violins, two violas and cello (in which form it is even better than the original). Inversely a number of Beethoven's works for other ensemble combinations were arranged as piano trios, including one from the second Symphony. Add to this that Beethoven composed a 'posthumous' Trio in E flat major, written probably about 1790 or 1791, where he used the designation 'scherzo', apparently for the first time. Add again that while at Bonn he wrote a set of variations for piano, violin and cello upon an original theme, published as Op. 44, a number which makes it look as if it belonged to his middle period. To complicate matters still further a manuscript in the British Museum (Add. 31748) contains, in addition to three piano duets, an incomplete piano trio, all described as autographs of Mozart. Saint-Foix decided that they were youthful works by Beethoven and published them as such in 1926. Unfortunately the duets turned out later to be arrangements of pieces from a ballet by Koželuh, while the attribution of the trio to Beethoven remains doubtful. In this welter the first landmarks are the three Trios in E flat major, G major and C minor, Op. 1. They are among the landmarks of Beethoven's life. Upon them he lavished the sum total of his powers during the first years in Vienna, and with them he made his début as a composer when they were produced at a soirée at Prince Lichnowsky's. They immediately 'commanded the most extraordinary attention.' Their beauty, mastery and boldness must have been a revelation, and I have sometimes thought the increased breadth and depth of Haydn's last trios may have been gained by contact with Beethoven's first. Haydn's warm admiration for the Trios in E flat and G major, and his distrust of the headlong C minor, at least show he knew them well.

Piano Trios

To us all three seem simple, and they are still beautiful—the E flat major with its Mozartian themes and clarity, but livelier humour; the G major, owing more to Haydn, especially in the slow movement and finale; and lastly the C minor, unmistakably Beethoven in its vehement beauty, daring modulations, little poem of a *menuetto* and the relentless finale illuminated by a divinely singing second subject.

Thereafter is a long gap till 1808, when Beethoven produced the pair of Trios in D major and E flat major, forming Op. 70. Stylistically they have a good deal in common with the A major cello Sonata, but are finer examples of middle period work.

For the D major Trio Beethoven employed the three-movement scheme. First a bright, tremendously decisive *allegro* with themes so noble in their sweep that even to look at them enlarges one's heart. Then a slow movement, D minor, *largo assai ed espressivo,* a tone picture without parallel in Beethoven's music. Its gloom, mystery and terror have earned the work the nickname of the 'Ghost' Trio. Very slow, haunted by a theme that moves across long, strange stretches of tremolo, now *sotto voce,* now rising to sudden flares of *fortissimo,* the poetic idea of this movement may well be what Beethoven's sketch-books seem to suggest—the Witches' scene from *Macbeth.*

The finale flanking it on the hither side apparently has no more poetic connection with the *largo* than the *allegro* that preceded it. The two bright movements, however, balance each other, the finale restoring the normal world, after the supernatural experience of the *largo,* in music akin to the finale of the cello Sonata in A.

Trio No. 6, in E flat major, is a sheerly happy work, a Virgilian Georgic, liberally planned with an introduction and four movements. The themes have an almost bucolic touch and the workmanship is fine, if not so striking as in the D major Trio.

Seven is said to be the perfect number. It is so here. The Trio in B flat major, No. 7, Op. 97, is the finest of the series, and one of the greatest works in existence. Beethoven surpassed even himself. Composed in 1811, it is sometimes known as the 'Archduke,' from a vague identification between its own greatness and the name of its dedicatee, the Archduke Rudolph. Beethoven once said that when the archduke had become fond of any of his works, he observed a gentle regret in his patron if the music was dedicated to any one else. The archduke's flair for masterpieces did him honour!

The first movement of this Trio is an instance of noble themes treated with a magnificent breadth, simplicity and strength of mass and design that set it in the same sort of relation to musical form as the great sculptures of the Parthenon to statuary in general. From the moment the piano begins this theme we are in the presence of something glorious. Note the *energy* obtained from the fairly rapid note values and the *dignity* from the slow pacing harmonies:

The more this marvellous movement is studied, the more is found in it. Here only pointers can be given to such things as Beethoven's remarkable scoring (with the daring *pizzicato* passages against the piano *staccato*), thinning out the tone to enhance the value of what had gone before and what is to come in the development; to the long fining down to a point of expectancy before the recapitulation; and to the superb coda.

The scherzo is again a superbly planned movement, with

an abundance of energy and enchanting tunes that, though lighter than those in the first movement, never lose their inherent nobility.

The third movement, *andante cantabile, ma però con moto,* is one of the finest sets of variations in existence on a theme which is the essence of all that is most lovely in a Beethoven slow movement. It requires the style of performance which the Germans call 'das Getragene'—the slow, deep-breathing, carried forward phrasing. But beyond all technical considerations it demands greatness of heart and soul in its interpretation. The wonderful theme is only heard once in its entirety. In the variations that follow it is as though Beethoven resolved the theme into its spiritual elements. Shakespeare's Cleopatra had not the celestial calm of this music, but her words fit these variations: 'I am fire and air; my other elements I give to baser life.'

For the finale Beethoven snatched back the work from far regions into bright day—music graceful, lively, expressive, yet with a pinch of devil in its odd little staccatos and sforzandos, and in the queer, wide, leaping intervals that I fancy came to his imagination when the physical joy of living ran strong.

Trio No. 8—'the little B flat' in one movement—was composed 'Vienna, 2nd June 1812. For my little friend Max. Brentano, to encourage her in pianoforte playing.' It is child's music, cheerful without vapidity.

Trio No. 9, the Bonn work in E flat major published posthumously, has already been mentioned; so too have the early variations. The works are negligible.

In 1816 Beethoven began sketching a Trio in F minor. It came to nothing. In 1823, in the thick of one of his 'variation' phases, he composed an 'Adagio, ten Variations on *Ich bin der Schneider Kakadu,* and Rondo,' Op. 121, for piano, violin and cello. Müller's trivial theme, thus surrounded by true Beethoven, has the effect of paste set in platinum. Perhaps Beethoven knew this.

Excluding the Quartet arranged from the piano Sonata, Op. 14, No. 1, and other arrangements already mentioned, Beethoven's works for strings alone consist of five string trios, one complete Quintet, a Quintet-Fugue in D for two violins, two violas and violoncello dating from 1817, and sixteen string quartets. Such is the official list, but a duet written in fun for viola and cello, 'with two eyeglasses *obbligato*,' may be mentioned as an extra, and there are also a number of minor pieces for two, three, four and five instruments.

The string trios all belong to the decade 1790–1800. To regard them as callow quartets is totally wrong. Designed for trios, as trios they stand or fall. They stand—and are models of what three-part string writing should be.

By the happy accident of the Abbé Dobbeler's journey to England with a copy of young Beethoven's string trio tucked into his violin case, we know that string Trio No. 1, in E flat major, existed as early as 1792. Beethoven probably revised it before publication in 1797, but from the outset its main characteristics of strong intellect, firmly handled harmonic form, warm feeling and charming fancy were apparent. The six movements are grouped as in the old *divertimenti,* but the *andante* (which comes second) is entirely Beethovenish and of a type to be met again in the scherzos of his C minor quartet, Op. 18, and his F major 'Rasumovsky,' Op. 59. Where a work is so perfectly adapted to its purpose as this string Trio it gives one rather a pang to find that it appeared in an arrangement for piano and cello.

The Serenade string trio, Op. 8 (1797), had a similar but more pardonable fate, being translated into a *Notturno* for piano and viola. Like Op. 3 it follows the *divertimento* scheme. The numerous movements are played in, and out, with a brisk march, yet the music itself is a little—dare I say it?—dull in comparison with the fine works by which Beethoven followed it up in the same year.

The three Trios in G major, D major and C minor for violin, viola and cello, together form Op. 9 (1796–8). Beethoven placed them high among his early works. Abandoning the loosely strung movements of *divertimento* form, he boldly employed the cyclic grouping of sonata form for them with extraordinary success. The music and its treatment are much stronger than in Op. 8. The G major Trio is a fascinating work; the D major is the weakest of the three; the C minor is generally considered the finest, but all are beautiful.

The string Quintet in C major for two violins, two violas and cello, Op. 29, composed in 1801, is sometimes called the 'Storm' quintet, from the semiquaver passages (like flashes of lightning) which stab across the almost orchestral tremolo of the accompaniment in the finale. The 'storm' is certainly a dramatic climax to a very beautiful work—beautiful both from its themes and the exquisite art with which the music and its medium are identified. The first theme of the first movement is too long to quote entire, but the opening must be given because it shows clearly a favourite device of Beethoven's for enhancing the beauty of a melody by adding a sort of mirrored melody beneath. Here it is in compressed score:

Beethoven came to quartet-writing comparatively late. He was nearing thirty. At a corresponding age Haydn had already about twenty quartets to his credit. But in Beethoven there was some instinct which withheld him from perpetrating crude work in this intimate medium, a feeling perhaps not unlike that from which he refused to revisit Wegeler and Eleonore,

except 'as a complete, ripe man.' Another curious circumstance is that, pupil of Haydn though he was, Beethoven
apparently owed little to the 'father of the string quartet.'
If we must judge by his own words, Aloys Förster was his
'old master.' Förster's quartets are said to be very Beethovenish,
and Beethoven certainly owed much to his friendship, example,
advice and the stimulus of the real quartet atmosphere to be
found at Förster's house, where Schuppanzigh, Weiss, Linke,
Mayseder, Hummel and others met twice a week for chamber
music. Yet the quartets of Haydn and Mozart did set a
mark on Beethoven, as we can well see, and he told Drouet
(the flute player) long after that without Haydn and Albrechts-
berger he would have committed many follies. One of them
was the overcrowding of 'material' in his early works.

The first impulse towards quartet writing seems to have
been given by Count Apponyi in 1795. Nothing came of it
at the time. In 1800, when the string Quartets forming Op. 18
were produced, the dedication went to Prince von Lobkowitz.

Six first-class quartets under one opus number seems to
the modern world mere squandering. Not so to the eighteenth
century, where the prodigal custom was to issue nearly all
chamber works in sets of three or six. Beethoven brought out
his Op. 18 in two sets, the first three being published by
Mollo of Vienna in the summer of 1801, and the last three in
October of the same year. The original manuscripts have
disappeared. From Beethoven's sketch-books and scraps of
historical information it is clear, however, that the present
order of the quartets does not represent the original order of
composition. Like Haydn before him, Beethoven rearranged
the six so that the finest works occupied the salient positions
and the weakest were 'skied' as third and sixth—that is to
say at the end of each published set. It is advisable to consider
them in their published order, which after all is Beethoven's
own choice. They also appeared arranged as piano trios.

The Quartet in F major, No. 1, planned in 1799, originally stood second and cost Beethoven much anxious thought. No less than sixteen pages of his sketch-books were devoted to chiselling the first subject, and when he entirely revised the Quartet in 1800 this theme came in for more retouching. As finally achieved it opens thus—beautifully incisive, harmonically clinched, rhythmically useful for every thematic, developmental or accompanying purpose:

Even a cursory glance at this Quartet shows how Beethoven granted equal rights to all four instruments—a democracy of style such as Haydn and Mozart had acknowledged but only partially adopted. Beethoven also displayed an almost orchestral daring in his scoring of the tragic D minor *adagio affettuoso ed appassionato* which (so he told Amenda) was a tone picture of the tomb scene in *Romeo and Juliet*. The scherzo and trio, at their face value, are less arresting. Nevertheless, when one thinks of Beethoven's later works, including the ninth Symphony, the leaping octave passages of the trio are a trait significant of vitality. The finale—a rondo—has curious affinities with *Prometheus* which can be well seen in its two fugato passages and in a certain melodic passage at bars 136–159.

The Quartet in G major, No. 2 (but composed third), is a deliciously happy work. Its nickname the 'Compliment' Quartet comes from a fancied resemblance in the opening phrases to a ceremonious greeting and reply between eighteenth century elegants, but it gives no idea of the charm and freshness of the music. Really the ornamental flourish in the first subject is most artfully contrived to beautify the dry arpeggio of G major, which at the touch of Beethoven's hand bursts into blossom, as Sir Henry Hadow says, adding that 'students of Bach will remember an exactly similar efflorescence in the theme of his D major fugue (No. 5 of the "48") presented in the same way and used for the same purpose.'

In the first, third and fourth movements of this Quartet Beethoven strengthens their relevance by forming each of their first subjects out of the tonic chord in arpeggio. For the slow movement, an *adagio cantabile* in C, he obtains his relevance more subtly, by letting the ornamental *gruppetto* which was a distinguishing feature of the first movement, expand into the lovely *fioritura* passages which 'grace' the first violin and cello parts. Old William Gardiner of Leicester was right when he discerned in the young Beethoven's music an intellect that opened a new world to him.

The Quartet in D major, No. 3, first in order of composition, is perhaps more tentative in workmanship than the others, but not less lovable in its ideas. The first subject of the first movement flows in poised on a dominant seventh, and the harmonic treatment develops a delicate edge of unexpectedness that removes insipidity from the smooth rhythm. The slow movement is practically in rondo form—an unusual choice for Beethoven. It decided him, after the scherzo, to cast his finale in sonata form, where the subjects tear along in a sublimated *gigue*.

The fine Quartet No. 4, in C minor, was supposed by Thayer to have been the last composed. That may well be, judging by the mature workmanship, but points of affinity with the two earlier string trios will not escape observation, any more than the premonitions of the later C minor violin Sonata and C minor Symphony. The choice of C (minor or major) as the key for the four movements may be a trace of the old code for suites and partitas, but the decision by which Beethoven substituted a scherzo for the slow movement and followed it by a *menuetto* was probably due to his feeling that some relief was needed from the passionate tension of the first and last movements.

Quartet No. 5, in A major, was begun fourth, but incorporates some earlier material dating perhaps from 1794, thus making the third movement—a theme with variations—the oldest thing in Op. 18. Of all the set it is the most Mozartian, especially in the last movement.

Quartet No. 6, in B flat major, is enigmatic. Thayer supposed that Beethoven wrote it among the last, yet the form, with its cluster of five movements, approximates to the suite, and the first subject is one of those stereotyped statements of the tonic chord that can be found by the hundred in symphonies and chamber music of the mid-eighteenth century. The fourth movement, called *La Malinconia,* is the most Beethovenish; a tone picture, with graphic touches, serving as an introduction to the cheerful finale. Yet it is not comparable to Beethoven's amazing portrait of a melancholic in the *largo* of the piano Sonata in D major, Op. 10. Can this B flat Quartet really have been written three years later than that Sonata?

Six years separated Beethoven's Op. 18 from his next set of Quartets—the three great works in F major, E minor and C major, Op. 59, composed in 1805-6 and dedicated to Count Rasumovsky. De Marliave may or may not be right in saying that the first sketches date back to 1804, but all the circumstances of the musical material and its treatment point to 1806 as the real period of composition. Formerly Beethoven, like Haydn and his contemporaries, had sought no more when arranging a set of quartets than that they should contrast well and follow each other agreeably. Now his instinct had advanced; he felt the need for unity in diversity. He therefore linked this set together by folksongs, though whether Beethoven or Count Rasumovsky was responsible for the idea is not clear. Count Rasumovsky, half Cossack by descent, was twice Russian ambassador to Austria, and a notable patron of the arts. Connected by marriage with the Lichnowsky family, himself a good musician and reputed to be one of the best connoisseurs and players of Haydn's quartets, it was natural he should commission a set of quartets from Beethoven.

That Beethoven was already interested in the use of folk-songs for sonata form is sure—witness his *Sonata Appassionata*, Op. 57, sketched in 1804, and his Septet of 1800; also, less provedly, his piano Sonata, Op. 54, of 1804. He would therefore welcome the Russian melodies with an open mind, seeing in them a connecting thread for his three Quartets. Czerny expressly states that Beethoven 'pledged himself to weave a Russian melody into every quartet,' and Czerny can be relied upon, says Thayer. The themes are easily traced in the F major and E minor quartets, because Beethoven attached the label 'Thème russe,' even if his harmonizations were so classically Viennese that their best friends would hardly recognize them through the disguise. The C major Quartet is a different affair. There Beethoven gave no passport of nationality, but naturalized the theme completely as his own. Lenz denied its Russian origin. To-day even the tradition of its Russian descent is forgotten, except by a few people who delve into the odd corners of history. Nevertheless I firmly believe tradition is right, and that the theme of the slow movement (*andante con moto quasi allegretto*) is a Russian folksong. Or shall I say *was* a folksong, since Beethoven handled it so freely? Yet at the back of his version there is still a character recognizable as Slavonic if one is acquainted with the folktunes of Russia and their melodic and rhythmic peculiarities. J. W. N. Sullivan, in his sincerely felt, sensitively written book on Beethoven, seems unaware of a possible Russian element in this movement. Yet his instinctive reaction to the music is that:

This movement, indeed, stands alone among Beethoven's compositions. . . . This strange slow movement, as more than one writer has remarked, makes on us the impression of something strictly abnormal. It is as if some racial memory had stirred in him, referring to some forgotten and alien despair. There is here a remote and frozen anguish, wailing over some implacable destiny. This is hardly human suffering; it is more like a memory from some ancient and starless night of the soul. What it is doing in this quartet we cannot imagine.

Could any words better describe immemorial Russia?

Nearly every one seems to have thought the Rasoumovsky Quartets odd when they were new. Felice Radicati, a good violinist and quartet composer, fingered them at Beethoven's request: 'I said to him that he surely did not consider these works to be music? Beethoven replied: "Oh, they are not for you but for a later age!" ' That later age now loves them as among the greatest works of music, wherein may be seen sonata form in its most splendid, almost dazzling manifestation; music whose regal harmonic advance and whose large, commanding gestures fill one with exultation at such glory.

The Quartet in F major (No. 1 of this set; No. 7 of the complete series) was begun, Beethoven notes, on 26th May 1806. The first movement, a noble *allegro* on most spacious lines, is followed by an *allegretto vivace e sempre scherzando* of the inimitable Beethoven type, where witty rhythms and peculiarly pithy staccato notes are features in a movement of an unusual design (see p. 258, Ex. 1). The slow movement in F minor is piercingly expressive and beautiful, one of the very finest of Beethoven's slow movements.

After the sketches for this *adagio* Beethoven added the note: 'A weeping willow or acacia tree over the grave of my brother.' Some biographers suggest the movement is an 'epitaph' on Karl van Beethoven's marriage, because Beethoven did not approve of the bride. As if an event and its expression in music must be simultaneous! Beethoven may well have had recollections of a time when—himself a boy—his little brother Georg had died at Bonn. To carry the music from such a mood to the brisk finale with its 'Thème russe' Beethoven employed a cadenza for the first violin in which the slow movement gently dissolves.

The Quartet in E minor, No. 2 (No. 8), is more constantly in the pathetic vein, and is shadowed with mystery in the first and second movements. About the slow movement, *molto adagio*, Beethoven once told Holz he conceived it as he gazed at the stars, 'contemplating the harmony of the spheres.' Here the solemn wonderment of man at death has merged with his solemn wonderment at the stars. It has done so with those many poets for whom Walt Whitman speaks when he says:

E minor Quartet, Op. 59, No. 2

This is thy hour, O soul, thy free flight into the worldless,

. . . . . .

Thee fully forth emerging, silent, gazing, pondering the themes
    thou lovest best,
Night, sleep, death and the stars.

Such words chime well with many slow movements by
Beethoven, but they fit especially with these two.

Another interesting point. If there is anything in the law
of mental association, then this starry *adagio* of Beethoven's
might suggest that the Rasumovsky Quartets and the letter to
the Immortal Beloved belong to the same summer. There
Beethoven said: 'When I consider myself in the setting of the
universe; what am I and what is that man—whom one calls
the greatest of men?' That is very much the mood of this movement, which is also linked with the slow movement of the
fourth Symphony through certain features of rhythm and
feeling. Even the key—E major—is worth noting. After
Beethoven became emancipated from the few conventions inherited from suite form (where all the movements were in the
same key) it was unusual for him to maintain one keynote—in
this case E (minor and major)—throughout a large work.
When he did so, he obviously had some special purpose. In
the A major Symphony, for example, he maintains the same
standpoint but seems to direct our thoughts down into the open
earth as into a grave, by setting the *allegretto* in A minor. In
this Rasoumovsky Quartet, while yet standing in the E minor
shadows of the first movement, he suddenly directs our gaze
upward by the change into E major, to behold the starry
heavens above.

The *allegretto* that follows, taking the place of a scherzo,
is so wistful that when a Russian tune is dragged in as the
trio, the effect is almost unnatural. It is in fact the very
tune which Mussorgsky used later in the first act of *Boris*

Godounov. A terrific finale, looking as if it began in C major, completes this wonderful work in E minor.

The C major Quartet, No. 3 (No. 9), is notable for the introduction. Beethoven deliberately leads in from silence, by harmonies so shifting that they seem 'like the baseless fabric of a vision,' into an *allegro* which is gloriously strong and clear. The *andante*, with its strange melody and mysterious *pizzicato* notes in the cello, has already been discussed. The *menuetto* is on the Haydn model, magnified. The great fugue finale, a combination of fugue and binary form, is the crowning glory of this Quartet. The rising passages (bars 144 to 176), where the instruments take it in turn to mount in fiery sequence, are indescribably exciting; indeed, the whole movement is so exciting that one forgets the enormous intellectual power controlling it.

Quartet No. 10, in E flat major, Op. 74, often called the 'Harp' from the long arpeggios in *pizzicato* of its first movement, was composed in 1809. It is glitteringly effective; the first violin part touches concerto technique and the second violin has a thrilling prominence. The slow movement is an *adagio* in A flat major in the mood that once inspired the slow movement of the *Sonate Pathétique,* but now stronger and less sentimental. The scherzo is built on one of those hammering rhythms Beethoven often associated with C minor, and the Quartet is completed by a graceful set of variations. A gallant work, a great work, but not one of his greatest because in its outward panoply of music there is a little more of the glory of this world than of the glory of the spirit.

Quartet No. 11—the *Quartetto serioso*—in F minor, Op. 95, which Beethoven composed in 1810 and dedicated to his old friend Zmeskall, forms a striking contrast. In Mendelssohn's opinion it was the most characteristic thing Beethoven ever wrote, and Mendelssohn was not far wrong, though some portions are amusingly like what Mendelssohn strove to be and was not. To enjoy the full flavour of this serious, passionate, hard-bitten work, with its rough humour, grimly pointed wit and strange flashes of tenderness, it should be studied in conjunction with Beethoven's letters to Zmeskall—the similarity in tone is striking. It is very much a man's quartet. It is also remarkable as belonging both to Beethoven's middle period and his last—a work which occupies much the same position in his career as an enharmonic modulation in his music.

The first movement begins with a short phrase, shot out by the instruments in pairs at the octave—just as Beethoven had done in his F major Quartet No. 1. The difference in mastery is amazing; the F major was clean and chiselled; but this F minor cuts like an acetylene flame. The leaping octave phrases and the tense compression of style give an extraordinary impression of Beethoven's vitality.

The *allegretto* in D major, which stands in place of a slow movement, has pensive sweetness. A descending passage for the cello recurring at intervals (like the scattered strands of an *ostinato*), and a soft fugato which the instruments sing gently to themselves, are features to notice. The scherzo is an alternation of recklessness and resignation—extremely hard to hold together in performance. The *larghetto espressivo*, prefacing the finale, packs as much tragedy into its seven bars as Shakespeare into the fourteen lines of a sonnet. The finale—*allegretto agitato*—is the Mendelssohnian movement, but with a sudden, swift Beethoven coda of forty-three bars which shocked d'Indy into calling it a light Rossinian operatic finale; adding that he thought 'no interpretation could palliate this error of a genius.' I still think Beethoven could have offered some convincing explanation for this coda if he had been allowed to do as he wished when he proposed writing down the meanings he had intended in each of his works. His friends, headed I think by Schindler, dissuaded him. No doubt Beethoven stands higher with the world for not having given away his secrets, since many musicians prefer 'absolute music' (so called)—but, all the same, there are times when one says: 'Bother Schindler!'

A little way back I likened Beethoven's F minor Quartet to an enharmonic modulation—one of those points of unity upon which two different worlds for the moment poise and synchronize their different terms of existence. By the time Beethoven completed his next Quartet, No. 12, in E flat major, Op. 127 (1825), he had travelled far from the world to which the 'Harp' Quartet belonged. The second great sorrow of his life had come to him, changing his relations to his fellow creatures. While at work on his *Missa Solennis* he had been studying the music of Palestrina and pure modal counterpoint, which wrought another change. The beauty of modal har-monies and the marvellous effects obtainable from the juxtaposition of common chords were revealed to him. The texture of sixteenth-century polyphony (with those melodies which are so much shorter than the 'subjects' of Viennese symphonic music and which yet are endless) modified his style perceptibly; so too did those permutations (which are the equivalent of development in counterpoint of the Golden Age) influence his style of development. Moreover, these things were confluent with the changes that had taken place in his own convictions and practice as the result of experiment.

Lastly there was the change in his spiritual perception. Years of pondering and experience, culminating in five years when his thoughts dwelt constantly on the truths expressed in the mass, had brought him to a position in which he had something of the vision and knowledge of Truth possessed by the great initiates. Life in its metaphysical reality had become clear to him.

Beethoven's last five string quartets emanate from this metaphysical world. They are not to be understood lightly. To approach them chronologically through his ninth Symphony is to come to them blindfold. They are best entered direct through the two masses.

They have become the testament of modern music. From them derive the methods which Wagner expanded to such glorious purpose in his *Ring, Tristan* and *Parsifal*; in them may be found the principles of César Franck's thematic metamorphosis and cyclical development; in the bare, sparing technique of Beethoven's last F major Quartet is the presage of Bartók, Stravinsky and all the schools of economists; in the *Grosse Fuge* is the triumphant assertion of linear counterpoint. Prince Galitsin's prophecy, made in 1824, has come true. 'Your genius is centuries in advance,' he wrote to Beethoven, 'and at the present time there is scarcely one hearer who would be sufficiently enlightened to enjoy the full beauty of this music; but posterity will pay homage to you and bless your memory more than your contemporaries are able to do.' Beethoven's last quartets are not the justification of modern music, but modern music has reached the point at which it justifies the quartets and proves Beethoven's genius to have been transcendental.

Whether Prince Galitsin had commissioned the quartets or not, string quartet form was the medium towards which Beethoven's instinct was already drawing him, as the only one sufficiently pure and flexible for the expression of the ideas now crowding upon him.

Prince Galitsin, a wealthy Russian amateur and patron of

music, had visited Vienna in 1822. He returned to St. Petersburg full of enthusiasm for Weber's *Freischütz,* then new, and equally anxious to get a score made for his own use. Zeuner, the viola player in Galitsin's quartet, suggested the money would be better spent by commissioning Beethoven to compose some new quartets. To the lasting glory of both, Galitsin took the advice and commissioned the quartets in November 1822. Later, when the quartets arrived, people were somewhat dismayed by them, and Galitsin's part of the transaction—the money—was only partially paid up at the time of Beethoven's death.

The Quartet in E flat major, Op. 127, was perhaps already taking shape in Beethoven's thoughts in 1822; in 1824 he wrote of it as finished; actually it was not completed till the end of that year or even the early months of 1825.

It is a glorious work, in which the gallantly ringing heroism of Beethoven's E flat mood is suffused by an indescribable happiness. Though the structure has been immensely expanded, it still bears a recognizable relation to the great quartets of the middle period. While far from being easy to understand, this work is simple and its main lines clear in comparison to its successors. The first movement, an *allegro* with singularly gracious, lovely subjects, is ushered in by a short prelude in E flat—*maestoso*—used twice again in G and C during the course of the movement, and always with an effect like the immense weight-bearing strength of Norman pillars and arches—one of its purposes being to determine the 'tonal structure' of the movement.

In the rhythmic tranquillity of the subject-matter of the first *allegro,* as in the opening of the *adagio* that follows, the Palestrina touch is seen. In these later years Beethoven loved to let his music become gradually perceptible to mortal sense, as it emerged from the metaphysical region of sound where his deafness had made him a permanent inhabitant. The

Palestrinian short point of imitation in the entry of the voices fitted perfectly with Beethoven's predilections. The theme for the marvellous set of variations in this Quartet emerges thus:

These variations contain a wealth of inspiration, expressed with consummate mastery. Students who wish to study them will find it a help to remember that Beethoven sometimes treated the theme as a concrete entity and sometimes as the soul of that entity. It is also helpful to recall the 'Benedictus,' the 'Agnus Dei' and the 'Dona nobis' of the *Missa Solennis* in conjunction with this movement.

The scherzo, though very extended, and even complex, is nearer to normal procedure. The finale, which is a compound of sonata and rondo form, has glorious melody and impulse swinging through it.

With the works immediately following Op. 127 Beethoven passed beyond any semblance of quartet form as it was then understood. For over a century his three greatest Quartets, in A minor, Op. 132, B flat major, Op. 130, and C sharp minor, Op. 131, remained more or less unsolved enigmas. The accident by which the A minor, the first composed, appeared with the highest opus number, while the C sharp minor, last composed, stood next below, has somewhat to answer for in obscuring the true sequence of Beethoven's ideas. Further, the dedication of the A minor and B flat major to Prince Galitsin made the Quartets appear as companions to the E flat major, Op. 127, in a set of three. They are not. In reality Opp. 130, 131 and 132 are the triptych, the true sequence being:

(*a*) Quartet in A minor, five movements;
(*b*) Quartet in B flat major, six movements;
(*c*) Quartet in C sharp minor, seven movements.

Their contents are so glorious, so inter-related and metaphysical, that one might almost think Beethoven regarded them as an ABC of the world to come.

For the sake of mental clarity I shall treat them in their true order.

The Quartet in A minor (No. 15), Op. 132, was mainly composed during the period March–August 1825, but sketches date from 1824, and work was interrupted in the spring of 1825 by Beethoven's severe illness—an event which left its impress on the music, as will presently be seen.

Simultaneously with the A minor quartet, Beethoven was evolving the great B flat major. It was finished about a month later. This relation went deeper than Beethoven's habit of working on several things at the same time; the two works are thematically joined, and so close is this connection that Beethoven was able to transfer a movement from one to the other—the *alla danza tedesca*—with perfect propriety. While still in the midst of the B flat Quartet he began to work on the C sharp minor, which occupied him till the summer of 1826.

Long ago he had linked his three Rasumovsky Quartets by the use of Russian folksong. Now he joined his great triad of quartets by a single fugal subject, which in the original or in a metamorphosis manifests itself in all three works. It forms the starting-point thus at the beginning of the A minor Quartet:

It recurs in many guises and adumbrations throughout the work; its rising sixth haunts the subject-matter of the B flat major Quartet and the theme, expanded, appears as one of the two subjects in the double fugue which originally formed the finale of the B flat major:

This *Grosse Fuge* was discarded as too long for its position on the advice of Beethoven's friends. But none the less he was right in feeling it to be the logical outcome of the Quartet. Finally the theme, now changed from an ascending sixth to a descending third, forms the fugue subject of the first movement and (reversed) the principal subject of the last movement of the C sharp minor Quartet:

FIRST MOVEMENT

LAST MOVEMENT

Once these facts are recognized, the quartets immediately become less bewildering, and individual study easier.

The A minor opens with the short introduction already quoted. This leads into an *allegro* of extraordinary, passionately regretful beauty, cast in the very remarkable form

Beethoven

(as d'Indy points out) of three expositions interrupted by developments of the introductory theme. The second move- ment, substituting a scherzo, is graceful and not very quick, with so much thematic relevance to the texture of the first movement that it seems rather another facet of the same personality than a contrast. The dreamy, floating *alternativo* which takes the place of the conventional trio, is derived from a German country dance, used by Beethoven in the seventeen- nineties for a ball at the Assembly Rooms. Towards the end the fugue theme throws its shadow upon the viola and cello.

The next movement is the famous 'Heiliger Dankgesang eines Genesenen an die Gottheit in der lydischen Tonart' (Holy Song of Thanksgiving to God from one healed of sickness, in the Lydian mode). It was probably added to the original scheme for the Quartet, and is the direct expression of Beethoven's gratitude for recovery from an illness in which he came near dying. (His canon, given to the doctor, will be remembered.) Apart from the high, austere loveliness of Beethoven's thank-offering to God, the use of the Lydian mode is memorable at a period when to musicians the modes were a book closed and obsolete. In re-opening it Beethoven showed a prophetic spirit. His modal melody is in five strains, prefaced and separated by two-bar interludes in which the instruments enter *sotto voce* with short imitational points, rather as in a Bach chorale-prelude, only here the subject- matter derives from the theme of the fugue motto of the whole. Beethoven alternates the Lydian sections with more human, personal sections in D major, and the movement is developed with a power and wealth of meaning that fill one with awe.

A short A major movement, *alla marcia,* leads to a bridge which contains a clear forecast of passages in the B flat major Quartet, but which also serves somewhat the same purpose as the famous bridge in the ninth Symphony. It leads indeed to the finale which Beethoven originally intended for the ninth

Symphony. Here it is transposed into A minor, a passionately beautiful movement, with a haunting theme that opens thus:

Following hard upon the A minor, the great B flat major Quartet (No. 13), Op. 130, was completed in 1825. Holz once said to Beethoven that it was the greatest of his quartets. Beethoven replied: 'Each in its way. Art demands of us that we shall not stand still. You will find a new manner of voice-treatment' (he meant the part-writing), 'and, thank God, there is less lack of fancy than ever before.'

That is an admirable summary of a composition almost terrifying in its vitality and grandeur.

The A minor had been designed in five movements that seemed rather to ray out fanwise from an unseen centre than to follow cyclic sonata form. This method is more apparent in the six movements of the B flat major. Bekker says: 'They do not stand in direct sequence, nor do they represent a continuous line of development; each from a different viewpoint relates directly to the close,' i.e. the *Grosse Fuge*.

The first movement, more or less in sonata form, is prefaced by an introduction which shows a version, an incarnation, call it what you will, of the fugue subject, and in the wonderful second subject, which, Dr. Walker well says, 'passes like a vision,' its veiled features are yet recognizable:

The whole movement repays closest study; its secrets, slow to yield, are noble to find. The dark, hushed, darting *presto* that follows is a miraculous little movement.

Third stands a long, wonderfully wrought *andante* in D flat, the texture presenting a tissue of melodies as smooth-pacing as Palestrina, as infinitely varied as Bach.

Movement four is the *alla danza tedesca,* originally destined for the A minor Quartet, but here transposed into G major.

Fifth comes the great cavatina, of which Beethoven himself said: 'Never did music of mine make so deep an impression upon me, even the remembrance of the emotions it aroused always costs me a tear.' It was one of his supreme inspirations; it must speak to each man according to his understanding.

Lastly in the original scheme came the *Grosse Fuge—tantôt libre, tantôt recherchée.* This gigantic movement, packed with ideas, was for long believed unplayable, grotesque, uncouth and cacophonous! The Archduke Rudolph, however, must have seen good in it, for when it was published separately he received the dedication. Beethoven's intellectual plan is almost staggering in its immensity. He begins with an overtura in which *the* fugue motto subject appears, its successive guises forecasting the nature of the three sections in which it will later be developed. At the commencement of the fugue a new theme appears, a leaping, leggy devil of a subject that assumes command as principal, the motto sinking to be the counter-subject:

Briefly, what follows is that the first section is a complete fugue in which the rhythmic theme is the subject; the second part is a short fugue wherein the melodic motto theme, which had served as counter-subject, now becomes the subject; in the third section both subjects are 'brought face to face,' and after a prolonged conflict the motto theme conquers, the leaping theme becomes the counter-subject, and the two end in a glorious apotheosis where opposition becomes harmonious co-operation. Thus the movement embodied some of Beethoven's most constant ideas. The 'two opposing principles' of his early poetic period, the linking of variation form with fugue (as once in the *Eroica*) and his final belief that a poetical element must be introduced into the traditional form of fugue—all are here.

That there is a poetic idea woven into the *Grosse Fuge* is apparent. Thanks to Schindler and Co. we are left to guess it. But I have sometimes wondered whether the invocation to 'bountiful Pan' which occupied Beethoven's thoughts in 1815 (as shown by his sketch-book) in connection with the projected Bacchus opera, may not have brought the Pan myth into his mind, to re-emerge years later in this terrifying movement, which might well be symbolic of the struggle between body and spirit, and the ultimate triumph of spirit.[1] Wrested from contact with the B flat major Quartet the *Grosse Fuge* loses the antecedents which make its conclusions logical. But the Quartet loses more. The cheerful, tripping finale which replaced the fugue was written by Beethoven in the autumn of 1826. It is the last thing he finished. In its own right the music is delightful music. Nevertheless it belies his original intentions and deflects our understanding.

[1] Pan, the god of flocks and herds, was also the god of travellers and identified with the Roman Faunus who assumed such various forms that it was hard to say whether he was one or many beings. The myth would be apt for Beethoven's purpose.

The C sharp minor Quartet (No. 14), Op. 131, held by
Beethoven to be his finest quartet, was dedicated by him to
Colonel Baron von Stutterheim out of gratitude for his having
taken the scamp, nephew Karl, into his regiment. The
pathos gives a queer twist at one's heart. And what did the
colonel make of this serene, other-world music? Here indeed
is the Palestrina style, miraculously translated into the language
of instruments, not human voices. If the preceding quartets
are difficult to grasp, the C sharp minor is doubly hard.
Vincent d'Indy speaks of it as absolutely new in conception and
in the resulting form. Dr. Walker says its pages seem to
shift and fade the more closely we regard them, and he considers no musical work has a more elusive character. But
I think Wagner's explanation of the nature of Palestrina's
music, 'where rhythm is only perceptible through changes in
the harmonic succession of chords,' gives some real assistance.

Unlike the fanwise form of the A minor and B flat major,
Beethoven wrote this Quartet in seven movements intended
to be played without a break, thus forming a perfect circle:

MOVEMENTS

No. 1	No. 2	No. 3	No. 4 Andante	No. 5
Fugue	Suite form	Recitative	with variations	Scherzo form

Keys

No. 6	No. 7
Aria form	Sonata form

The key scheme beneath these movements is very subtle; so
too is the design of the successive movements. They may be
summarized as above, adopting Vincent d'Indy's nomenclature

though not quite his key-sequence, as he does not reckon the B minor recitative a separate movement, thereby missing the very note in the plan which provides the rising sixth of the motto theme. So here we have *seven* (the perfect number in the lore of numbers), forming a circle (which is a symbol of eternity), and the motto fugue theme (probably symbolizing Life) all combined by Beethoven. Still further, the motto theme with its characteristic interval of the sixth is now below the threshold of consciousness, merged as it were in the new order, but in its reversed form—with the *third* as its characteristic, it dominates the thematic matter of the Quartet. Thus the third (which might symbolize God since it is the number of the Trinity) and its inversion the sixth—Man—are seen like reality and its reflection.

The first movement is a slow fugue on the subject already quoted, a transformation of the motto theme of the A minor and B flat Quartets. This noble, gravely beautiful fugue is succeeded by movements which represent a steadily ascending line. The last, in sonata form, attains the elevation Beethoven aimed at in the finale of the ninth Symphony. I know of few things in music which seem so to transcend temporal existence as the passage beginning at bar 56 and its counterpart later on:

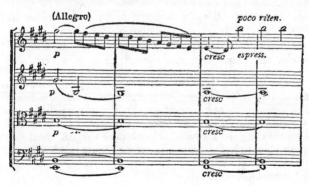

As at the beginning, so at the end of these three Quartets, one comes back to the question of Beethoven's meaning. How far was he the unconscious channel for these great works (and his ideas never came more freely than when composing them) and how far was he their arbiter? That cannot be argued here. Whatever the relation, he was a willing co-operator, not a trance medium. As to Beethoven's meaning, each person must take or make their own share of it from the music. For myself, after long thought, I believe these three string Quartets replaced Beethoven's intention of composing three masses, and it seems possible to me that the C sharp minor Mass—projected and apparently abandoned—became the C sharp minor Quartet.[1] Beethoven's ultimate religion was very much that of the great initiates and the Greek philosophers. In the words on the nature of God which he wrote out and kept constantly on his desk, in the esoteric passage he copied [2] on the immateriality of God and His omniscience, for which 'there is no threefold existence' —in these sentences are to be found, I believe, the clue to the three Quartets in so far as we shall ever have it. Analogies and explanations must not be pressed too precisely. The music, like God in Herrick's definition, is best known by not defining it. But we shall not be far wrong, if we see in the fugue motto theme a symbol of Life, eternal and unchangeable behind the shifting phenomena of the temporal world, and manifesting itself through them, now here, now

---

[1] After that idea occurred to me, Beethoven's words, written on the score of the C sharp minor Quartet when he sent it to Schott the publisher, seemed a corroboration: 'Zusammengestohlen aus Verschiedenem Diesem und Jenem' (Put together from pilferings from one thing and another). Schott became alarmed. Beethoven assured him he had said it in joke and the Quartet was brand new. But *both* sayings were true.

[2] Reproduced on p. 124.

there. The fugue, indeed, in the *Missa Solennis,* already stood to Beethoven as the symbol of life everlasting. The three Quartets might well symbolize body, soul and spirit. Beethoven once called the B flat major the 'Leibquartett.' It may also well be that the quartets stand for the threefold life of past, present and future. The A minor Quartet, retrospect; the B flat major, the present; the C sharp minor, the life of the world to come. It would be like Beethoven to use C sharp here—the enharmonic equivalent of D flat, *seen from the other side.* Whatever his meaning, one thing is sure: we are always safe in knowing that with Beethoven it will be the greater, not the lesser idea.

Last in order comes the Quartet in F major, Op. 135. It was to Beethoven much what the Requiem was to Mozart, and the *Four Serious Songs* to Brahms. Begun somewhere about July, and completed at Gneixendorf in the October of 1826, its composition covers the appalling period of Karl's attempted suicide and Beethoven's first steps upon the un-returning road of death. A short work, it was originally designed to be yet shorter, since it is believed Beethoven introduced a fourth movement only as an afterthought. The scheme as it now stands consists of (1) an *allegretto* in F major; (2) a *vivace,* also in F major; (3) a *lento assai cantante e tranquillo* in D flat major; and (4) a finale which alternates between F minor and major. Most biographers imagine the D flat slow movement was the interpolation. I do not believe that, because without the *lento* the Quartet would have been entirely in F major (excluding the internal modulations of the move-ments), and Beethoven was far less likely to adopt the mono-tonous key scheme of a single tonic than one which gave him F—D flat—F as his three established, contrasting points. Further, on the analogy of such a three-movement work as his D major Trio, Op. 70, Beethoven would more probably set a slow movement between two quick ones than three

quick ones in succession. Still further, the 'poetic idea' of
the Quartet is complete without the *vivace*. Finally, in performance it is the *vivace* which one senses as diverging from the
direct progress of Beethoven's idea. That idea is inevitable
from the opening of the Quartet, though it does not find words
till the superscription of the finale: 'Der schwer gefasste
Entschluss' (The Resolution hard to take):

Der schwer gefasste Entschluss

Muss es sein?   Es muss sein!   Es muss sein!

'Must it be? It must be! It must be!' The phrase had
begun in joke months earlier over a money payment; it continued as a jesting tag among his friends. But to Beethoven,
bluffing the world with the joke, already a sick man, the
words came to have an ominous ring. They were his own
question and answer to death. In music he debated the matter
he would not admit openly. With the very first notes of the
first movement—a phrase fatalistically made from the falling
fourth of 'Es muss sein,' expressed in the chord of B flat minor
(his black key)—the shadow of death lies upon the threshold:

Throughout this movement and the *vivace* the music is limned with bare, spare lines that give more the impression of a charcoal drawing than of colour. One passage indeed (it begins at the seventy-eighth bar after the double bar in the *vivace* and runs on for about forty-six bars) is next to unplayable for the first violin, but immensely impressive.

'The tree of man was never quiet,' says Housman in one of his poems. The words fit this strange scherzo. Following the scherzo comes a slow movement, among the loveliest ever composed, where the instruments enter one by one, and as if out of the void a presence wavers together and stands there. The key, D flat major, shows what it is. Beethoven's words, written against a sketch for this movement, confirm it: 'Süsser Ruhegesang oder Friedensgesang' (Sweet song of rest or peace). Here is the supreme rest, such as Brünnhilde invokes in her farewell to the dead hero of *Götterdämmerung*: 'Ruhe, ruhe, du Gott.'

The finale is haunted again by the questioning, the recoil of the human heart from death. In two passages of intense drama the phrase 'Muss es sein?' approaches threateningly, and the answer is given like a pass-word: 'Es muss sein! Es muss sein!' Yet at the end Beethoven deliberately brushes aside the menace and dissolves the answer into shadows. He goes to face the Unseen with gaiety.

Closing the pages of this F major Quartet to gaze in retrospect upon Beethoven's whole career, his words take on a new meaning. 'Muss es sein?' Destiny seems to brood over the composer as over his compositions. Beethoven the man had to be; his music had to come into being. Everything is as it should be. 'Es muss sein,' we say quietly, and that answer is true, for it is not of Death, but of Life.

APPENDICES

APPENDIX A

CALENDAR

(Figures in brackets denote the age reached by the person mentioned during the year in question.)

Year	Age	Life	Contemporary Musicians
1770		Ludwig van Beethoven born Dec. 16, at Bonn, son of Johann van Beethoven (*c.* 30), musician in the court band of the Elector of Cologne.	Tartini (78) dies, Feb. 26. Albrechtsberger aged 34; Arne 60; Bach (C. P. E.) 56; Bach (J. C.) 35; Bach (W. F.) 60; Boccherini 27; Cherubini 10; Cimarosa 21; Clementi 18; Dittersdorf 31; Dussek 9; Galuppi 64; Gaveaux 9; Gluck 56; Gossec 36; Grétry 29; Hasse 71; Haydn 38; Jommelli 56; Koželuh 16; Kreutzer (R.) 4; Lesueur 10; Martini 64; Méhul 7; Monsigny 41; Mozart 14; Paisiello 29; Piccinni 42; Salieri 20; Schenk 9; Steibelt 5; Vogler 21; Wagenseil 55; Weigl 4; Winter 15; Zelter 12; Zingarelli 18.
1771	1		Paer born, June 1.
1772	2		Daquin (78) dies, June 15.
1773	3	Death of grandfather, Louis van Beethoven (61), Dec. 24.	Catel born, June 10; Quantz (76) dies, July 12.
1774	4		Gassmann (51) dies, Jan. 22; Jommelli (60) dies,

278

Appendix A—Calendar

Year	Age	Life	Contemporary Musicians
			Aug. 25; Spontini born, Nov. 14.
1775	5	Begins to be taught by his father.	Boieldieu born, Dec. 16; Crotch born, July 5.
1776	6	Makes rapid progress on violin and piano.	
1777	7	Enters school.	Wagenseil (62) dies, March 1.
1778	8	Makes his first appearance at a concert, March 26. Van den Eeden, court organist, offers to give him lessons, but the arrangement does not last long.	Arne (68) dies, March 5; Hummel born, Nov. 14.
1779	9	The tenor, Pfeiffer, undertakes his musical education.	Boyce (69) dies, Feb. 7.
1780	10	The B. family is befriended by Cressener, the English *chargé d'affaires*.	
1781	11	Becomes a pupil of C. G. Neefe (33). Leaves school to concentrate on music. Begins to learn the organ with Father Willibald Koch, and later with Zenser, organist of the Minster. Obtains a tiny post as organist of the Minorite Church, and assistant to Father Koch. Rovantini gives him lessons on the violin and viola until his death, Sept.	
1782	12	Deputizes for Neefe (34) at the organ at the Electoral Chapel.	Auber born, Jan. 29; Bach (J. C.) (47) dies, Jan. 1; Field born, July 26.

Beethoven

Year	Age	Life	Contemporary Musicians
		First published composition, Variations on a March by Dressler.	
1783	13	Appointed cembalo player in the court orchestra and accompanist at the theatre (35), April 26. Two Rondos for piano composed.	Hasse (84) dies, Dec. 16.
1784	14	B. receiving no salary, the family lives in very straitened circumstances, his father being more given to drink than to work. Death of the Elector Maximilian Friedrich, April 15, and dismissal of the opera company. New elector, Max Franz, reorganizes the musicians and appoints B. second court organist with a salary. A piano Concerto composed.	Bach (W. F.) (74) dies July 1; Martini (78) dies, Oct. 3; Onslow born, July 27; Ries born, Nov.; Spohr born, April 5.
1785	15	Studies the violin under Franz Anton Ries (30), a good friend of the B. family. Three piano Quartets composed.	Galuppi (79) dies, Jan. 3.
1786	16		Bishop born, Nov. 18; Sacchini (52) dies, Oct. 7; Weber born, Dec. 18.
1787	17	Visit to Vienna and meeting with Mozart (31). Death of B.'s mother (40), July 17. Ries (32) assists the family.	Gluck (73) dies, Nov. 15.

Year	Age	Life	Contemporary Musicians
1788	18	Acquaintance with the von Breuning family and with Count Waldstein (26). B. plays viola in the opera orchestra.	Bach (C. P. E.) (74) dies, Dec. 15.
1789	19	Part of the salary is withdrawn from B.'s dissolute father and paid to him as the head of the family. Two Preludes for piano (Op. 39).	
1790	20	Haydn (58), on his way to England, entertains the Bonn musicians, including B., to dinner, Dec. 25. Cantatas on death of Emperor Joseph II (49) and accession of Leopold II (43).	
1791	21	Visits of the electoral court to Mergentheim and Aschaffenburg. Meeting with Sterkel (41). *Ritter-ballet,* ostensibly composed by Waldstein (29), but really by Beethoven.	Czerny born, Feb. 20; Hérold born, Jan. 28; Meyerbeer born, Sept. 5; Mozart (35) dies, Dec. 5.
1792	22	Second visit of Haydn (60) to Bonn. He praises a cantata by B. Variations for piano; Songs; Octet for wind (Op. 103); (?) Variations for piano trio (Op. 44). The elector sends B. to Vienna, Nov., where he begins to study counterpoint under Haydn. Death	Potter born, Oct. 2; Rossini born, Feb. 29.

Year	Age	Life	Contemporary Musicians
		of his father (*c.* 52) at Bonn, Dec. 18. String Trio, E flat major (Op. 3).	
1793	23	Gives up Haydn's (61) lessons and goes to Schenk (32). Acquaintance with Prince Lichnowsky (35) and Baron van Swieten (59).	
1794	24	Begins to study under Albrechtsberger (58), Jan. He also submits Italian vocal pieces to Salieri (44) and studies quartet writing under Aloys Förster (46). Bonn being occupied by the French, B. decides to remain in Vienna.	
1795	25	Parts with Albrechtsberger (59). First public appearance in Vienna, March 29, with the piano Concerto, B flat major (Op. 19). Three piano Trios (Op. 1); 3 piano Sonatas (Op. 2), dedicated to Haydn (64); *Adelaide* and other songs.	Marschner born, Aug. 16.
1796	26	Visits to Prague, Feb., and Berlin, spring. Quintets for strings (Op. 4) and for piano and wind (Op. 16); 2 cello Sonatas (Op. 5); piano Sonata (Op. 7); Rondo for piano, C major (Op. 51, No. 1).	Loewe born, Nov. 30; Umlauf (39) dies, June 8.

Year	Age	Life	Contemporary Musicians
1797	27	Publications and lessons improve his financial position.	Donizetti born, Nov. 25; Schubert born, Jan. 31.
1798	28	Meeting with Wölfl (26), who dedicates three sonatas to him. Publication of 3 string Trios (Op. 9), 3 piano Sonatas (Op. 10) and clarinet Trio (Op. 11). B. meets R. Kreutzer (32) at the house of Bernadotte (35), who is French ambassador to Vienna.	Gaveaux (37) produces the opera, *Léonore, ou l'Amour conjugal,* in Paris.
1799	29	Publication of 3 violin Sonatas (Op. 12); *Pathétique* Sonata for piano (Op. 13); 2 piano Sonatas (Op. 14).	Dittersdorf (60) dies, Oct. 24; Halévy born, May 27.
1800	30	Gives a concert, April 2, at which the Septet (Op. 20) and the first Symphony, C major (Op. 21), are performed. Horn Sonata (Op. 17) first performed at Punto's (45) concert, April 18. B. defeats Steibelt (35) at an improvising contest. Czerny (9) becomes his pupil. Composition of 6 string Quartets (Op. 18), piano Sonata (Op. 22), piano Concerto No. 3, C minor (Op. 37) and Ballet, *Die Geschöpfe des Prometheus* (Op. 43).	Piccinni (72) dies, May 7.
1801	31	The Ballet produced at the	Bellini born, Nov. 1;

Year	*Age*	*Life*	*Contemporary Musicians*
		Burg Theatre, March 28. Alarming signs of deaf, ness begin to show them, selves. Composition of piano Sonatas (Opp. 26–28); violin Sonatas (Opp. 23, 24); string Quintet, C major (Op. 29). Op. 27, No. 2 is dedicated to Giulietta Guicciardi, with whom B. is in love. Ries (17) becomes B.'s pupil.	Cimarosa (52) dies, Jan. 11; Lanner born, April 11; Paer (30) produces the opera, *Achilles,* in Vienna, a funeral march in which incites B. to write that in the piano Sonata, Op. 26.
1802	32	Symphony No. 2, D major (Op. 36), com, pleted at Heiligenstadt, autumn, where he suffers much from depression and writes the 'Heiligenstadt Testament,' Oct. 6. 3 piano Sonatas (Op. 31).	Sarti (73) dies, July 28.
1803	33	Oratorio, *Christus am Öl, berge*, produced, April 5. Violin Sonata, A major (Op. 47), dedicated to R. Kreutzer (37), performed by B. and Bridgetower (24), May 17. Visit to Baden and Ober,Döbling for his health, summer. Meeting with Vogler (54) and his pupil Weber (17) in Vienna, winter. B. and Clementi (51) meet, but do not become acquainted. Publication of 3 violin	Adam born, July 24; Berlioz born, Dec. 9; Glinka born, May 20/June 2; Lortzing born, Oct. 23; Süssmayer (37) dies, Sept. 16.

Year	Age	Life	Contemporary Musicians
		Sonatas (Op. 30); piano Sonatas (Op. 31, Nos. 1 and 2); Bagatelles for piano (Op. 33); Variations for piano (Opp. 34–5); Romance for violin and orchestra, G major (Op. 40).	
1804	34	Symphony No. 3, E flat major (Op. 55) completed, April. It is intended as homage to Napoleon Bonaparte (35), but when he assumes the title of Emperor, May, B. withdraws the dedication and calls the work *Sinfonia eroica*. Piano Sonatas (Opp. 53, 54) composed at Ober-Döbling, summer. Piano Sonata (Op. 31, No. 3) published.	Benedict born, Nov. 27; Paer (33) produces the opera, *Eleonora, ossia l' Amore conjugale*, based on the work of Gaveaux (see 1798), at Dresden; Strauss (J. i) born, March 14.
1805	35	Composition of the opera, *Leonore, oder die eheliche Liebe*, begun, spring. Meeting with Cherubini (45), July. First performance of the opera as *Fidelio*, Nov. 20. It is withdrawn after three performances and revised. Piano Sonata, F minor (*Appassionata*) (Op. 57) completed.	Boccherini (62) dies, May 28.
1806	36	*Fidelio* revived in its revised form, with the overture, *Leonora* No. 3, March 29.	

Year	Age	Life	Contemporary Musicians
		First performance of violin Concerto (Op. 61) by Clement (26), Dec. 23.	
1807	37	Symphony No. 4, B flat major (Op. 60) produced, spring. Copyright in piano Concerto No. 4, G major (Op. 58), 3 string Quartets (Op. 59), fourth Symphony and violin Concerto sold to Clementi (55) for publication in London, April. Mass, C major (Op. 86), finished at Heiligenstadt, summer. First performance of *Coriolan* Overture (Op. 62), Dec.	
1808	38	Summer spent at Heiligenstadt, where he finishes the Symphonies Nos. 5 and 6 (Opp. 67–8), 2 piano Trios (Op. 70) and the choral Fantasia(Op.80.) B. is offered an appointment at the court of Jerome Bonaparte (24), King of Westphalia, at Cassel, but delays its acceptance.	Balfe born, May 15.
1809	39	The Archduke Rudolph, who has become B.'s pupil, joins the Princes Kinsky and Lobkowitz in guaranteeing him a small income to keep him in Vienna.	Albrechtsberger (73) dies, March 7; Haydn (77) dies, May 31; Mendelssohn born, Feb. 3.

Year	Age	Life	Contemporary Musicians
		Piano Sonata, E flat major (Op. 81A) (*Les Adieux, l'Absence et le Retour*), dedicated to Rudolph on his departure before the French occupation of Vienna, May. Piano Sonata, F sharp major (Op. 78), dedicated to Countess Therese von Brunswick, with whom he had been deeply in love. Piano Concerto No. 5, E flat major (Op. 73) ('Emperor'); string Quartet, E flat major (Op. 74). Publication of cello Sonata, A major (Op. 69).	
1810	40	Meeting with Bettina Brentano (25), May. Visit to Baden for a cure, Aug., his hearing having now alarmingly deteriorated. Music to Goethe's (61) *Egmont* (Op. 84); string Quartet, F minor (Op. 95).	Chopin born, Feb. 22; Nicolai born, June 9; Schumann born, June 8.
1811	41	Piano Trio, B flat major (Op. 97) finished, March. Music for two pieces by Kotzebue (50) for the opening of a new theatre at Pesth, *King Stephan* and *The Ruins of Athens*. B. becomes acquainted with	Hiller born, Oct. 24; Liszt born, Oct. 22.

Year Age	Life	Contemporary Musicians
	Mälzel (39), the inventor of the metronome. First visit to Teplitz.	
1812 42	Symphony No. 7, A major (Op. 92), finished, May. B.'s health being very precarious, he goes to the Bohemian baths in the summer: Teplitz, Carlsbad and Franzensbrunn. Meeting with Goethe (63), Brentano (34), his sister Bettina von Arnim (27) and Varnhagen von Ense (27), also the singer Amalie Sebald, with whom he falls in love. Visit to his brother Johann at Linz, autumn, where he finishes the Symphony No. 8, F major (Op. 93). Violin Sonata, G major (Op. 96), finished and played by Rode (38) and the Archduke Rudolph.	Dussek (51) dies, March 20.
1813 43	B. again visits Baden in the hope of curing his deafness. *The Battle of Vittoria* (Op. 91) composed there. That work and the seventh Symphony performed in Vienna, Dec. 8.	Dargomizhsky born, Feb. 2/14; Grétry (72) dies, Sept. 24; Verdi born, Oct. 10; Wagner born, May 22; Wanhal (74) dies, Aug. 26.
1814 44	*Fidelio* again revised, and produced in the new form, May 23. *Fidelio* Overture	Vogler (65) dies, May 6.

Year	Age	Life	Contemporary Musicians
		in E major added after first performance. Piano Sonata, E minor (Op. 90); overture, *Namensfeier* (Op. 115); cantata, *Der glorreiche Augenblick*.	
1815	45	Death of B.'s brother Karl, Nov. 15, whose son, Karl (9), falls to his charge. 2 cello Sonatas (Op. 102). Setting of Goethe's (66) *Meeresstille und glückliche Fahrt* (Op. 112), dedicated to the poet.	Franz born, June 20; Heller born, May 15.
1816	46	Obtains legal authority for taking Karl (10) out of his mother's care and placing him in an institution, Feb.; but later in the year she succeeds in her appeal against the decree, on the grounds that his deafness unfits him for his duties as guardian. *Liederkreis* (Op. 98). Piano Sonata, A major (Op. 101).	Paisiello (75) dies, June 5.
1817	47	Becomes involved in a long lawsuit concerning his nephew (11); he is much depressed and his health is greatly impaired.	Gade born, Feb. 22; Méhul (54) dies, Oct. 18; Monsigny (88) dies, Jan. 14.
1818	48	Broadwood piano presented to B. Friendship with Potter (26).	Gounod born, June 17; Koželuh (46) dies, May 7.

Year	Age	Life	Contemporary Musicians
1819	49	Piano Sonata, B flat major (Op. 106) finished, March, and published Sept. *Missa Solennis*, D major (Op. 123), begun.	Offenbach born, June 21.
1820	50	The lawsuit against his brother's widow decided in his favour. Karl (14) is again in his charge and gives him more pain and trouble than ever.	Serov born, Jan 11/23; Vieuxtemps born, Feb. 20.
1821	51	Piano Sonata, E major (Op. 109), published, Nov.; piano Sonata, A flat major (Op. 110), finished, Dec. 25.	
1822	52	Rossini (30), who has a great success in Vienna, meets B. and Schubert (25) calls with a set of Variations he has dedicated to him. Piano Sonata, C minor (Op. 111), finished, Jan. 13. Overture, *Die Weihe des Hauses* (Op. 124), composed at Baden, summer.	Franck born, Dec. 10; Raff born, May 27.
1823	53	*Missa Solennis*, D major (Op. 123) finished, Feb. 27. 33 Variations for piano on a theme by Diabelli (42) (Op. 120). Weber (37) and Benedict (19) visit B. at Baden, Oct. 5. B. accepts an	Lalo born, Jan. 27; Liszt (12) gives a concert in Vienna, at which B. is present, April 13; Steibelt (58) dies, Sept. 20.

Year	Age	Life	Contemporary Musicians

opera libretto, *Melusine,*
from Grillparzer (32).

1824 54 Symphony No. 9 and part
of *Missa Solennis* performed,
May 7. B. conducts, but
hears neither the performance nor the applause.
Invitation from the London
Philharmonic Society falls
through, May. B. con-
tinues to be much worried
by his nephew (18) and
is severely ill. String
Quartet, E flat major
(Op. 127), finished dur-
ing the winter.

Contemporary Musicians: Bruckner born, Sept. 4;
Cornelius born, Dec. 24;
Reinecke born, June 23;
Smetana born, March 2;
Viotti (71) dies, March 3.

1825 55 Still unwell, B. goes to
Baden, May, and recovers.
String Quartet, A minor
(Op. 132), composed
there. The finale is
written from the sketches
originally intended for an
instrumental finale to the
ninth Symphony. Kuhlau
(39) and George Smart
(49) visit B. at Baden.

Contemporary Musicians: Gaveaux (64) dies; Salieri
(75) dies, May 7; Strauss
(J. ii) born, Oct. 25;
Winter (70) dies, Oct. 17.

1826 56 First performance of string
Quartet, B flat major (Op.
130), March 21. The
finale is the *Grosse Fuge,*
afterwards published separately (Op. 133). B.'s
nephew (20) fails in his
examinations and attempts

Contemporary Musicians: Weber (40) dies, June 4/5.

Year Age	Life	Contemporary Musicians

suicide; B.'s health breaks down completely. String Quartet, C sharp minor (Op. 131), finished, *c.* Sept. B. takes Karl to his brother Johann at Gneixendorf, where he writes the string Quartet, F major (Op. 135), and a new finale for Op. 130. Return to Vienna, Dec. He catches cold on the journey and develops pneumonia and dropsy.

1827 57 Confined to his bed, B. receives £100 from the London Philharmonic Society on account of a concert to be given by them, March 1. He proposes to work up the sketches for his tenth Symphony for them. Schubert (30), Hummel (49) and his pupil Hiller (16) visit B., March.

Beethoven dies, March 26.

Seyfried (51) writes a *Libera me* for B.'s funeral. Auber aged 45; Balfe 19; Bellini 26; Benedict 23; Berlioz 24; Bishop 41; Boieldieu 52; Bruckner 3; Catel 54; Cherubini 67; Chopin 17; Clementi 75; Cornelius 3; Czerny 36; Dargomizhsky 14; Donizetti 30; Field 45; Franck 5; Glinka 24; Gossec 93; Gounod 9; Halévy 28; Hérold 36; Hummel 49; Kreutzer (R.) 61; Kuhlau 41; Liszt 16; Loewe 31; Lortzing 24; Marschner 32; Mendelssohn 18; Meyerbeer 36; Paer 56; Potter 35; Ries 43; Rossini 35; Schenk 66; Schubert

Year	Age	Life	Contemporary Musicians
			30; Schumann 17; Smetana 3; Spohr 43; Spontini 53; Verdi 14; Wagner 14; Weigl 61; Zelter 69; Zingarelli 75.

APPENDIX B

CATALOGUE OF WORKS

The unenclosed figures in the left-hand column are the opus numbers under which the works were originally published. The figures in brackets are the numbers assigned to 'Werke ohne Opuszahl' (WoO, Works without opus number) by Georg Kinsky & Hans Halm, *Das Werk Beethovens. Thematisch-bibliographisches Verzeichnis seiner sämtlichen vollendeten Kompositionen* (Munich, 1955).

I. DRAMATIC WORKS
1. Operas

Op.

— *Vestas Feuer* (1803). First scene of an opera (Schikaneder).

— *Fidelio, oder die eheliche Liebe* (1805). Opera in 3 acts (Sonnleithner, after Bouilly's *Léonore, ou l'amour conjugal*). Called *Leonore* by the composer.

— *Fidelio, oder die eheliche Liebe* (1806). Opera in 2 acts. Revised version of the preceding (text revised by Breuning).

72 *Fidelio, oder die eheliche Liebe* (1814). Opera in 2 acts. Final revision of the preceding (text revised by Treitschke).

2. Ballets

(1) *Musik zu einem Ritterballet* (1790–1).

43 *Die Geschöpfe des Prometheus* (1800–1).

3. Incidental Music

(91) Two arias for *Die schöne Schusterin* by Ignaz Umlauf (1796):
O welch ein Leben!
Soll ein Schuh nicht drücken.

84 *Egmont* (Goethe) (1810).

113 *Die Ruinen von Athen* (Kotzebue) (1811).

117 *König Stephan, oder Ungarns erster Wohltäter* (Kotzebue) (1811).

Appendix B—Catalogue of Works

Op.
(2) Triumphal march and (?) introduction to Act II for Kuffner's play *Tarpeja* (1813).

(94) *Germania,* final chorus for *Die gute Nachricht* by Georg Friedrich Treitschke (1814).

(96) *Leonora Prohaska* (Duncker) (1815).

(97) *Es ist vollbracht,* final chorus for Treitschke's *Die Ehrenpforten* (1815).

124 *Die Weihe des Hauses* (Meisl) (1822), including adaptations
114 and revisions from *Die Ruinen von Athen.*
(98)

II. CHORAL MUSIC
1. *With orchestra*
(a) Sacred

85 *Christus am Ölberge* (Huber) (1803, revised 1804). Oratorio.

86 Mass, C major (1807).

123 *Missa solennis,* D major (1819–23).

(b) Secular

(87) Cantata on the death of the Emperor Joseph II (Averdonk) (1790).

(88) Cantata on the accession of Leopold II (Averdonk) (1790).

80 Fantasia for piano, chorus and orchestra (Kuffner) (1808).

136 *Der glorreiche Augenblick* (Weissenbach) (1814).

(95) *Chor auf die verbündeten Fürsten* (Bernard) (1814).

112 *Meeresstille und glückliche Fahrt* (Goethe) (1815).

— *Opferlied* (Matthisson) (1822). First choral setting.

122 *Bundeslied* (Goethe) (1822–3).

121b *Opferlied* (Matthisson) (1824). Second choral setting.

125 Choral Symphony. *See* Symphonies.

2. *With piano*

(109) *Trinklied* (c. 1787).

(122) *Kriegslied der Österreicher* (Friedelberg) (1797).

(111) *Punschlied* (c. 1790).

(117) *Der freie Mann* (Pfeffel) (1791–2).

Beethoven

Op.

(119) *O care selve* (Metastasio) (1795).

(103) *Un lieto brindisi* (Bondi) (1814).

(105) *Hochzeitslied* (Stein) (1819).

(106) *Lobkowitz-Kantate* (1823).

III. VOCAL ENSEMBLE
1. *With orchestra*

(93) *Nei giorni tuoi felici* (Metastasio) (1802–3). Duet.

116 *Tremate empi, tremate* (Bettoni) (1814). Trio.

118 *Sanft wie du lebtest* (1814). Quartet.

2. *With piano*

100 *Merkenstein* (Rupprecht) (1814–15). Duet. *See also* Solo Songs.

3. *Unaccompanied*

(99) 26 Italian duets, trios and quartets (Metastasio) (1792– c. 1802).

(100) *Lob auf den Dicken* (Beethoven) (1801).

(101) *Graf, Graf, liebster Graf* (Beethoven) (1802).

(102) *Abschiedsgesang* (Seyfried) (1814).

(104) *Gesang der Mönche* (Schiller) (1817).

(159– 48 canons for 3 to 6 voices (words by various authors)
198,   (1795–1826).
203)

IV. SOLO SONGS
1. *With orchestra*

(89) *Prüfung des Küssens* (c. 1790).

(90) *Mit Mädeln sich vertragen* (Goethe) (c. 1790)

65 *Ah perfido!* (Metastasio) (1796).

(92) *Primo amore* (c. 1800).

(92a) *No, non turbati* (Metastasio) (1801–2).

2. *With piano*

(107) *Schilderung eines Mädchens* (1783).

(108) *An einen Säugling* (Döhring) (1783).

Appendix B—Catalogue of Works

Op.

(110) *Elegie auf den Tod eines Pudels* (*c.* 1787).

(112) *An Laura* (Matthisson) (*c.* 1790).

(113) *Klage* (Hölty) (1790).

52 8 songs (*c.* 1790–2):
> *Urians Reise um die Welt* (Claudius).
> *Feuerfarb'* (Mereau).
> *Das Liedchen von der Ruhe* (Ueltzen).
> *Maigesang* (Goethe).
> *Mollys Abschied* (Bürger).
> *Die Liebe* (Lessing).
> *Marmotte* (Goethe).
> *Das Blümchen Wunderhold* (Bürger).

(114) *Selbstgespräch* (Gleim) (1792).

(115) *An Minna* (1792–3).

(116) *Que le temps me dure* (Rousseau) (1792–3).

— *Traute Henriette* (*c.* 1793).

(118) *Seufzer eines Ungeliebten* and *Gegenliebe* (Bürger) (1794–5).

(120) *Man strebt die Flamme zu verhehlen* (*c.* 1795).

46 *Adelaide* (Matthisson) (1795–6).

82 4 *ariette* and a duet (Metastasio) (1795–6, revised 1809).

(121) *Abschiedsgesang an Wiens Bürger* (Friedelberg) (1796).

(126) *Opferlied* (Matthisson) (1796, revised 1798).

(123) *Zärtliche Liebe* (Herrosee) (*c.* 1797).

(124) *La partenza* (Metastasio) (1797–8).

(125) *La tiranna* (1798).

(128) *Plaisir d'aimer* (1798–1800).

48 6 songs (Gellert) (1803):
> *Bitten.*
> *Die Liebe des Nächsten.*
> *Vom Tode.*
> *Die Ehre Gottes aus der Natur.*
> *Gottes Macht und Vorsehung.*
> *Busslied.*

(129) *Der Wachtelschlag* (Sauter) (1803).

88 *Das Glück der Freundschaft* (1803).

(130) *Gedenke mein* (1804).

Beethoven

Op.

32 *An die Hoffnung* (Tiedge) (1805). First setting.
(132) *Als die Geliebte sich trennen wollte* (Breuning) (1806).
(133) *In questa tomba oscura* (Carpani) (1807).
(134) *Sehnsucht* (Goethe). 4 settings (1807–8).
(136) *Andenken* (Matthisson) (1809).
(137) *Lied aus der Ferne* (Reissig) (1809).
(138) *Der Jüngling in der Fremde* (Reissig) (1809).
(139) *Der Liebende* (Reissig) (1809).
75 6 songs (1809):
    Mignon (Goethe).
    Neue Liebe, neues Leben (Goethe).
    Es war einmal ein König (Goethe).
    Gretels Warnung (Halem).
    An den fernen Geliebten (Reissig).
    Der Zufriedene (Reissig).
(135) *Die laute Klage* (Herder) (?1809).
83 3 songs (Goethe) (1810):
    Wonne der Wehmut.
    Sehnsucht.
    Mit einem gemalten Band.
(140) *An die Geliebte* (Stoll). 2 settings (1811).
(141) *Der Gesang der Nachtigall* (Herder) (1813).
94 *An die Hoffnung* (Tiedge) (1813). Second setting.
(142) *Der Bardengeist* (Hermann) (1813).
(143) *Des Kriegers Abschied* (Reissig) (1814).
(144) *Merkenstein* (Rupprecht) (1814). For the duet version *see*
    Vocal Ensemble.
(145) *Das Geheimnis* (Wessenberg) (1815).
(146) *Sehnsucht* (Reissig) (1815–16).
98 *An die ferne Geliebte* (Jeitteles) (1816). Song cycle.
99 *Der Mann von Wort* (Kleinschmid) (1816).
(147) *Ruf vom Berge* (Treitschke) (1816).
(148) *So oder so* (Lappe) (1817).
(149) *Resignation* (Haugwitz) (1817).
(150) *Abendlied unterm gestirnten Himmel* (Goeble) (1820).
— 2 Austrian folksongs (1820):

Appendix B—Catalogue of Works

Op.

Das liebe Kätzschen.
Der Knabe auf dem Berge.

128 *Der Kuss* (Weisse) (1822).
(151) *Der edle Mensch* (Goethe) (1823).

3. Arrangements, with piano, violin and cello

(152) 25 Irish songs (1810–13).
(153) 20 Irish songs (1810–13).
(154) 12 Irish songs (1810–13).
(155) 26 Welsh songs (1810–14).
(157) 12 popular songs of various origin (1814–15).
108 25 Scottish songs (1815–16).
(158) 23 popular songs of various countries (1816–18).
(156) 12 Scottish songs (1817–18).

V. ORCHESTRA
1. Symphonies

21 No. 1, C major (1799–1800).
36 No. 2, D major (1801–2).
55 No. 3, E flat major (*Eroica*) (1803).
60 No. 4, B flat major (1806).
67 No. 5, C minor (1804–8).
68 No. 6, F major (*Pastoral*) (1807–8).
92 No. 7, A major (1811–12).
93 No. 8, F major (1812).
125 No. 9, D minor (1822–4). The finale is a setting for soloists and chorus of Schiller's *An die Freude*.

2. Overtures

138 *Leonore No. 1* (1805). Intended for the first performance of *Fidelio* but abandoned as unsuitable.

72a *Leonore No. 2* (1805). Played at the first performance of *Fidelio*.

72a *Leonore No. 3* (1806). Written for the second version of *Fidelio*.

62 *Coriolan* (1807). Overture to the play by Heinrich Joseph von Collin.

Beethoven

Op.
115 *Zur Namensfeier* (1815).
(For the remainder *see* Dramatic Works)

3. *With solo instruments*
(a) Piano

(4) Concerto, E flat major, piano part only (1784).
(6) Rondo, B flat major (1794–5). Possibly intended for the first version (lost) of Concerto No. 2.
15 Concerto No. 1, C major (1798).
19 Concerto No. 2, B flat major (second version, 1798–1801).
37 Concerto No. 3, C minor (1800).
58 Concerto No. 4, G major (1805–6).
80 Fantasia, C minor. *See* Choral Works, 1(b).
73 Concerto No. 5, E flat major (*Emperor*) (1809).

(b) Violin

40 Romance, G major (?1802).
50 Romance, F major (?1802).
61 Concerto, D major (1806). Also arranged for piano (1807).

(c) Piano, violin and cello

56 Concerto, C major (1803–4).

4. *Miscellaneous*

(7) 12 minuets (1795).
(8) 12 German dances (1795).
(12) 12 minuets (1799).
(13) 12 German dances (*c.* 1800).
(14) 12 *Contretänze* (1800–1).
(16) 12 *Écossaises* (?1806).
91 *Wellingtons Sieg, oder die Schlacht bei Vittoria* (1813).
(3) *Gratulations-Menuett*, E flat major (1822).

5. *Military Band*

(18) March No. 1, F major (3 versions, 1809, 1810, 1823 with trio).
(19) March No. 2, F major (3 versions, 1810, 1810, 1823 with trio).

Appendix B—Catalogue of Works

Op.

(20) March, C major (1809–10).
(21) Polonaise, D major (1810).
(22) *Écossaise,* D major (1810).
(24) *Marsch zur grossen Wachtparade,* D major (1816).

VI. CHAMBER MUSIC
1. *Strings*
(a) Quintets

4   E flat major (1795–6). Adaptation of the Wind Octet, Op. 103.
29   C major (1801).
104   C minor (1817). Arrangement of the Piano Trio, Op. 1, no. 3.
—   Movement in D minor (1817).
137   Fugue, D major (1817).
—   Movement in C major (1826). Known only from a piano arrangement.

(b) Quartets

—   Minuet, A flat major (*c.* 1794).
—   2 preludes and fugues: (1) F major, (2) C major (1794–1795).
18   6 quartets: F major, G major, D major, C minor, A major, B flat major (1798–1800).
—   F major (1801–2). Arrangement of the Piano Sonata, Op. 14, no. 1.
59   3 quartets (*Rasumovsky*): F major, E minor, C major (1805–1806).
74   E flat major (*Harp*) (1809).
95   F minor (1810).
127   E flat major (1822–5).
132   A minor (1825).
130   B flat major (1825; new finale 1826).
133   *Grosse Fuge,* B flat major (1825). Original finale of Op. 130.
131   C sharp minor (1826).
135   F major (1826).

Op.

(c) Trios

3   E flat major (1792).

(9) 6 minuets (*c.* 1795). 2 violins and cello.

8   Serenade, D major (1796–7).

9   3 trios: G major, D major, C minor (1796–8).

—   Prelude and fugue, E minor (?). 2 violins and cello.

(15) 6 *Ländlerische Tänze* (1802). 2 violins and cello.

(d) Duos

(32) *Duett mit zwei obligaten Augengläsern,* E flat major (*c.* 1795–8). Viola and cello.

(34) Short piece, A major (1822). 2 violins.

(35) Canon, A major (1825). 2 violins.

2. Wind

(27) 3 duets for clarinet and bassoon: C major, F major, B flat major (*c.* 1790–2).

(26) Duet, G major, for 2 flutes (1792).

103 Octet, E flat major, for 2 oboes, 2 clarinets, 2 horns and 2 bassoons (1792).

(25) *Rondino,* E flat major, for 2 oboes, 2 clarinets, 2 horns and 2 bassoons (1792).

87   Trio, C major, for 2 oboes and cor anglais (1794).

71   Sextet, E flat major, for 2 clarinets, 2 horns and 2 bassoons (1796).

(28) Variations, C major, on 'Là ci darem la mano' from Mozart's *Don Giovanni,* for 2 oboes and cor anglais (1796–7).

(29) March, B flat major, for 2 clarinets, 2 horns and 2 bassoons (?1807).

(30) 3 *Equali* for 4 trombones: D minor, D major, B flat major (1812).

—   Adagio for 3 horns (1815).

3. Strings and wind

81b Sextet, E flat major, for 2 horns and string quartet (1794–5).

25   Serenade, D major, for flute, violin and viola (1795–6).

Appendix B—Catalogue of Works

Op.

20 Septet, E flat major, for clarinet, horn, bassoon, violin, viola, cello and double bass (1799-1800).

(17) 11 dances (*Mödlinger Tänze*) for 2 clarinets, 2 horns, 2 violins and bass (1819).

4. Strings and piano
(a) Quartets

(36) 3 quartets: E flat major, D major, C major (1785).

16 E flat major (1796). Arrangement of the Quintet for piano and wind, Op. 16.

(b) Trios

— Movement in E flat major (1783).

44 14 variations on an original theme, E flat major (?).

(38) E flat major (*c.* 1790-1).

1 3 trios: E flat major, G major, C minor (1793-4).

— D major (1805). Arrangement of Symphony No. 2.

70 2 trios: D major, E flat major (1808).

97 B flat major (*Archduke*) (1811).

(39) Movement in B flat major (1812).

121a Variations, G major, on Wenzel Müller's song 'Ich bin der Schneider Kakadu' (1815-16).

(c) Duos
i. Violin and piano

(40) 12 variations, F major, on 'Se vuol ballare' from Mozart's *Le nozze di Figaro* (1792-3).

(41) Rondo, G major (1793-4).

(42) 6 Allemandes (1795-6).

12 3 sonatas: D major, A major, E flat major (1797-8).

23 Sonata, A minor (1800-1).

24 Sonata, F major (1800-1).

30 3 sonatas: A major, C minor, G major (1802).

47 Sonata, A major (*Kreutzer*) (1802-3).

96 Sonata, G major (1812).

Beethoven

ii. Viola and piano

42 Notturno, D major (?1796). Arrangement of the Serenade for string trio, Op. 8.

iii. Cello and piano

5 2 sonatas: F major, G minor (1796).

(45) 12 variations, G major, on 'See the conquering hero comes' from Handel's *Judas Maccabaeus* (?1796).

66 12 variations, F major, on 'Ein Mädchen oder Weibchen' from Mozart's *Die Zauberflöte* (1798).

(46) 7 variations, E flat major, on 'Bei Männern, welche Liebe fühlen' from Mozart's *Die Zauberflöte* (1801).

69 Sonata, A major (1807-8).

102 2 sonatas: C major, D major (1815).

iv. Mandoline and piano

(43) Adagio, E flat major (1796).

(43) Sonatina, C minor (*c.* 1796).

(44) Sonatina, C major (1796).

(44) *Andante con variazioni,* D major (1796).

5. Wind and piano

(37) Trio, G major, for piano, flute and bassoon (1786-7).

16 Quintet, E flat major, for piano, oboe, clarinet, horn and bassoon (1796-7).

17 Sonata, F major, for piano and horn (1800).

41 Serenade, D major, for piano and flute (1803). Arrangement of the Trio for flute, violin and viola, Op. 25.

105 6 variations (5 on Scottish tunes) for piano and flute (or violin) (1817-18).

107 10 variations (on Scottish, Russian and Tirolese tunes) for piano and flute (or violin) (1817-18).

6. Strings, wind and piano

11 Trio, B flat major, for piano, clarinet (or violin) and cello (1798).

Appendix B—Catalogue of Works

Op.

38 Trio, E flat major, for piano, clarinet (or violin) and cello (1802–3). Arrangement of the Septet for wind and strings, Op. 20.

VII. PIANO SOLO
1. *Sonatas*

(47) 3 sonatas: E flat major, F minor, D major (1782–3).

(50) F major (2 movements) (*c.* 1788–90).

(51) C major (2 movements, the second completed by Ries) (1791–2).

2 3 sonatas: F minor, A major, C major (1794–5).

49/2 G major (1796).

7 E flat major (1796–7).

10 3 sonatas: C minor, F major, D major (1796–8).

49/1 G minor (1798).

13 C minor (*Pathétique*) (1798–9).

14 2 sonatas: E major, G major (1798–9).

22 B flat major (1799–1800).

26 A flat major (1800–1).

27/1 E flat major (*quasi una fantasia*) (1800–1).

27/2 C sharp minor (*quasi una fantasia*) (1801).

28 D major (1801).

31 3 sonatas: G major, D minor, E flat major (1801–2).

53 C major (*Waldstein*) (1803–4).

54 F major (1804).

57 F minor (*Appassionata*) (1804–5).

78 F sharp major (1809).

79 G major (1809).

81a E flat major (*Les Adieux, l'absence et le retour*) (1809–1810).

90 E minor (1814).

101 A major (1816).

106 B flat major (*Hammerclavier*) (1817–19).

109 E major (1820).

110 A flat major (1821).

111 C minor (1821–2).

Beethoven

2. *Variations*

(63) 9, C minor, on a march by Ernst Christoph Dressler (1782).

(64) 6, F major, on a Swiss air (for piano or harp) (*c.* 1790).

(65) 24, D major, on the *arietta* 'Venni amore' by Vincenzo Righini (1st version, lost, 1790; 2nd version, 1802).

(66) 13, A major, on 'Es war einmal ein alter Mann' from Dittersdorf's *Das rote Käppchen* (1792).

(68) 12, C major, on the 'Minuett à la Viganò' from the ballet *Le nozze disturbate* by Jakob Haibel (1795).

(69) 9, A major, on 'Quant'è più bello' from Paisiello's *La Molinara* (1795).

(70) 6, G major, on the duet 'Nel cor più non mi sento' from Paisiello's *La Molinara* (1795).

(71) 12, A major, on a Russian dance from *Das Waldmädchen* by Paul Wranitzky (1796).

(72) 8, C major, on the romance 'Une fièvre brûlante' from Grétry's *Richard Cœur de Lion* (1796–7).

(73) 10, B flat major, on 'La stessa, la stessissima' from Salieri's *Falstaff* (1799).

(75) 7, F major, on the quartet 'Kind, willst du ruhig schlafen' from *Das unterbrochene Opferfest* by Peter von Winter (1799).

(76) 6, F major, on the trio 'Tändeln und scherzen' from *Soliman II* by Franz Xaver Süssmayr (1799). In later editions Variation VI was divided into three, making eight in all.

(77) 6, G major, on an original theme (1800).

34 6, F major, on an original theme (1802).

35 15 and fugue, E flat major, on a theme from the ballet *Die Geschöpfe des Prometheus* (1802).

(78) 7, C major, on 'God save the king' (1803).

(79) 5, D major, on 'Rule, Britannia' (1803).

(80) 32, C minor, on an original theme (1806).

76 6, D major, on a theme from *Die Ruinen von Athen* (1809).

120 33, C major, on a waltz by Anton Diabelli (1823).

Appendix B—Catalogue of Works

Op.

3. Miscellaneous

(48) Rondo, C major (1783).

(49) Rondo, A major (1783).

(82) Minuet, E flat major (?1785).

(55) Prelude, F minor (?1786–7).

39   2 preludes in all the major keys (1789).

(54) *Lustig-traurig*, C major and minor (?1790).

—   2 exercises: C major, B flat major (*c.* 1790).

—   Andante, C major (*c.* 1793).

—   Minuet, F major (*c.* 1794).

—   Minuet, C major (1794–5).

—   *Drei kleine Nachahmungssätze:* F major, F major, C major (*c.* 1794).

—   Fugue, C major (?).

129   *Rondò a capriccio*, G major (*Alla ungherese quasi un capriccio*) (*c.* 1795).

(10) 6 minuets (1795).

51/1 Rondo, C major (1796–7).

—   Allegretto, C minor (*c.* 1797).

(52) Bagatelle, C minor (1797).

(53) Allegretto, C minor (2 versions, 1796–8).

(11) 7 *Ländlerische Tänze* (1798).

(81) Allemande, A major (*c.* 1800).

—   *Anglaise*, D major (*c.* 1800).

51/2 Rondo, G major (1800).

—   2 Bagatelles: C major, E flat major (1800).

—   Canon, G major (1802).

33   7 Bagatelles: E flat major, C major, F major, A major, C major, D major, A flat major (1802).

—   Waltz, C minor (1803).

—   Canon, A flat major (1803).

—   Theme and variations, A major (1803).

(57) Andante, F major (*Andante favori*) (1803–4). Originally the slow movement of Sonata, Op. 53.

(56) Bagatelle, C major (1803–4).

(83) 6 *Écossaises*, E flat major (?1806).

Op.

77 Fantasia, G minor (1809).

(58) 2 cadenzas for Mozart's Piano Concerto in D minor, K.466 (*c.* 1809).

— Cadenzas for the piano concertos Op. 15, 19, 37, 58 and 61 (arrangement of Violin Concerto) (*c.* 1809).

(59) Bagatelle, A minor (1810). Published by Nohl in 1867 with the title *Für Elise*. Since the original manuscript, which has disappeared, belonged to Therese von Malfatti, it is thought that the title should read *Für Therese*.

(23) *Écossaise,* G major (*c.* 1810).

— 2 German dances: F major, F minor (*c.* 1811).

89 Polonaise, C major (1814).

(200) Theme, 'O Hoffnung' (1818). For the Archduke Rudolph, who wrote 40 variations on it.

(60) Piece, B flat major (1818).

— *Kleines Konzertfinale,* C major (1820). Arrangement of the last section (Presto) of the C minor Piano Concerto, Op. 37, made for Friedrich Starke's *Wiener Pianoforte-Schule*, Part III.

(61) *Allegretto für Piringer,* B minor (1821). Written for the amateur musician Ferdinand Piringer.

119 11 Bagatelles: G minor, C major, D major, A major, C minor, G major, C major, C major, A minor, A major, B flat major (1820–2).

— Bagatelle, C major (1823–4).

126 6 Bagatelles: G major, G minor, E flat major, B minor, G major, E flat major (1823–4).

(84) Waltz, E flat major (1824).

(61a) Piece, G minor (1825). Written for Charles Burney's granddaughter Sarah Burney Payne.

(85) Waltz, D major (1825).

(86) *Écossaise,* E flat major (1825).

VIII. PIANO DUET

(67) 8 variations, C major, on a theme by Count Waldstein (1791–2).

Appendix B—Catalogue of Works

Op.

6   Sonata, D major (c. 1796–7).

(74) Song, 'Ich denke dein' (Goethe), with 6 variations (1799–1804).

45   3 marches: C major, E flat major, D major (1802–3).

134 Fugue, B flat major (1826). Arrangement of the *Grosse Fuge* for string quartet, Op. 133.

IX. ORGAN

(31) Fugue, D major (1783).

X. MECHANICAL INSTRUMENTS

(33) *Allegro non più molto* and *Allegretto*, C major for an unspecified instrument (?).

(33) 3 pieces for a musical clock: Adagio, F major; Scherzo, G major; Allegro, G major (1799).

—   Grenadiers' march, F major, for a musical clock (1807–18).

APPENDIX C

PERSONALIA

Albrechtsberger, Johann Georg (1736–1809), German composer in Vienna who taught Beethoven counterpoint.

Amenda, Karl F. (1771–1836), good violinist, student of theology. Became an intimate friend of Beethoven's in Vienna, 1798.

Arnim, Bettina von, née Brentano (1785–1859), poetess. Friend of Beethoven and Goethe.

Artaria, Domenico (1775–1842), founded the well-known publishing house in Vienna.

Averdonk, Johanna Helena, court singer; pupil of Johnan van Beethoven.

Bach, Carl Philipp Emanuel (1714–88), second son of J. S. Bach; clavier player and composer of church music, symphonies, concertos and sonatas.

Beckenkamp, painter who resided in Bonn 1784–5 and is supposed to have painted the portraits of Beethoven's father and mother.

Belseroski, Joseph Clement, viola player in the elector's band at Bonn. One of the witnesses of Johann van Beethoven's marriage, 1767.

Bigot, Marie (1786–1820), Alsatian pianist. Wife of the librarian to Count Rasoumovsky and friend of Beethoven.

Bouilly, Jean-Nicolas (1763–1842), administrator of a department near Tours during the Terror. Wrote the libretti for Cherubini's *Water Carrier* and Gaveaux's *Léonore*.

Braun, Baron, a grandee with a private orchestra. At one time manager of the Theater-an-der-Wien.

Braun, Baroness. Beethoven dedicated the horn Sonata, Op. 17, to her.

Breitkopf & Härtel, publishing firm at Leipzig, founded in 1719 by Bernhardt Christoph Breitkopf (1695–1777).

Brentano, Maximiliane, daughter of Franz Brentano and his wife Antonie, née von Birkenstock. Beethoven wrote the little Trio in B flat (1812) to encourage his 'little friend' in piano playing; later he dedicated the Sonata in E major (Op. 109) to her.

Bridgetower, George Augustus Polgreen (*c.* 1779–1860), violinist, a mulatto, son of an African father (known in London as the 'Abyssinian Prince') and a German or Polish mother. Met Beethoven in Vienna and Teplitz, and played the Kreutzer Sonata with him at a concert on 17th May, 1803.

Bürger, Gottfried August (1748–94), German romantic poet.

Clementi, Muzio (1752–1832), Italian pianist and teacher. Met Beethoven in Vienna in 1804. Contracted with him for the publication of certain works and reported to his partner, F. W. Collard, in a letter dated 1807. They were tardy in their payment. Beethoven thought highly of his piano studies and gave them to Gerhard von Breuning.

Collard, firm of pianoforte makers, in direct succession through Clementi to Longman and Broderip, music publishers in Cheapside since 1767. F. W. Collard's name appears in the Patent Office in 1811 in connection with improvements in pianofortes.

Collin, Heinrich Joseph von (1771–1811), Austrian poet. Author of play on the subject of Coriolanus.

Cramer, Johann Baptist (1771–1858), German pianist settled in London. Studied under Clementi; self-taught in theory and composition.

Czerny, Karl (1791–1857), pianist and composer in Vienna. Beethoven gave him lessons from 1800 to 1803, and he became a passionate admirer of his. He also studied with Hummel and Clementi. He was reluctant to perform in public, but was besieged by pupils. He only accepted those of special talent, among them being Liszt.

Diabelli, Anton (1781–1858), head of the firm of Diabelli, music publishers in Vienna, and a minor composer.

Dragonetti, Domenico (1763–1846), Italian double bass player, the greatest of his time.

Dressler, Ernst Christoph (1734–79), composer and singer, member of the court chapels at Bayreuth and Gotha; later *Kapellmeister* at Wetzlar; finally opera singer in Vienna and Cassel.

Dussek, Jan Ladislav (1761–1812), Czech pianist and composer whose works were noteworthy in the development of pianoforte style.

Eeden, Gilles (or *Heinrich*) *van den* (died 1782), second court organist at Bonn.

Elssler, Johann, valet and copyist to Haydn; father of Fanny Elssler, a famous dancer.

Förster, Emanuel Aloys (1748–1823), Silesian composer settled in Vienna, whom Beethoven called his 'old master.' He influenced Beethoven's chamber music, and his own compositions are said to be Beethovenish in character.

Galitsin, Prince Nicolas Borissovich (1794–1866), Russian nobleman and patron of Beethoven.

Gardiner, William, of Leicester. Author of *Italy, her Music, Arts and People.* Enthusiastic amateur of music. First became acquainted with Beethoven's string Trio in E flat, Op. 3, in 1793. Great admirer also of Haydn, to whom he sent the famous present of six pairs of stockings into which were woven themes by Haydn.

Gelinek, Joseph (1758–1825), Bohemian secular priest, pianist and composer for his instrument, famous as an improviser.

Gellert, Christian Fürchtegott (1715–69), German poet.

Grétry, André Ernest Modeste (1741–1813), Belgian composer settled in Paris and an eminent member of the French school of comic opera.

Grillparzer, Franz (1791–1872), the greatest dramatic poet of Austria. He wrote Beethoven's funeral oration and was one of the torch-bearers at the ceremony.

Holz, Karl (1798–1858), an able violinist; second violin in Schuppanzigh's quartet in Vienna.

Huber, Franz Xaver, a popular author for the Vienna stage, a poet, and the author of the text of *Christus am Oelberge.*

Hummel, Johann Nepomuk (1778–1837), pianist and composer, pupil of Mozart.

Jeitteles, Alois, a poet of whom little is known. Author of the lyrics *An die ferne Geliebte* which Beethoven set to music.

Kant, Immanuel (1724–1804), German philosopher. His *Natural*

History and Theory of the Firmament was among the books in Beethoven's library.

Kempis, Thomas à (c. 1380–1471), a Dutch Augustinian canon and writer, Thomas Hammerken, went to the school at Deventer, thence to the convent of Mount St. Agnes at Zwolle. He was known as Thomas from Kempen (his birthplace), and became a monk in 1399; later sub-prior of his monastery. His book, *The Imitation of Christ*, was in Beethoven's library.

Kiesewetter, Raphael Georg (1773–1850), settled in Vienna, 1794, as a law-student. One of Beethoven's amateur musical friends and a bass singer. Later became a writer on musical history.

Klopstock, Gottlieb Friedrich (1724–1803), German poet. His complete works were in Beethoven's library.

Kotzebue, August Friedrich Ferdinand von (1761–1819), German dramatist whose works were fashionable in their time.

Koželuh, Leopold (1754–1818), Bohemian composer, settled first at Salzburg, then in Vienna; Mozart's successor in the office of imperial chamber composer.

Kreutzer, Rodolphe (1766–1831), French violinist and composer to whom Beethoven dedicated the Sonata, Op. 47.

Krumpholz, Johann Baptist (1745–90), harpist and composer. For some years at Esterház and took lessons from Haydn.

Krumpholz, Wenzel (1750–1817), one of the first violins at the court opera at Vienna and among the first to recognize Beethoven's genius and inspire others with his enthusiasm. He also played the mandoline and Beethoven wrote a sonata in one movement for piano and mandoline for him.

Lesueur, Jean François (1760–1837), French composer and theorist, professor of composition at the Paris Conservatoire from 1818.

Linke, Joseph (1783–1837), violoncellist of the Schuppanzigh Quartet in Vienna.

Mälzel, Johann Nepomuk (1772–1838), German musician and inventor of the metronome. Beethoven and he arranged to give concerts together, but they quarrelled and parted company.

Matthisson, Friedrich von (1761–1831), poet; author of the words of *Adelaide* and the *Opferlied*.

Beethoven

Mayseder, Joseph (1789–1863), Austrian violinist and composer. One of the *habitués* at Aloys Förster's quartet meetings. When Schuppanzigh was appointed leader of Count Rasumovsky's Quartet, he frequently played second violin.

Méhul, Etienne Henri (1763–1817), French composer, organist and pianist. Inspector at the Paris Conservatoire.

Monsigny, Pierre Alexandre (1729–1817), French composer, mainly of comic operas.

Moscheles, Ignaz (1794–1870), pianist and composer for his instrument. Born in Prague, but lived mainly in London and Leipzig.

Müller, Wenzel (1767–1835), Moravian composer in Vienna. Wrote 227 light and popular compositions, from one of which Beethoven took a melody, *Ich bin der Schneider Kakadu,* and wrote ten variations on it.

Neate, Charles (1784–1877), English pianist, pupil of Field, the first to introduce into England Beethoven's E flat major Concerto.

Neefe, Christian Gottlob (1748–1798), came to Bonn, 1779; court organist there from 1783.

Pachler-Koschak, Marie, pianist. Beethoven met her in 1817, and again at Baden in 1823. He gave her an autographic souvenir— a setting of 'The beautiful to the good,' the concluding words of the *Opferlied.*

Paer, Ferdinando (1771–1839), Italian opera composer settled in Paris in 1807 as *maître de chapelle* to Napoleon.

Pleyel, Ignaz (1757–1831), Austrian composer. Pupil of Haydn. Founded the Parisian firm of pianoforte makers and publishers Pleyel et Cie.

Punto, Giovanni (Johann Wenzel Stich, known as *Punto*) (1755–1803), horn player. Beethoven composed his Sonata for piano and horn, Op. 17, for him.

Radicati, Felice Alessandro (1778–1823), Italian violinist, pupil of Pugnani. Married Teresa Bertinotti (1776–1854). At Beethoven's request fingered the Rasumovsky Quartets.

Ramm, Friedrich (born 1744), famous oboe player. Friend of Mozart.

Reicha, Anton (1770–1836), played flute in Elector Max Franz's band. He went to Vienna and was one of Beethoven's intimates. Later succeeded Méhul at the Paris Conservatoire.

Reicha, Joseph (1746–95), director of Elector Max Franz's *Hofschau-spieler*, in the band of which Beethoven played viola, and uncle of Anton.

Ries, Ferdinand (1784–1838), pianist and composer, son of Franz Anton Ries, pupil of Beethoven and author of *Biographische Notizen* about him.

Ries, Franz Anton (1755–1846), violinist, learnt from Salomon (q.v.) and became an infant prodigy. He played in the elector's band at Bonn and remained there and at Godesberg as teacher.

Rochlitz, Johann Friedrich (1769–1842), critic and founder of the *Allgemeine musikalische Zeitung*.

Rode, Pierre (1774–1830), French violinist, pupil of Viotti. Beethoven finished the Sonata in G, Op. 96, expressly for him when he was on a visit to Vienna.

Romberg, Andreas (1767–1821), violinist in Elector Max Franz's orchestra, 1789. Cousin of Bernhard Romberg.

Romberg, Bernhard (1767–1841), violoncellist in Elector Max Franz's orchestra, 1789. Became famous as soloist. Composed much.

Salieri, Antonio (1750–1825), Italian composer settled in Vienna in 1766, appointed court composer in 1774 and musical director to the court in 1788.

Salomon, Johann Peter (1745–1815), violinist whose parents lived at Bonn in Beethoven's childhood. Settled in London in 1781 and introduced Haydn to England in 1790.

Schikaneder, Emanuel (1748–1812), theatrical impresario, actor and singer in Vienna. Engaged Beethoven to compose operas for the Theater-an-der-Wien.

Schindler, Anton (1796–1864), Austrian writer; friend of Beethoven and his 'Boswell.'

Schlösser, Louis. Visited Beethoven in 1823 and wrote descriptions of his visits and conversations.

Schuppanzigh, Ignaz (1776–1830), violinist and director of the Augarten concerts in Vienna. Gave Beethoven violin lessons in 1794. His quartet the first to play Beethoven's string quartets.

Sebald, Amalie, singer, member of a family who had for years furnished members to Fasch's Singakademie. Said to have a 'fascinatingly lovely singing voice.' Among the friends of C. M. von Weber in Berlin in 1812.

Simrock, Nikolaus (1752–1834), horn player at Bonn and founder of a publishing house there.

Sonnleithner, Joseph von (1766–1835), secretary of the Court Theatre in Vienna. First librettist of *Fidelio.*

Steibelt, Daniel (1755–1823), pianist and composer for his instrument. Came to Vienna in 1800 with a great reputation.

Sterkel, Johann Franz Xaver (1750–1817), secular priest and pianist, famous as an improviser.

Streicher, Nanette (Maria Anna), née Stein (1769–1838), pianist and wife of the piano-maker Johann Andreas Streicher (1761–1833).

Stumpff, Johann Andreas (1769–1846), harp manufacturer, born in Thuringia, but lived in London. Among the visitors at Baden who were admitted to intimate association with Beethoven. Gave him Handel's scores. Wrote a long account of his meeting and intercourse with Beethoven at Baden.

Swieten, Gottfried von, Baron (1734–1803), Austrian diplomat, physician and musical amateur in Vienna. Friend of Haydn and Mozart. Beethoven dedicated his first Symphony to him.

Thomson, George (1759–1851), Scotch publisher for whom Beethoven wrote arrangements of folksongs.

Todi, Luiza Rosa d'Aguiar (1753–1833), Portuguese mezzo-soprano singer.

Treitschke, Georg Friedrich (1776–1842), poet and stage-manager of German court opera in Vienna. Revised the libretto of *Fidelio.*

Umlauf, Ignaz (1756–96), popular dramatic composer in Vienna.

Unger, Caroline (1805–77), singer; studied both soprano and contralto parts of the ninth Symphony and the Mass in D.

Varnhagen von Ense, Karl August (1785–1858), biographer and part editor of the *Musenalmanach.*

Vogler, Georg Joseph (1749–1814), secular priest, organist, pianist and composer. Played in Bonn (1790 or 1791). Engaged to write operas in Vienna in 1801 by Schikaneder. He is the subject of Browning's well-known poem, *Abt Vogler*.

Weigl, Joseph (1766–1846), composer in Vienna. Appointed musical director, 1792, to the Royal Imperial National Court Theatre.

Weiss, Franz (1788–1830), viola player, member of Rasumovsky's string quartet.

Winter, Peter von (1755–1825), composer at Mannheim and Munich; composer of operas, including *Das unterbrochene Opferfest*.

Wölfl, Joseph (1772–1814), pianist and composer for his instrument.

APPENDIX D

BIBLIOGRAPHY

BEETHOVEN literature has assumed proportions that make a complete bibliography out of the question here. The following list which is intended for students and does not represent the sources of this volume, merely aims at giving the best-known and most useful biographies and books of reference, together with a selection of recent works from various countries.

Abraham, Gerald, 'Beethoven's Second-Period Quartets' (the 'Musical Pilgrim' series). (Oxford University Press, 1942.)

Beethoven, L. van, 'The Letters of Beethoven.' Translated and edited by Emily Anderson. 3 vols. (Macmillan, London, 1961.)

Bekker, P., 'Beethoven.' (Schuster & Loeffler, Berlin, 1911; now published by Deutsche Verlags-Anstalt, Stuttgart.) English translation by M. M. Bozman. (Dent, 1925.)

Berlioz, Hector, (a) 'Étude analytique des Symphonies de Beethoven', in 'Voyage Musical,' Vol. I. (Paris, 1844.) (b) Articles on Beethoven's Symphonies, Trios, Sonatas, *Fidelio,* etc., in 'A Travers Chants.' (Calmann Lévy, Paris, 1862.)

Biamonti, G., 'Catalogo cronologico e tematico delle opere di Beethoven.' (Ilte, Turin, 1968.)

Bilancioni, G., 'La Sordità di Beethoven.' (Formiggini, Rome, 1921.)

Blom, Eric, 'Beethoven's Pianoforte Sonatas Discussed.' (Dent, London, 1938.)

Boettcher, H., 'Beethoven als Liederkomponist.' (B. Filser, Augsburg, 1928.)

Boyer, Jean, 'Le "Romantisme" de Beethoven.' (Didier, Paris, 1939.)

Braunstein, J., 'Beethovens Leonore-Ouvertüren.' (Breitkopf & Härtel, Leipzig, 1927.)

Breuning, Gerhard von, 'Aus dem Schwarzspanierhause.' New edition. (Schuster & Loeffler, Berlin, 1907.)

Brümmer, E., 'Beethoven im Spiegel der zeitgenössischen rheinischen Presse.' (Triltsch, Würzburg, 1933.)

Bücken, Ernst, 'Ludwig van Beethoven.' (Athenaion, Potsdam, 1934.)

Chantavoine, J., 'Louis van Beethoven.' (Alcan, Paris, 1907.)

Closson, E., 'L'Elément flamand dans Beethoven.' (Imprimerie Veuve Monnom, Brussels, 1929.)

—— 'The Fleming in Beethoven.' Translated by Muriel Fuller (Oxford University Press, 1936.)

Cobbett, Walter Willson, 'Cobbett's Cyclopedic Survey of Chamber Music,' Vol. I. Articles: 'Beethoven,' by Vincent d'Indy; 'Beethoven,' by W.W. Cobbett. (Oxford University Press, 1929.)

Cockshoot, J. V., 'The Fugue in Beethoven's Piano Music.' (Routledge, London, 1959.)

Cooper, M., 'Beethoven: the Last Decade, 1817–1827.' (Oxford University Press, London, 1970.)

Dickinson, A. E. F., 'Beethoven.' (Nelson, London, 1941.)

Engelmann, W., 'Beethovens Kompositionspläne, dargestellt in den Sonaten für Klavier und Violine.' (B. Filser, Augsburg, 1931.)

Evans, Edwin, sen., 'Beethoven's Nine Symphonies Fully Described and Annotated.' 2 vols. (W. Reeves, London, 1923–4.)

Fishman, N., ed., 'Kniga eskisov sa 1802–03.' (Sketchbook from the years 1802–3.) 3 vols. (Glinka Museum, Moscow, 1962.)

Fiske, Roger, 'Beethoven's Last Quartets' (the 'Musical Pilgrim' Series). (Oxford University Press, 1940.)

Frimmel, T. von, 'Ludwig van Beethoven.' (Schlesische Verlagshandlung, Berlin, 1922.)

—— 'Beethovens äussere Erscheinung.' (G. Müller, Munich, 1905.)

—— 'Beethoven im zeitgenössischen Bildnis.' (K. König, Vienna, 1928.)

—— 'Beethoven‑Handbuch.' 2 vols. (Practically a Beethoven encyclopaedia.) (Breitkopf & Härtel, Leipzig, 1926.)

—— 'Beethoven‑Jahrbuch.' 2 vols. (G. Müller, Munich, 1908–9.)

Grace, Harvey, 'Ludwig van Beethoven.' (Kegan Paul, now Routledge & Co. Ltd.; J. Curwen & Sons Ltd., London, 1927.)

Grove, Sir G., 'Beethoven and his Nine Symphonies.' (Novello, London, 1906.)

—— Article on 'Beethoven' in Grove's 'Dictionary of Music and Musicians,' 4th edition. (Macmillan & Co. Ltd., 1940.)

Haas, W., 'Systematische Ordnung Beethovenscher Melodien.' (Quelle & Meyer, Leipzig, 1932.)

319

Hadow, Sir W. H., 'Beethoven's Op. 18 Quartets' (the 'Musical Pilgrim' Series). (Oxford University Press, 1926.)

—— 'The Oxford History of Music.' (*a*) Vol. V. 'The Viennese Period.' (Clarendon Press, Oxford, 1904.) (*b*) Collected Essays. (Oxford University Press, 1928.)

Heer, Josef, 'Der Graf von Waldstein und sein Verhältnis zu Beethoven.' (Quelle & Meyer, Leipzig, 1933.)

Helm, T., 'Beethovens Streichquartette.' Third edition. (Siegel, Leipzig, 1921.)

Herriot, E., 'La Vie de Beethoven.' (Nouvelle Revue Française, Paris, 1929.)

Herriot, E., 'The Life and Times of Beethoven.' Translated by Adelheid I. Mitchell and William J. Mitchell. (Macmillan, New York, 1935.)

Herwegh, M., 'Technique et interprétation sous forme d'essai d'analyse psychologique expérimentale appliquée aux sonates pour piano et violon de Beethoven.' (P. Schneider, Paris, 1926.)

Hess, W., 'Beethoven.' (Gutenberg, Zürich, 1956.)

—— 'Beethovens Oper Fidelio und ihre drei Fassungen.' (Atlantis, Zürich, 1953.)

—— 'Verzeichnis der nicht in der Gesamtausgabe veröffentlichten Werke Ludwig van Beethovens.' (Breitkopf & Härtel, Wiesbaden, 1957.)

Hevesy, A. de, 'Beethoven. Vie intime.' (Emile-Paul frères, Paris, 1926.)

—— 'Beethoven the Man.' English translation by F. S. Flint. (Faber & Gwyer, London, 1927.)

Hopkinson, Cecil, and *Oldman, C.B.,* 'Thomson's Collections of National Song, with Special Reference to the Contributions of Haydn and Beethoven.' (Bibliographical Society, Edinburgh, 1940.)

Howes, Frank, 'Beethoven' (the 'Musical Pilgrim' Series). (Oxford University Press, 1933.)

Huschke, K., 'Beethoven als Pianist und Dirigent.' (Schuster & Loeffler, Berlin, 1919.)

Indy, Vincent d', 'Beethoven. Biographie critique.' (H. Laurens, Paris, 1911, 'Les Musiciens célèbres.')

—— Article in 'Cobbett's Cyclopedic Survey of Chamber Music.' (Oxford University Press, 1929.)

Appendix D—Bibliography

James, B., 'Beethoven and Human Destiny.' (Dent, London, 1960.)

Jolivet, A., 'Ludwig van Beethoven.' (Richard-Masse, Paris, 1955.)

Kalischer, A. C., 'Beethovens Frauenkreis.' 2 vols. (Schuster & Loeffler, Berlin, 1909.)

Kaznelson, S., 'Beethovens ferne und unsterbliche Geliebte.' (Standard Buch, Zürich, 1954.)

Kerman, J., 'The Beethoven Quartets.' (Oxford University Press, London, 1967.)

—— ed., 'Ludwig van Beethoven: Autograph Miscellany from *circa* 1786 to 1799.' 2 vols. (British Museum, London, 1970.)

Kerst, F., ed., 'Die Erinnerungen an Beethoven.' 2 vols. (J. Hoffmann, Stuttgart, 1925.)

Kinsky, G., & Halm, H., 'Das Werk Beethovens. Thematisch-bibliographisches Verzeichnis seiner sämtlichen vollendeten Kompositionen.' (Henle, Munich, 1955.)

Köhler, K.-H., & Herre, G., eds., 'Ludwig van Beethovens Konversationshefte', I, IV and V. (Deutscher Verlag für Musik, Leipzig, 1968–72.)

Kufferath, M., 'Fidelio de L. van Beethoven.' (Fischbacher, Paris, 1912.)

Laisné, H., 'Le Message de Beethoven.' 2 vols. (Editions de la 'Schola Cantorum,' Paris, 1929.)

La Mara (Maria Lipsius), 'Beethovens unsterbliche Geliebte.' (Breitkopf & Härtel, Leipzig, 1908.)

—— 'Beethoven und die Brunsviks.' (Siegel, Leipzig, 1920.)

Landon, H. C. Robbins, 'Beethoven: a Documentary Study.' (Thames & Hudson, London, 1970.)

Lederer, Felix, 'Beethovens Bearbeitungen schottischer und anderer Volkslieder.' (Neuendorff, Bonn, 1934.)

Leitzmann, A., ed., 'Ludwig van Beethoven: Berichte der Zeitgenossen. Briefe und persönliche Aufzeichnungen.' 2 vols. (Insel-Verlag, Leipzig, 1921.)

Lenz, W. von, 'Beethoven et ses trois styles.' (St. Petersburg, 1852; Paris, 1855; new edition, Legouix, Paris, 1909.)

—— 'Beethoven. Eine Kunststudie.' 5 parts. (E. Balde, Cassel; Hoffmann & Campe, Hamburg; 1855–60.)

Levien, J. Mewburn, 'Beethoven and the Philharmonic Society.' (Novello, London, 1927.)

Ley, S., 'Beethoven als Freund der Familie Wegeler-von Breuning.' (F. Cohen, Bonn, 1927.)

—— ed., 'Beethovens Leben in authentischen Bildern und Texten.' (B. Cassirer, Berlin, 1925.)

—— 'Wahrheit, Zweifel und Irrtum in der Kunde von Beethovens Leben.' (Breitkopf & Härtel, Wiesbaden, 1955.)

McEwen, Sir John B., 'Beethoven: An Introduction to an Unpub-lished Edition of the Pianoforte Sonatas.' (Oxford University Press, 1932.)

Marliave, Joseph de, 'Beethoven's Quartets.' With introduction and notes by Jean Escaria and a preface by Gabriel Fauré. Translated by Hilda Andrews. (Oxford University Press, 1928.)

Marx, A. B., 'Anleitung zum Vortrag Beethovens Klavierwerke.' New edition by Schmitz. (G. Bosse, Regensburg, 1912.) Also new edition by Behncke. (O. Janke, Berlin, 1912.)

—— 'Ludwig van Beethoven. Leben und Schaffen.' 2 vols. (O. Janke, Berlin, 1911.)

Mersmann, H., 'Beethoven. Die Synthese der Stile.' (J. Bard, Berlin, 1922.)

Mies, Paul, 'Die Bedeutung der Skizzen Beethovens zur Erkenntnis seines Stiles.' (Breitkopf & Härtel, Leipzig, 1925.)

—— 'Beethoven's Sketches: an Analysis of his Style based on a Study of his Sketch-Books.' Translated by Doris L. Mackinnon. (Oxford University Press, 1929.)

Mikulicz, K. L., ed., 'Ein Notierungsbuch von L. van Beethoven.' (Breitkopf & Härtel, Leipzig, 1927.)

Milne, A. Forbes, 'Beethoven: The Pianoforte Sonatas.' 2 vols. The 'Musical Pilgrim' Series. (Oxford University Press, 1925 and 1928.)

Misch, L., 'Beethoven Studies.' (University of Oklahoma Press, Norman, 1953.)

'*Music & Letters,*' Beethoven Double Number, April 1927. ('Music & Letters,' London, 1927.)

Nagel, W., 'Beethoven und seine Klaviersonaten.' 2 vols. Second edition. (H. Beyer & Söhne, Langensalza, 1923.)

Appendix D—Bibliography

Nef, K., 'Die neun Sinfonien Beethovens.' (Breitkopf & Härtel, Leipzig, 1928.)

Nettl, P., 'Beethoven Encyclopedia.' (Philosophical Library, New York, 1956.)

Newman, Ernest, 'The Unconscious Beethoven.' (Parsons, London, 1927.)

Nohl, L., 'Beethovens Leben.' 3 vols. (Markgraf & Müller, Vienna; J. E. Günther, Leipzig; 1864–77.)

Nohl, W., 'Ludwig van Beethoven als Mensch und Musiker im täglichen Leben.' Second edition, enlarged. (C. Grüninger Nachf., Stuttgart, 1927.)

—— 'Ludwig van Beethoven. Aus seinem Leben und Wirken.' (M. Galle, Berlin, 1927.)

—— 'Beethoven, Geschichten und Anekdoten.' (Union Zweig-niederl, Berlin, 1927.)

—— 'Goethe und Beethoven.' (G. Bosse, Regensburg, 1927.)

—— 'Ludwig van Beethovens Konversationshefte.' (O. C. Recht-Verlag, Munich, 1923.)

Nottebohm, G., 'Beethoveniana.' 2 vols. (Peters, 1925.)

—— 'Zwei Skizzenbücher von Beethoven aus den Jahren 1801 bis 1803.' (Breitkopf & Härtel, 1924.)

Oulibischeff, A. D., 'Beethoven, ses critiques et ses glossateurs.' (Brockhaus, Leipzig, 1857.)

Prod'homme, J. G., ed., 'Beethoven, raconté par ceux qui l'ont vu.' (Librairie Stock, 1927.)

—— 'La Jeunesse de Beethoven.' (Payot, Paris, 1920; Librairie Delagrave, Paris, 1927.)

—— 'Les Symphonies de Beethoven.' (Delagrave, Paris, 1926.)

Radcliffe, P., 'Beethoven's String Quartets.' (Hutchinson, London, 1965.)

Riezler, Walter, 'Beethoven.' Translated by G. D. H. Pidcock. (Forrester, London, 1938.)

Rolland, Romain, 'Beethoven.' Translated by L. Langnese-Huc. (Rotapfel-Verlag, Zürich, 1927.)

—— 'Beethoven.' 2 vols. (Editions du Sablier, Paris, 1928.)

—— 'Beethoven. Les grandes époques créatrices.' (Editions du Sablier, Paris, 1929.)

—— 'Beethoven the Creator. I. From the Eroica to the Appassion‑ ata.' Translated by Ernest Newman. (Gollancz, London, 1929.)

—— 'Goethe und Beethoven.' French original in the periodical 'Europe.' (May and June 1927.) German translation by Kippenburg. (Rotapfel‑Verlag, Zürich, 1928.) English trans‑ lation by Pfister and Kemp. (Hamish Hamilton, London, 1931.)

Sandberger, A., ed., 'Neues Beethoven‑Jahrbuch.' (B. Filser, Augsburg, 1924; H. Litolff, Brunswick, 1933–8.)

—— 'Ausgewählte Aufsätze zur Musikgeschichte. Bd. 2. For‑ schungen, Studien und Kritiken zu Beethoven und zur Beethovenliteratur.' (Drei Masken Verlag, Munich, 1924.)

Schauffler, Robert Haven, 'Beethoven, the Man who Freed Music.' 2 vols. (Curtis Brown, London; Doubleday, Doran & Co., Garden City, New York; 1929.)

Schenker, H., 'Ludwig van Beethoven: IX Sinfonie.' (Universal Edition, Vienna, 1912.)

Schering, A., 'Beethoven in neuer Deutung.' (Kahnt, Leipzig, 1934.)

Scherman, T. K., & Biancolli, L., eds., 'The Beethoven Companion.' (Doubleday, New York, 1972.)

Schiedermair, L., 'Der junge Beethoven.' (Quelle & Meyer, Leipzig, 1925.)

Schindler, A., 'Beethoven‑Biographie.' (1st edition, Münster, 1840.) Neudruck herausgegeben von Dr. A. C. Kalischer. (Schuster & Loeffler, Berlin, 1909.)

—— 'Beethoven as I knew him.' Edited by D. W. MacArdle. Translated by C. S. Jolly. (Faber, London, 1966.)

Schmidt‑Görg, J., ed., 'Drei Skizzenbücher zur Missa solemnis.' 3 vols. (Beethovenhaus, Bonn, 1968–70.)

—— *& Schmidt, H.,* eds., 'Ludwig van Beethoven.' (Pall Mall Press, London, 1970.)

Schmitz, A., 'Beethoven: unbekannte Skizzen und Entwürfe.' (Beethovenhaus, Bonn, 1924.)

Schweisheimer, W., 'Beethovens Leiden, ihr Einfluss auf sein Leben und Schaffen.' (G. Müller, Leipzig, 1922.)

Smolle, K., 'Beethovens unsterbliche Geliebte.' (Vienna, 1947.)

—— 'Wohnstätten Ludwig van Beethovens von 1792 bis zu seinem Tod.' (Beethovenhaus, Bonn, 1970.)

Sonneck, O. G., 'Beethoven, Impressions of Contemporaries, collected by O. G. Sonneck. (Oxford University Press, 1927; G. Schirmer, New York, 1926.)

—— 'Beethoven Letters in America.' (Beethoven Association, New York; Hawkes, London; 1927.)

—— 'The Riddle of the Immortal Beloved.' (G. Schirmer, New York, 1927.)

Specht, R., 'Bildnis Beethovens.' (Avalun-Verlag, Hellerau, 1931.)

—— 'Beethoven as he Lived.' Translated by Alfred Kalisch. (Macmillan, London, 1933.)

Steinitzer, M., 'Beethoven.' (Reclam's Universal-Bibliothek; replaces the volume by Nohl in this series; 1927.)

Sterba, E. & R., 'Beethoven and his Nephew.' (Pantheon, New York, 1954.)

Sullivan, J. W. N., 'Beethoven: his Spiritual Development.' (Jonathan Cape, London, 1927.)

Tenger, Mariam, 'Beethovens unsterbliche Geliebte nach persönlichen Erinnerungen.' (F. Cohen, Bonn, 1903; 1st edition 1890.) English translation by Gertrude Russell; 'Recollections of Countess Therese Brunswick.' (Fisher Unwin, London, 1898.)

Thayer, A. W., 'Ludwig van Beethovens Leben.' Translated into German and edited by H. Deiters. Revised and completed by H. Riemann. 5 vols. (Breitkopf & Härtel, Leipzig, 1907–17.)

—— 'The Life of Ludwig van Beethoven.' Revised English edition by H. E. Krehbiel. 3 vols. (The Beethoven Association, New York, 1921.)

—— 'Life of Beethoven.' Revised and edited by Elliot Forbes. 2 vols. (Princeton University Press, 1964.)

Thomas-San-Galli, W. A., 'Die unsterbliche Geliebte Beethovens, Amalie Sebald.' (O. Hendel, Halle, 1909.)

—— 'Ludwig van Beethoven.' (R. Piper & Co., Munich, 1920.)

Thompson, Herbert, Article on Beethoven in 'The Heritage of Music.' (Oxford University Press, 1927.)

Tovey, Donald Francis, 'A Companion to Beethoven's Pianoforte

Sonatas.' Complete analysis. (The Associated Board of the R.A.M. and the R.C.M., London, 1931.)

Tovey, Donald Francis, 'Beethoven's Ninth Symphony.' (Oxford University Press, 1928.)

—— 'Essays in Musical Analysis.' (Oxford University Press, 1934.)

Turner, W. J., 'Beethoven. The Search for Reality.' (Benn, London, 1927; new edition 1933.)

Tyson, A., 'The Authentic English Editions of Beethoven.' (Faber, London, 1963.)

Unger, M., 'Beethovens Handschrift.' (Beethovenhaus, Bonn, 1927.)

—— 'Auf Spuren von Beethovens unsterblicher Geliebten.' (Beyer & Söhne, Langensalza, 1911.)

Unverricht, H., 'Die Eigenschriften und die Originalausgaben von Werken Beethovens in ihrer Bedeutung für die moderne Textkritik.' (Bärenreiter, Cassel, 1960.)

Veidl, T., 'Der musikalische Humor bei Beethoven.' (Breitkopf & Härtel, Leipzig, 1929.)

Wagner, R., 'Schriften über Beethoven.' (Breitkopf & Härtel, Leipzig, 1916.)

Walker, E., 'Beethoven.' ('Music of the Masters.') 3rd edition. (John Lane, London, 1920.)

Wasielewski, J. W. von, 'Ludwig van Beethoven.' 2 vols. (Brachvogel & Ranft, Berlin, 1888.)

Weber, W., 'Beethovens Missa Solemnis.' (F. E. C. Leuckart, Leipzig, 1908.)

Wegeler, F. G., and *Ries, F.,* 'Biographische Notizen über Ludwig van Beethoven.' (1st edition, Koblenz, 1838.) Neudruck mit Ergänzungen und Erläuterungen von Dr. A. C. Kalischer, (Schuster & Loeffler, Berlin, 1906.)

Weingartner, F., 'Ratschläge für Aufführungen klassischer Symphonien.' Vol. I. 'Beethoven.' Second edition revised. (Breitkopf, Leipzig, 1916; 1st edition 1906.) English translation by Jessie Crosland: 'On the Performance of Beethoven's Symphonies.' (Breitkopf & Härtel, 1907.)

Weise, D., ed., 'Ein Skizzenbuch zur Chorfantasie op. 80 und zu anderen Werken.' (Beethovenhaus, Bonn, 1957.)

Appendix D—Bibliography

—— 'Ein Skizzenbuch zur Pastoralsymphonie op. 68 und zu den Trios op. 70.' (Beethovenhaus, Bonn, 1961.)

Willetts, P. J., 'Beethoven and England. An Account of Sources in the British Museum.' (British Museum, London, 1970.)

Wyzewa, Téodor de, 'Beethoven et Wagner.' (Perrin et Cie, Paris, 1898; new edition, 1914.)

INDEX

Abercrombie, General, 161
Adagio for string quartet, 250
Adagio, Variations and Rondo
  for piano, violin and cello
  (Op. 121), 249
Adelaide, song, 42, 210
Aerde, R. van, 6
Aeschylus, 50
Ah! perfido, scena and aria, 42,
  211
Albrechtsberger, 38, 156, 252,
  310
Albumblatt für Elise, for piano,
  114
Alexander I, Tsar, 238
Amati, Nicholas, 98
Amenda, Karl, 37, 45, 48, 253,
  310
Andante favori, for piano, 141
An die ferne Geliebte, song cycle,
  211, 212
Anschütz, actor, 88
Apponyi, Count, 252
Arnim, Achim von, 67
Arnim, Bettina von. *See* Bren-
  tano
Artaria, Domenico, 24, 101, 310
Augustus, Emperor, 86
Averdonk, Johanna Helena, 16

Bach, 3, 20, 37, 78, 81, 115-18,
  144, 149, 208, 224, 254, 271
Bach, C. P. E., 111, 114, 116,
  310
Bacon, 12

Bagatelles: (Op. 33), 148
  (Op. 119), 148
  (Op. 126), 148
Bartók, Béla, 263
Battle of Vittoria, The, 69, 70,
  150-2
Baum, Heinrich, 25
Baums, Gertrud, 11
Beckenkamp, painter, 27, 310
Beer, clarinettist, 233
Beethoven, Henri-Adelard van, 6
Beethoven, Johann van (father),
  7-9, 11-13, 15-19, 24, 26-8,
  35, 100
Beethoven, Johann van
  (brother), 14, 15, 35, 41, 49,
  68-9, 83-4, 99-100
Beethoven, Johanna van, 62-3,
  72-3, 78-9, 100
Beethoven, Karl van (brother),
  13, 15, 26, 35, 41, 49, 62, 66,
  69, 71, 72, 101, 258
Beethoven, Karl van (nephew),
  26, 63, 71-5, 77-9, 82-5, 87,
  93, 95, 101-3, 207, 272, 275
Beethoven, Louis van, 6-9, 11,
  13, 16
Beethoven, Ludwig Maria van,
  11
Beethoven, Maria Josepha van, 6
Beethoven, Maria Magdalena
  van, 7, 8, 11, 15, 18, 19,
  24-7, 100
Beethoven, Maria Margaretha
  Josepha van, 25, 27

Index

Beethoven, Michel van, 6
Beethoven, Therese van, 69, 100
Bekker, Paul, 127, 130, 144, 146, 151, 160, 182, 195, 200, 204, 205, 208, 215, 223, 230, 239, 269
Belderbusch, minister, 13, 21
Belseroski, J. C., 8, 310
Berlioz, 157, 161, 169, 171, 181, 201
Bernadotte, General, 40, 52, 159
Bertolini, Dr., 97
Bigot, Marie, 105, 310
Bouilly, J. N., 191, 310
Brahms, 181, 214, 235, 275
Brauchle, tutor, 73
Braun, Baron, 191, 310
Braunhofer, Dr., 213
Breitkopf & Härtel, 66, 68, 101, 107, 114, 116, 120, 218, 310
Brentano, Bettina (von Arnim), 42, 65, 67, 125, 152, 310
Brentano, Maximiliane (Max), 249, 310
Brentano, Mme, 105
Breuning, Christoph von, 28
Breuning, Eleonore von, 28, 29, 34, 60, 92, 132, 194, 203. See also Wegeler
Breuning, Frau von, 28, 29
Breuning, Gerhard von, 84, 95
Breuning, Lorenz von (nephew), 28, 37
Breuning, Lorenz von (uncle), 28
Breuning, Stephan von, 28, 37, 53, 54, 58, 84, 86, 95, 194
Breuning, von, court councillor, 15

Breuning, von (family), 30, 33, 104
Bridges, Robert, 212
Bridgetower, G. A., 110, 241, 311
Browning, 19, 106, 112, 146
Brunswick, Charlotte von, 56
Brunswick, Franz von, 62, 105, 143
Brunswick, Josephine von, 47. See also Deym
Brunswick, Therese von, 47, 54–6, 59–65, 86, 87, 143
Bundeslied, 216
Bürger, G. A., 185, 311
Byron, 87

Campe, 95
Cantata for Cressener, 18, 127
Cantata for Prince Lobkowitz, 215
Cantata on the Accession of Leopold II, 32, 180, 214
Cantata on the Death of Joseph II, 32, 203, 214
Capell, Richard, 202
Cherubini, 104, 111, 195, 197
Chopin, 148
Christus am Ölberge, oratorio, 51, 52, 192, 216–18
Cicero, 95
Clasen, 2, 3
Clemens, August, elector, 4, 5
Clement, Franz, 110, 186
Clementi, 114, 115, 133, 138, 153, 311
Closson, Ernest, 9, 194
Coleridge, 167, 241
Collard, F. W., 115, 311

Colles, H. C., 159
Collin, Heinrich von, 205, 311
Concerto for piano, violin and cello (Op. 56), 186
Concertos for piano:
  No. 1, C major (Op. 15), 42, 182
  No. 2, B flat major (Op. 19), 42, 182
  No. 3, C minor (Op. 37), 52, 182, 183
  No. 4, G major (Op. 58), 65, 183
  No. 5, E flat major ('Emperor') (Op. 73), 67, 183-6, 238
  E flat major (early), 132, 182
  D major (early), 132, 182
  D major (sketch), 185
Concertos for violin:
  C major (fragment), 182
  D major (Op. 61), 65, 169, 186-7
Consecration of the House, The, overture, 114, 207-8
Contredanse, E flat major, 152
Coriolan, overture, 65, 190, 205
Courtin, Frau, 11
Cramer, J. B., 113, 137, 311
Cranz, publisher, 138, 142
Cressener, George, 18
Cucuel, Georges, 15, 114
Czerny, 99, 111, 112, 115, 137, 138, 139, 241, 256, 311

Debussy, 138
Degenharth, 232
Deym, Josephine von (*née* von Brunswick), 54-7, 59, 64, 65

Diabelli, A., 149, 311
Dittersdorf, 132
Dobbeler, Abbé, 32, 250
Dragonetti, Domenico, 70, 110, 311
Dressler, E. C., 21, 127, 128, 129, 147, 311
Drouet, flute player, 252
Droz, Gustave, 10
Duet for viola and cello, 250
Duo, G major, for two flutes, 232
Duo for musical box(?), 232
Duos for clarinet and bassoon, 232
Duport, Jean Pierre, 243
Dussek, 70, 136, 312

Eeden, Gilles van den, 16, 17, 312
Egmont, incidental music, 190, 205, 220
Eichoff, 27
Elegie auf den Tod eines Pudels, song, 210
Elegischer Gesang, quartet, 215
Elgar, 181, 189
Elssler, Johann, 38, 312
Eppinger, Heinrich, 37
Equali for trombones, 67, 88, 234, 235
Erdödy, Countess, 73, 96, 105
Ertmann, Dorothea von, Baroness, 105
Es ist vollbracht, chorus, 207
Esterházy, Prince, 38, 218, 219
Evans, Edwin, sen., 169

Fantasy for piano (Op. 77), 143

Index

Fantasy for piano, chorus and orchestra (Op. 80), 66, 175, 180, 185
Fasch, 42
Feuerfarb', song, 174
Fidelio, opera, 15, 29, 57–8, 70, 78, 81, 86, 104, 114, 169, 180, 191–204, 205, 214, 217, 220. See also *Leonora*
Fischenich, 174
Fischer, Cäcilia, 9
Fischer, Gottfried, 8, 9, 16, 19
Flecker, James Elroy, 47
Förster, Aloys, 38, 118, 252, 312
Fox Strangways, A. H., 107 n.
Franck, César, 191, 263
Frederick William II of Prussia, 12, 112, 243
Friess, Count, 101
Frimmel, Th. von, 90
Fugue for string quintet, 71

Galitsin, Prince, 81, 263, 264, 266, 312
Gallenberg, Count, 48
Gänsbacher, 112
Gardiner, William, 32, 254, 312
Gaveaux, Pierre, 192
Gegenliebe, song, 185
Gelinek, Joseph, 41, 312
Gellert, 211, 312
German Dances for violin and piano, 235
Germania, wie stehst du, chorus, 207
Gesang der Nachtigall, song, 172
Gleichenstein, Baron von, 37
Glorreiche Augenblick, Der, cantata, 214

Gluck, 89, 91, 112, 115, 119, 190, 195, 197, 200, 203, 242
Goethe, 67, 68, 81, 95, 96, 100, 125, 171, 202, 205, 215
Gounod, 164
Gratulations Menuett, 152
Grétry, 114, 312
Grillparzer, 88, 312
Grove, George, 122, 156, 172, 174, 180
Guarnerius, Andreas, 98
Guarnerius, Joseph, 98
Guicciardi, Giulietta, 47, 48, 54, 60, 63, 86, 95

Hadow, W. H., 133 n., 254
Handel, 85, 115, 208, 209, 210, 217, 243
Hanzman, Father, 19
Hardy, Thomas, 128, 229
Häring, 37
Haydn, 1, 2, 6, 24, 32, 35–40, 66, 69, 85, 89, 91, 112, 118, 130, 132–4, 142, 151, 154, 155, 157, 158, 165, 168, 174, 181, 183, 191, 197, 200, 210, 213, 231, 233, 235, 236, 239, 241, 244, 246, 247, 252, 253, 255, 256, 260
Heller, Ferdinand, 22
Hellmesberger, Joseph, 182
Herder, 33, 172
Herrick, 274
Herzog, musical director, 81
Hevesy, 73
Hofmeister, publisher, 116, 182
Holz, Karl, 82, 84, 101, 105, 107, 245, 258, 269, 312
Homer, 50

d'Honrath, Jeannette, 29
Horneman, C., 90
Horsalka, musician, 80
Houdon, sculptor, 89
Housman, A. E., 277
Huber, F. X., 216, 312
Hulin, General, 57
Hummel, 37, 86, 88, 218, 252, 312
Hüttenbrenner, Anselm, 87

d'Indy, Vincent, 262, 268, 272
In questa tomba, arietta, 211

Jeitteles, A., 211, 312
'Jena' symphony, 156
Jerome Bonaparte, King of Westphalia, 66
Joachim, Joseph, 187, 243
Joseph Clemens, elector, 4
Joseph II, emperor, 24, 32, 203, 214
Junker, chaplain, 31

Kanne, August, 117
Kant, 95, 163, 312
Keglevics, Babette von, Countess, 135
Kempis, Thomas à, 313
Kerich, Abraham von, 28
Keverich, Heinrich, 7
Kiesewetter, R. G., 37, 313
King Stephan, overture, 206
Kinsky, Prince, 66, 69, 105
Klein, sculptor, 89
Klinger, Max, 90
Klöber, August von, 90, 92
Klopstock, 46, 95, 313
Koch, Willibald, 18, 20

Kotzebue, 206, 313
Koželuh, 213, 246, 313
Kretzschmar, Hermann, 169
Kreutzer, R., 88, 110, 241, 313
Krumpholz, Wenzel, 37, 245, 313
Kügelgen, G. von, 10
Kyd, Major-General, 97

La Fontaine, 95
La Mara, 60
Lampi, painter, 64
Languider, Karoline, 63
Laym, Joseph, 7
Laym, Maria Magdalena. *See* Beethoven
Lenz, Wilhelm von, 256
Leonora Overture, No. 1; 57, 195, 196
—— No. 2; 57, 58, 118, 190, 196, 197
—— No. 3; 57, 65, 118, 155, 169, 190, 194, 196, 197
Leonora Prohaska, incidental music, 206
Leopold II, emperor, 32, 182, 214
Lesueur, 171, 313
Levin, Rahel, 67
Libisch, oboist, 34
Lichnowsky, Moritz, Count, 37, 144
Lichnowsky, Prince, 35-7, 41, 44, 52, 57, 98, 104, 116, 141, 246, 256
Lichnowsky, Princess, 57, 104
Linke, Joseph, 245, 252, 313
Liszt, 43, 87

Index

Lobkowitz, Prince Franz Joseph, 37, 53, 66, 104, 112, 213, 252

Lobkowitz, Prince Ferdinand, 215

Louis Ferdinand, Prince of Prussia, 53

Lyser, J. P., 90

Mähler, W. J., 90

Maine, Basil, 189

Malfatti, Therese von, 60, 65

Malfatti, von, Dr., 65, 85, 86

Mälzel, J. N., 69, 70, 151, 173, 313

Marches for military band, 152

Maria Theresa, Empress, 21

Maschek, Vincenz, 175

Masefield, John, 133

Marliave, Joseph de, 255

Mass, C major, 65, 217–22, 224–5

Mass, C sharp minor (sketch), 228, 274

Mass, D major (*Missa Solennis*), 78–9, 82, 90, 131–2, 146, 148, 209, 210, 222–9, 275

Matari, 25

Matthisson, Friedrich von, 215, 313

Maximilian Franz, elector, 21, 23, 26–7, 31, 33, 35–6, 223, 231, 232

Maximilian Friedrich, elector, 13–14, 16, 21, 127, 130

Mayseder, Joseph, 252, 314

Meeresstille und glückliche Fahrt, cantata, 215

Méhul, 195, 197, 314

Meisl, Carl, 207

Mendelssohn, 76, 148, 164, 171, 260, 261

Mendelssohn, Fanny, 196

Metastasio, 36

Meyerbeer, 70, 171

Meynell, Alice, 126

Michelangelo, 94

Milton, 175

Missa Solennis. See Mass, D major

Mit Mädeln sich vertragen, song, 210

Mollo, publisher, 252

Monk's Song from *Wilhelm Tell,* 216

Monsigny, 15, 114, 314

Montagu, Lady Mary Wortley, 4

Moscheles, 85, 86, 314

Moussorgsky, 259, 260

Mozart, 1, 11, 18, 23, 24, 36, 38, 39, 52, 56, 73, 80, 88, 91, 113, 118–21, 132–4, 142, 150, 161, 180–3, 190, 191, 195, 208, 231, 232, 235, 236, 238, 243, 246, 247, 252, 253, 255, 275

Müller, Dr., 92

Müller, Wenzel, 249, 314

Murat, 57

Murillo, 10

Namensfeier, overture, 152

Napoleon, 40, 52, 53, 57, 66, 67, 70, 89, 143, 159–61, 184, 214, 229

Neate, Charles, 119, 205, 314

Neefe, C. G., 19, 20, 114, 116–117, 314

Neidl, J., 90

Newman, Ernest, 122, 128
Nottebohm, Gustav, 135, 149

Obermeyer, Therese. *See* Beethoven
Octet, E flat major (Op. 103), 231
Ode to Joy, 194
Oliva, Franz, 206
Opferlied, chorus, 215
Overture on the name BACH (sketch), 116, 117

Pachler-Koschak, Marie, 105, 314
Paer, 118, 192, 314
Palestrina, 262, 264, 265, 271, 272
Parry, Hubert, 133, 137, 142, 150, 171, 178
Pestalozzi, 64
Peters, Hofrat, 79
Pfeiffer, Tobias, 17
Philharmonic Society, London, 78, 85, 86, 97
Pleyel, Ignaz, 70, 112, 213, 314
Plutarch, 46, 95, 162, 164
Poll, Maria Josepha. *See* Beethoven
Polonaise for piano, 148
Preludes for piano, 131, 142, 147
Prod'homme, J. G., 114
Prometheus, ballet, 30, 39, 40, 51, 148, 152–7, 159, 160, 161, 168, 172, 190, 191, 196, 198, 207, 253
Prüfing des Küssens, song, 210
Punto, Giovanni, 110, 234, 314
Quartets (strings), 123, 146, 251

F major (Op. 18, No. 1), 48, 110, 252, 253, 261
G major (Op. 18, No. 2), 110, 145, 252, 253, 254
D major (Op. 18, No. 3), 110, 252, 254
C minor (Op. 18, No. 4), 110, 250, 252, 254, 255
A major (Op. 18, No. 5), 110, 165, 252, 255
B flat major (Op. 18, No. 6), 110, 252, 255
F major (Op. 59, No. 1), 59, 62, 65, 110, 169, 250, 255–8, 266
E minor (Op. 59, No. 2), 59, 62, 65, 163, 255–60, 266
C major (Op. 59, No. 3), 59, 62, 65, 255, 256, 257, 260, 266
E flat major (Op. 74), 260
F minor (Op. 95), 76, 260–2
E flat major (Op. 127), 82, 262, 264, 265
B flat major (Op. 130), 146, 265, 266, 267, 269–73
C sharp minor (Op. 131), 83, 118, 217, 265, 266, 267, 272–5
A minor (Op. 132), 82, 265, 266–70, 272, 273–5
Grosse Fuge, B flat major (Op. 133), 263, 267, 269–71
F major (Op. 135), 83, 263, 275–7
Quartets (with piano) (1784), 132, 134, 135
Quintet, E flat major, for piano and wind (Op. 16), 232, 235

Quintet, C major, for strings (Op. 29), 101, 251

Radicati, F. A., 257, 314
Radoux, court painter, 6
Ramm, F., 110, 314
Rasumovsky, Count, 255, 256
Recke, Elise von der, 67
Reicha, Anton, 37, 110, 314
Reicha, Joseph, 315
Reiss, Johanna. *See* Beethoven
Ries, Ferdinand, 38, 53, 92, 101, 105, 232, 240, 315
Ries, Franz, 25, 38, 315
Righini, Vincenzo, 132, 147
Rio, Fanny del, 74
Rio, Giannatasio del, 74, 76
Ritterballet, 30, 150, 190
Rochlitz, J. F., 68, 95, 99, 315
Rode, Pierre, 110, 236, 241, 242, 315
Rolland, Romain, 60, 64, 91, 113, 194, 195, 197
Romances for violin and orchestra (Opp. 40 and 50), 186
Romberg, A., 31, 70, 110, 315
Romberg, Bernhard, 31, 110, 315
Rondino for wind instruments, 231
Rondo, A major, for piano, 131
Rondo, G major, for piano, 48
Rondo, G major, for violin and piano, 235
Rondo, *Rage over a Lost Penny,* 148
Rossini, 262
Rovantini, Franz, 17, 19

Rudolph, Archduke, 66, 78, 105, 123, 144, 223, 241, 248, 270
Ruggieri, Vincenzo, 98
Ruins of Athens, The, incidental music, 198, 206–8

Sacred Songs (Gellert), 211
Saint-Foix, Georges, 246
Salieri, 38, 70, 191, 210, 236, 315
Salomon, J. P., 2, 3, 315
Salomon, Philipp, 8
Satzenhofen, Caroline von, Countess, 13
Schaden, von, Dr., 24, 26
Schall, Count Marschall von, 27
Schenk, Johann, 38
Schikaneder, Emanuel, 52, 56, 191, 315
Schiller, 81, 95, 100, 142, 174, 175, 194, 203, 204, 216
Schiller, Charlotte von, 174
Schimon, Ferdinand, 90
Schindler, Anton, 23, 60, 75, 82, 86, 105, 109, 136, 144, 204, 207, 224, 262, 271, 315
Schlesinger, publisher, 213
Schlösser, Louis, 121, 315
Schmidt, Dr., 48
Schmitz, Arnold, 195, 197
Schopenhauer, 25
Schott, publisher, 274 n.
Schubert, 81, 85, 87, 131, 148, 202, 210–11
Schulz, 209
Schumann, 25, 148, 181, 211, 223, 235
Schumann, Clara, 25, 243

Schuppanzigh, Ignaz, 37, 62, 70, 82, 106, 110, 245, 252, 315

Sebald, Amalie, 60, 65, 67, 68, 75, 174, 316

Septet, E flat major (Op. 20), 233, 234, 256

Serenade for string trio (Op. 8), 42, 250

Serenade, D major, for flute, violin and viola (Op. 25), 232, 233

Seume, 48

Sextet, E flat major, for strings and horns, 232

Sextet, E flat major, for wind instruments, 232

Shakespeare, 12, 46, 47, 95, 133, 142, 143, 192, 193, 205, 232, 249, 261

Shedlock, J. S., 103, 124, 153

Simrock, N., 98, 108, 316

Smart, George, 85

Sonata, F major, for horn and piano (Op. 17), 234

Sonatas (piano):
3 early Sonatas, 127, 130, 136
F minor (Op. 2, No. 1), 42, 132–4
A major (Op. 2, No. 2), 42, 132–4
C major (Op. 2, No. 3), 42, 132–4
E flat major (Op. 7), 42, 134
C minor (Op. 10, No. 1), 42, 135
F major (Op. 10, No. 2), 42, 135
D major (Op. 10, No. 3), 42, 135, 255

C minor (*Pathétique*) (Op. 13), 42, 130, 136, 260
E major (Op. 14, No. 1), 42, 136, 250
G major (Op. 14, No. 2), 42, 136
B flat major (Op. 22), 136
A flat major (Op. 26), 118, 137, 162, 206
E flat major (Op. 27, No. 1), 138
C sharp minor ('Moonlight') (Op. 27, No. 2), 48, 94, 130, 138, 144
D major ('Pastoral') (Op. 28), 138
G major (Op. 31, No. 1), 139, 238
D minor (Op. 31, No. 2), 139, 142, 238, 240
E flat major (Op. 31, No. 3), 140, 238
G minor (Op. 49, No. 1), 140
G major (Op. 49, No. 2), 140, 141, 233
C major (*Waldstein*) (Op. 53), 114, 141, 142
F major (Op. 54), 141, 142, 256
F minor (*Appassionata*) (Op. 57), 57, 141, 239, 256
F sharp major (Op. 78), 64, 143
G major (Op. 79), 143, 144, 150
E flat major (*Lebewohl*) (Op. 81A), 143–4
E minor (Op. 90), 144

Sonatas (piano)—*continued*
 A major (Op. 101), 71, 145
 B flat major (*Hammerclavier*)
  (Op. 106), 78, 145, 160
 E major (Op. 109), 79, 118,
  123, 146, 148
 A flat major (Op. 110), 79,
  145, 146
 C minor (Op. 111), 79, 105,
  123, 146
Sonatas (violin and piano), 236
 D major (Op. 12, No. 1), 42,
  236
 A major (Op. 12, No. 2), 42,
  236, 237
 E flat major (Op. 12, No. 3),
  42, 236, 237, 238
 A minor (Op. 23), 238
 F major (Op. 24), 238
 A major (Op. 30, No. 1),
  238, 239, 240
 C minor (Op. 30, No. 2),
  238, 239, 240, 254
 G major (Op. 30, No. 3),
  238, 239
 A major (Kreutzer) (Op. 47),
  52, 110, 238, 240, 242
 G major (Op. 96), 67, 110,
  118, 236, 241, 244
Sonatas (violoncello and piano),
  243
 F major (Op. 5, No. 1), 42,
  243, 244
 G minor (Op. 5, No. 2), 42,
  243, 244
 A major (Op. 69), 66, 244,
  247
 C major (Op. 102, No. 1),
  245

 D major (Op. 102, No. 2),
  245
Sonatina for mandoline and
  piano, 245
Sonatinas for piano (early), 132
Sonnleithner, Joseph von, 191,
  ·192, 194, 316
Sophocles, 50
Specht, Richard, 60, 72, 98,
  104
Spohr, 70, 110
Spontini, 191
Squire, Wm. Barclay, 90
Stainhauser, painter, 10, 90
Starcke, Friedrich, 148
Steibelt, Daniel, 37, 316
Stein, Fritz, 156
Sterkel, J. F. X., 32, 132, 316
Stieler, J. C., 90
Strauss, Richard, 151, 181
Stravinsky, Igor, 263
Streicher, Andreas, 71
Streicher, Nanette, 71, 76, 105,
  316
Stumpff, J. A., 85, 115, 126,
  316
Stutterheim, Baron von, 272
Sullivan, J. W. N., 256
Swieten, G. van, Baron, 37, 316
Symphonies:
 No. 1, C major (Op. 21), 42,
  51, 52, 118, 155, 157
 No. 2, D major (Op. 36), 51,
  52, 158, 159, 174, 238, 246
 No. 3, E flat major (*Eroica*)
  (Op. 55), 35, 49, 52–3, 70,
  118, 122, 147, 148, 152,
  153, 156, 159–67, 175, 179,
  192, 203, 205, 271

Symphonies—*continued*
No. 4, B flat major (Op. 60), 57, 65, 168–70, 179, 259
No. 5, C minor (Op. 67), 65, 170–2, 217, 254
No. 6, F major (Pastoral) (Op. 68), 65, 114, 115, 152, 172, 212
No. 7, A major (Op. 92), 67, 70, 172, 173, 259
No. 8, F major (Op. 93), 67, 172–4, 223
No. 9, D minor (Choral) (Op. 125), 15, 33, 47, 51, 79, 81, 114, 123, 146, 148, 158–60, 167, 174–80, 203, 204, 214, 223, 229, 253, 263, 268, 269, 273
No. 10 (sketch), 85

Tchaikovsky, 181
Teimer, brothers, 232
Thayer, A. W., 23, 38, 48, 60, 73, 92, 95, 100, 108, 152, 154, 196, 254, 255, 256
Thomson, George, 213, 316
Tiedge, 67
Todi, Luiza Rosa, 32, 316
Tolstoy, 240
Tomaschek, J. W., 111
Tovey, D. F., 132, 136, 141, 177, 180, 225, 227, 229
Treitschke, G. F., 192, 194, 203, 207, 316
Trio for piano, clarinet and cello (Op. 11), 233
Trio for piano, flute and bassoon, 232

Trio for two oboes and cor anglais, 232
Trios (piano, violin and cello), 246
E flat major (Op. 1, No. 1), 42, 246, 247
G major (Op. 1, No. 2), 42, 246, 247
C minor (Op. 1, No. 3), 42, 246, 247
D major (Op. 70, No. 1), 66, 247, 248, 275
E flat major (Op. 70, No. 2), 66, 247, 248
B flat major (Op. 97), 67, 215, 248–50
B flat major (one movement), 67, 249
E flat major (early), 246, 249
F minor (sketch), 249
Trios (strings), 250
E flat major (Op. 3), 32, 42, 250
D major (Serenade) (Op. 8), 42, 250. *See also* Serenades
G major (Op. 9, No. 1), 42, 251
D major (Op. 9, No. 2), 42, 251
C minor (Op. 9, No. 3), 42, 251
Triumphal March for *Tarpeja*, 206
Turner, W. J., 176
Tuscany, Grand Duke of, 59
Tuscher, von, councillor, 78

Umlauf, Ignaz, 82, 191, 316
Unger, Caroline, 82, 316

Index

Van den Eeden. *See* Eeden
Variations (piano), 146
  God save the King, 147
  March by Dressler, 21, 127,
    129, 147
  Original Theme, C minor,
    21, 128, 148
  Original Theme, F major
    (Op. 34), 147
  Prometheus theme (Op. 35),
    147, 148, 152
  Righini's *Venni Amore*, 132,
    147
  Rule, Britannia, 147
  Theme by Dittersdorf, 132
  Theme by Waldstein, 132
  Turkish March, 206
  Waltz by Diabelli (Op. 120),
    149
Variations on Mozart's *Là ci
  darem*, for two oboes and cor
  anglais, 232
Variations on Mozart's *Se vuol
  ballare*, for violin and piano,
  235
Variations on National Themes,
  234, 235
Variations on Original Theme
  for piano, violin and cello
  (Op. 44), 246
Varnhagen von Ense, K. A.,
  67, 316
Vigano, Salvatore, 154
Virgil, 50, 99
Vogler, G. J., 112, 147, 317
Voltaire, 204

Wagner, 172, 174, 204 n., 209,
  231, 263, 272

Waldstein Ferdinand von,
  Count, 30, 33, 36, 132, 141,
  150
Walker, Ernest, 132, 134, 135,
  140, 173, 184, 239, 244, 269,
  272
Wawruch, Professor, 84
Weber, 264
Wegeler, Eleonore, 46, 58,
  251
Wegeler, F. G., 23, 28, 29, 37,
  41, 45-6, 54, 58, 83, 104, 121,
  132, 251
Weigl, Joseph, 233, 317
*Weihe des Hauses, Die. See Con-
  secration of the House*
Weiss, Franz, 110, 252, 317
Wellington, Duke of, 69-70
*Wellington's Victory. See Battle
  of Vittoria*
Wesendonck, Mathilde, 25
Westerhold, Count, 232
Westerhold, Fräulein, 29
Whitman, Walt, 164, 258
Willmann, Magdalene, 41-2,
  44-5
Winter, Peter von, 175, 317
Witt, Friedrich, 156
Wölfl, Joseph, 37, 111, 317
Wordsworth, 119
Wurzer, 17-18
Wyzewa, T. de, 114

Zenser, organist, 18
Zeuner, violist, 264
Zmeskall von Domanowecz,
  Freiherr, 37, 40, 76, 81, 87,
  105, 107, 260, 261